D0501362

Wallace Stevens

THE POET AND HIS CRITICS

Wallace Stevens

THE POET AND HIS CRITICS

ABBIE F. WILLARD

AMERICAN
LIBRARY
ASSOCIATION
CHICAGO
1973

PS
3537
T4753
295

THE POET AND HIS CRITICS

A series of volumes on the meaning of the
critical writings on selected modern British
and American poets.

Edited by CHARLES SANDERS, University of Illinois, Urbana

Robert Frost by Donald J. Greiner
William Carlos Williams by Paul L. Mariani
Dylan Thomas by R. B. Kershner, Jr.
Langston Hughes by Richard K. Barksdale

Grateful acknowledgment is made to Alfred A. Knopf, Inc., for
permission to quote from the copyrighted works of Wallace Stevens.
Journal entries from SOUVENIRS AND PROPHECIES: THE
YOUNG WALLACE STEVENS by Holly Stevens, pp. 55, 107, and
109-10 are reproduced by permission of The Huntington Library,
San Marino, California.

LIBRARY OF CONGRESS CATALOGING IN PUBLICATION DATA
Willard, Abbie F
    Wallace Stevens : the poet and his critics.
    (The Poet and his critics)
    Bibliography: p.
    Includes index.
    1. Stevens, Wallace, 1879–1955—Criticism and
    interpretation—History.
PS3537.T4753Z95   811'.5'2   78-8150
ISBN 0-8389-0267-7

Copyright © 1978 by the American Library Association

All rights reserved. No part of this publication may be reproduced
in any form without permission in writing from the publisher,
except by a reviewer who may quote brief passages in a review.

Printed in the United States of America

For
A.K.W.
and
G.W.W.

11-13-81 /bry ATcS

Contents

Acknowledgments

Grateful acknowledgment must be made to Professor Charles Sanders of the University of Illinois whose enthusiasm was matched only by his patience in editing and his encouragement to the author. And, special thanks also go to Christine Burroughs, librarian at the University of Georgia, for her aid in securing necessary periodicals and research space.

Preface

Unlike most artists, Wallace Stevens was successful as both a business executive and a poet. During his lengthy career as vice president of the Hartford Accident and Indemnity Company he continued to write verse, persisting in both vocations until shortly before his death. Because of his dual role, and because of his prolific publications, critics have been attracted to him as an anomaly and as an important force in twentieth-century poetry. Yet, in over fifty years of criticism all that has been definitively decided is Stevens's important place in modern literature. How he developed, what influenced him, whom he emulated, how he viewed the world, or even what form he chose for his art are still issues for debate. Stevens himself contributed to the speculations when he varied, qualified, explained, or evaded his own previous statements. Because of the continuing debate and Stevens's role in it, this study examines the major issues of critical concern, but also discusses Stevens's contribution to the interpretation of his own work. The study is not an annotated bibliography but rather a selective and evaluative study, divided into chapters according to the issues most frequently discussed in Stevens criticism. The chapters are arranged for smoothest thematic transition and move from the most basic concern, Stevens's development as a poet, gradually into broader, more complex themes which conclude with the poet speaking for himself on those themes.

Chapter 1 discusses Stevens's chronological development from the three perspectives most frequently encountered in studies about Stevens. These perspectives include those critics who contend that Stevens progressed, those who argue that any change in theme or technique was caused by pressures of the age, and those who suggest that the poet's work never changed. Chapter 2 examines the influences on Stevens's development with particular emphasis on the literary movements that affected the poet. These movements

and schools include the American Adamic tradition, the French
Symboliste and British Romantic movements, as well as the modernist and metaphysical schools. Chapter 3 builds on the first two
by seeking to define the aesthetic forms Stevens chose for the basis
of his evolving style. Because of the poet's experimentation with
different modes, any analysis of his form requires a discussion of
the various genres with which he experimented. Throughout his
career, Stevens borrowed techniques and themes from genres other
than his own. To best describe this tendency, chapter 3 examines
the criticism on Stevens as philosophical poet, painterly poet, musical poet, and psychological poet.

Inherent in the poet's manipulation of genre, one finds a world
view that seeks to integrate the forces of reality and imagination.
Chapter 4 discusses Stevens's world view as it has been paraphrased
and interpreted by critics. The poet's way of conceptualizing and
communicating his multidisciplinary world required an ambiguous,
often diffuse, rhetorical style. Faced with this difficult style, many
critics attempt to explicate Stevens's theory of poetry, his poetic
practice, and his definition of man, but they seldom advance beyond mere quotation or restatement of the poet's original source.
Chapter 5 then reviews the original sources, Stevens's own comments on himself and his world. In lecture, essay, and letter form,
he provides an example of self-criticism at its best and worse.

Within each chapter individual studies are arranged thematically
rather than chronologically and are subsumed under major chapter
divisions and more specific subdivisions that are noted only when
clear distinctions in focus or differences of opinion surface in the
review of a particular thematic area in the criticism. This structure
is utilized because the critics very quickly aligned themselves with
one another on the questions of development, influence, genre, and
world view. A chronological review of the same criticism, except
where noted, reveals no decisive trends in mass critical thinking.
Most studies, because of diversity in many critics' comments,
could be included under numerous thematic categories. Such
studies are placed, according to their primary focus, in chapters
most appropriate for that focus. Where critics have made penetrating comments in more than one area of concern, they are included in more than one chapter. Following each chapter, a list of
references is included, and at the end of the book a list of selected
additional readings that includes checklists, bibliographies, special
issues, and collections on Stevens may be found. Individual studies
from many of these special issues and collections are often discussed within particular chapters. Such studies were chosen for

inclusion because of their relevance to the themes predominating in Stevens criticism and because of their contribution to the body of critical information. Where entire journal issues or collections are devoted to one such Stevens theme, that issue, in its entirety, is included in the appropriate chapter. Book reviews of Stevens's various volumes are also included only when they provide unique, noteworthy, or insightful comments on the important Stevens themes. When reviews or longer studies are reprinted in other than original sources, the most accessible source is usually noted. Because many such reviews and studies focus on one specific poem but add little to the general understanding of Stevens, explication notes are included only when they discuss themes of greater import.

In general, WALLACE STEVENS: THE POET AND HIS CRITICS is a study prepared for the educated or novice reader of literature and for the merely interested or specialist in poetry as well. While bibliographical completeness is sacrificed for thematic coherence, comprehensiveness is attempted in a thorough review of all criticism pertinent to the predominant issues in Stevens's poetry. This study then selects, arranges, and assesses criticism that continues to proliferate as the poet's reputation grows. Responding to this increasing volume, directions for future study are also suggested. If Wallace Stevens's poems in their development are the beginning point of this study, his comments on their method and substance, his prose, should provide not an end, but a direction for future critical analysis.

CHAPTER 1

Chronology

> When one is young everything is
> physical; when one is old every-
> thing is psychic.
>
> WALLACE STEVENS "ADAGIA"

Wallace Stevens's development as a poet has been a source of repeated critical examination because of the length of his poetic career spanning over half a century, and because of Stevens's own insistence that poetry like life must acknowledge and accommodate constant fluctuation in man's experience and his perceptions of that experience. The chronology of Stevens's development has therefore been a source of inquiry: does the poet's skill steadily increase or decrease; is his long career divisible by phases of varying style and theme; do his poems, life, and times interact in any meaningful way; or do his numerous poems in varying forms simply expound on variations of a single theme? The critics are still debating, but have delineated two opposing perspectives on the chronological development of Stevens's oeuvre. By far the majority, many critics have examined the canon as exemplary of a poet who progressed through several distinct phases of development. Others, in a far more limited minority that focuses primarily on common themes and techniques throughout the poet's work, view Stevens as an artist who created, without change or development, a unified grand poem. These two different approaches to Stevens's chronology will be discussed in the descending order of their popularity, and will be followed by a brief discussion of critics who review not the development of a poet, but the chronology of their own criticism on that poet.

The Phases of Development:
A Poet in Progressive Change

Many of the studies that examine Stevens's work attempt to discuss and explain the total gestalt of the poet's career. In order to structure such mammoth overviews, critics have arranged their

1

attempts by introducing biographical background as it relates to the poetry; by tracing in their comments the chronology of the poetry's developing techniques and theory; or by emphasizing specific periods of development.

Chronology Examined through Biography

The biographically oriented critics are best represented by Samuel French Morse, the poet's official biographer and the critic who most explicitly extends chronology into the realm of biography. Morse's study, *Wallace Stevens: Poetry As Life* (1970), in the Pegasus American Author's series is based on the premise that Stevens's life and poetry are closely integrated. Although Morse's study was to have been a definitive biography, the critic's attention to poetic technique and development far exceeds his efforts in unearthing lost details of the poet's life. Yet, Morse attempts throughout his study to relate individual poems to specific periods and phases in Sevens's life. Morse is therefore an exemplary biographically oriented critic, though he is hardly a biographer. What emerges in Morse's work to make it most illustrative of biographical criticism is the critic's contention, appropriate to Stevens's own beliefs, that being and creation are interrelated and that ultimately life and poetry issue from the same source.

Appropriate to this thesis, Morse divides the poet's life/art into four phases: juvenilia of 1879–1916, *Harmonium* years 1914–30, reevaluation period 1930-45, and the mellowed late poems of 1945-55. In each of these phases Morse notes a predominant poetic concern. Stevens's attention to manipulations of color, light, images, and words in the "gaudy" poems such as "Sea Surface Full of Clouds" and "The Emperor of Ice-Cream" of the *Harmonium* period are replaced by a transitional reexamination of poetic techniques as Stevens reevaluated art itself in the 1930s volumes *Owl's Clover* and *The Man with the Blue Guitar*. Morse assesses the attempts of this decade as poetic failures and explains poems of the 1940s such as "Notes Toward a Supreme Fiction" as works in which the poet is attempting to reestablish his relation to the world and to preserve the artistic self as well as the value of the external world which seemed so threatened by the political events of the 1930s. The final phase, evident in poems such as those in *The Rock* group, focuses on the actuality of everyday life, the transparent world view of the poet, and the poet's acceptance of the intermingling reality and imagination. While these phases provide the very structure and substance of Morse's study, they also indicate the divisions most critics acknowledge in Stevens's work. Throughout his discussion of phases and poems, Morse examines the poems as illustrations and records of actual moments (or the desire to achieve such moments) in the poet's life. He derives this approach from Stevens's claim that being and creating extensions of imaginative reality were the stuff of life and of art; and Morse develops this approach by intermingling facts of the poet's life and criticism of the poet's art.

In Stevens's earliest phase, 1879–1916, Morse finds evidence of Stevens's positive regard for his home, parents, and Dutch heritage, translated in later poems to a respect for ancestral values. In Stevens's *Harmonium* years of 1914–30, Morse notes the wit and playfulness of a youthful Harvard man and the poetic concern with "things as they are" and "things as they seem." So interrelated are Stevens's life and art during this period, that the poet compiles "The Little June Book" of verse for his future wife, but also publishes five selections from this in his "Carnet de Voyage," his first group of post-Harvard verse to become public. Morse extends his dual glance at the poet's life and art in this phase when he labels "Peter Quince at the Clavier" as Stevens's version of a law-yer's love poem. If the poet's chosen vocation of law interacted at all with his avocation, poetry, it did so as a stimulus for activity beyond that of a law office, for Morse perceptively tells us that Stevens failed at his first job, journalism, because it was too mundane for his poetic tastes.

In the third phase of development, 1930–45, because he was gaining professional and financial security, Stevens returns to his art after a lengthy dormant period. The events of the poet's life then, according to Morse, inspire the poet's values that led to the creation of a complacent art apart from the demands of politics and social order. The security which Stevens experienced during this period also provided him with the time and predisposition to reexamine and reevaluate his own work and the function of art. This obviously led, in poems and correspondence between 1935–41, to a more theoretical poetry. Similarly, in this period, the poet's interest in art led not only to his acquisition of paintings by Brianchon, Cavallés, Brayer, Marchand, Ceria, Lebasque, and Labasque, but also to a growing emphasis on the visual image and perception in his verse. The relationship between art and life is here so close, according to Morse, that Stevens recreates a painting he acquired by Tal Coat in his own poem "Angel Surrounded by Paysans."

Finally, in the last phase, the late years 1945–55, Stevens turns, in Morse's view, to a gentler, more discursive verse communicated in the "plainness of speech" that the aging process brought on Stevens as man and artist. While such relations between biography and poetic development concern Morse, as critic he also evaluates the artistic themes and techniques in the phases of development. Stevens's first published volume *Harmonium* is labeled witty and irreverent by Morse, with an "essential gaudiness" in its nature emphasized by the arrangement of the poems. Of the 1930s poems, Morse judges "Owl's Clover" and "The Man with the Blue Guitar" pivotal poems because of their reexamination of the artist's role. The former defies the world pressures of the 1930s to make poetry the poet's personal outpouring of suffering, misery, or injustice; and the latter examines the poet's task as a painter's task of realization. Morse suggests that Stevens was forced to further artistic evaluation in the 1940s when Hi Simons, a Chicago publisher, became interested in Stevens's work while preparing a bibliography of the poet. Simons's letters of inquiry to Stevens stimulated Stevens to turn his attention from stylistic maneuvers to aesthetic considerations. Morse perceptively notes that the figure of the poet began to appear as persona in the poetry about the time of this correspondence between Stevens and Simons. According to Morse, when Stevens began his early 1940s poems, the persona is not readily identifiable, and the poems therefore seem to lack a recognizable human voice. These poems also turn their attention to things and to defining the role of a poet in times hostile to poetry, but lack, in Morse's view, the brilliance of *Harmonium* and the mellowed discursiveness of the last years.

Morse seems most positive toward the final poems and finds them so complete in their integration of poetry and poet's life that he notes the poems and letters of this period preclude the need for biography. Here the reader of Morse feels cheated. If the juvenilia and early volumes were influenced by the experiences and acquaintances of Stevens, the activities and friends of the aging poet are no less relevant to his poetic confrontation with and acceptance of the natural world and man's mortal place in it. Morse terms Stevens's latest poems in *The Rock* the poet's ultimate triumph of grandeur through simplicity, and yet he tells us less about the world and life of the poet during this period of "triumph" than about any other phase in Stevens's long career.

The examination of juvenilia in Morse's study distinguishes this critic's approach from many others. Morse's book is one of the few to describe Stevens's Harvard poems as important to the poet's published canon, but like many other studies, Morse's accurately notes the importance of George Santayana to the Stevens of the

Harvard years and later. Morse's comments, however, are most helpful not in tracing the influence of this philosopher and critic teaching at Harvard while Stevens was a student there, but in describing how Stevens's writings in these early years prefigure the later published verse. Morse praises the comic stories which, like Stevens's later work, are concerned with things as they are and things as they seem, but Morse distinguishes these in quality from the more maudlin and mimetic sonnets of the same college years. In the six Stevens poems published in 1900, selections from "Ballade of the Pink Parasol," "Outside the Hospital," and "Street Songs" indicate to Morse the first hint of *Harmonium*'s greatness.

In the next period of Stevens's life, 1914–30, Morse lodges the first obvious evidence of Stevens's originality and promise. Reviewing a poem from this period, "For an Old Woman in a Wig," Morse discusses the poet's growing mastery of craft and subject matter as well as the seldom mentioned link from juvenilia to *Harmonium*. According to this critic, "For an Old Woman in a Wig" not only provides a transition from the Harvard sonnets to the masterful and sophisticated "Sunday Morning" or "A High-Toned Old Christian Woman," but also prefigures, in its terza rima form, the tristich stanza, a hallmark of Stevens verse.

Morse juxtaposes such analyses with bits of information about the poet's life and with speculative interpretations of the poet's motives in that life and art. The critic delves into such speculation when he notes that Stevens, like the poet's father, felt a need for privacy. He speculates even further about the poet's relationship with his mother, noting that the years 1910–15 are sparsely documented. The lack of documentation, an inherent problem with biographical criticism, reveals Morse at his weakest. Yet Morse's discussion of Stevens's brief career with the *Herald Tribune* in New York; his analysis of Stevens's feeling of warmth toward his ancestral and familial Dutch heritage; his account of Elsie, Stevens's wife, as the model for the bust on the 1916 "liberty head" dime and half-dollar; and his reliance on the personal recollections of such Stevens acquaintances as Carl Van Vechten and Alfred Kreymborg provide, as any biographical approach should, a sense of the human in the artist.

If Morse does evade extensive discussion of the life and art of the aging poet, he is certainly more detailed in his anecdotes from the early years and his attempts to relate life and art in the middle years. Yet, the reader cannot help asking for more about Stevens the man and less about the poems as art. Because the Morse study is the only one to date purported to be biographical in emphasis, it is the only key to the man apart from his art. Morse's assumption, that for Stevens poetry and life are one, is a valid one and demands a critical approach that combines the two. Yet a discussion that completely equates Stevens's life and art, as appropriate as it is to Stevens's aesthetic theory, does not provide the full perspective on the life of the man. Instead, it simply combines an analysis of selected poems with bits of biographical fact and speculation. The result is an interesting though sketchy approach to the poet, but not a fully developed and thorough account of the man's life.

Like Morse, Frank Kermode in *Wallace Stevens* (1960) provides a general overview that intermingles well-founded explication, a touch of biography, some discussion of Stevens's poetic philosophy, and some analysis of his poetic techniques. This and Kermode's brief review of important criticism might provide the novice reader of Stevens with a guide to important issues, but unfortunately those issues are not appropriately emphasized or related. Unlike Morse, Kermode fails to specify why he freely mixes discussion of various elements in the poet's life and art. In one paragraph alone he describes Stevens's physical appearance; recalls Harriet Monroe's impression of the poet; considers two of the poet's plays; notes influences in symbolist theory, Mallarmé, and Japanese Nō drama; and jumps into a summary of the mature verse. Here, as elsewhere in Kermode, varying themes are noted but immediately discarded without development, expansion, or clear specification of their relationships to one another. And, unlike Morse, Kermode fails to sustain a discussion of biography and chronology, because Kermode, in approaching this theme and others, seems to lose interest in such a structured approach.

Kermode devotes his opening chapter to a discussion of the poet's life including Stevens's dictate that poetry, the material for poetry, and reality are interrelated. After this brief introduction, Kermode's study provides a loose chronological description of the *Harmonium* years (chapter 2), the middle years (chapter 3), the prose works (interjected as chapter 4 because most were written in the forties and early fifties), the maturing years (chapter 5), and the last poems (chapter 6). Unlike Morse, Kermode begins with the Stevens life and art of the *Harmonium* period, and only briefly alludes to an earlier publishing life for the poet, waving away any consideration of this period by relying solely on Stevens's parable of Zeller life (his maternal grandparents) found in *The Necessary Angel*. This nonchalant approach to early Stevens influences Kermode's judgment of the poetry itself. He criticizes the early manner as "gaudy" and as "Imagist scraps," thereby underestimating the innovativeness of Stevens's *Harmonium* work, but qualifying this assertion with praise for the "gaiety," "variety," and "power" of these poems.

According to Kermode, in *Harmonium* Stevens defines the outlines of his world as a nonrational world in which reality arranges itself into poems with a gaudy texture necessary to communicate the strangeness of that reality. Kermode does not use the adjective "gaudy" pejoratively but rather as a synonym for the gaiety and precision of Stevens's language. He also stresses the importance of recognizing the *Harmonium* themes that bind the great early poetry with the greater poetry of old age. The themes and images common throughout Stevens's poetry are, according to Kermode, the seasons as an analogue for the cyclical nature of human life and the creative imagination; the imagination as man's defense against the "poverty of fact"; and the sense of loss in the face of death and decay. In *Ideas of Order* Kermode finds this elegiac acceptance of mortality becoming more prevalent while foreshadowing the meditations of the last poems. He describes the meditative mode that in "The Idea of Order at Key West" of this volume "quietly breeds its own richness of internal reference" (p. 57). In comparison, the poems of *Owl's Clover* are "total failures" followed by an advance toward mature form found in *The Man with the Blue Guitar*. He praises the title poem of this volume for its rhythm, diction, and couplet form, but notes that it lacks the "emotional progression" of the later *Notes Toward a Supreme Fiction*. Although *Parts of a World* is an indispensable prelude to *Notes*, according to Kermode, it is hardly his favorite volume. But he does, despite this fact, objectively identify its developing elements so important to *Notes:* the theme of reality and the hero interacting, the fortuity of poetic discovery, the imagery of changing weather, and the complementary nature of animal consciousness imposing order while human consciousness discovers it.

Kermode examines *Transport to Summer* and *The Auroras of Autumn* as manifestations of Stevens's most prolific period, but he criticizes the multiple short poems for diluting metaphysics with fable and praises the longer "Credences of Summer." "Notes toward a Supreme Fiction" is undoubtedly Stevens's masterpiece, in Kermode's view, because it blends the fortuitous and the meditative as well as intensifies the themes and doctrines of earlier poems. Kermode extends his praise to the final volume, *The Rock*, in which he finds twenty-five poems of "undiminished power."

Among the best of all Stevens's works are the late "To an Old
Philosopher in Rome," "The World as Meditation," and "The
Rock," but these poems are to Kermode simply completed elab-
orations on the skeletal structure erected in *Harmonium*.

Although such opinions are well-founded, Kermode's main contribution to Stevens criticism is his attempt to move beyond biography and chronology by relating Stevens's prose to his poetry.
While many critics mention such a relationship, Kermode refines
the combined theory and practice approach by integrating specific Stevens lectures and essays with specific poems. This and
Kermode's summary of some fundamental characteristics of Stevens as artist are quite helpful; but his lack of explicit emphasis on
defined relationships between events in Stevens's life and art makes
his intermingling of biography, criticism, and chronology appear
at times to approach chaos.

In a later study, *Continuities* (1968, pp. 77-91), Kermode extends his analysis of the relationship between poetry and prose by
examining the chronology of the *Collected Letters* as a parallel to
the poetry. He views these letters as crucial, not for elucidating
specific poems but as indications of Stevens's preoccupation with
the nature of modern poetry; and he views them as part of a "paraphilosophical game" in which Stevens thinks on paper as he does
in some of the poems. The early letters expose Stevens as a very
private person speculating about life, but the letters of the war
years after his self-confessed failure, *Owl's Clover*, steadily increase
in their attention to the theory of poetry. According to Kermode,
Stevens achieved his "most authentic and fluent speech" in this
period of examination, the period in which he wrote *Notes
Toward a Supreme Fiction*. Kermode boldly and accurately asserts that criticism has failed to explain this poetry because most
critics treat the entire oeuvre rather than single poems, thereby
forcing discreet poems into one false whole; strip Stevens's world
then attempt to reassemble it; or attempt to explain the cognitive
thought in his poetry that defies exposition. To remedy this, Kermode calls for a focus on the particulars of each poem and the
self within it. In *Continuities*, as in his earlier book, Kermode
merges scholarship and informal style in an appealing and absorbing mixture. His unique way of noting and communicating relationships between disparates, as well as his irreverent and atraditional approach to criticism are refreshing. He mixes freely the
diction of speech, poetry, and scholarship to describe an intermingling of life, letters, poems, and language in the poet he discusses. And because he confines himself to a brief examination of

parallel chronological development in the poems and letters, Kermode does not weaken this study with undeveloped emphasis and unspecified relationships as he does in his earlier work.

Aside from these two critics who devote book-length stud.es to the interrelated biographical and chronological development of the poet, numerous reviewers have noted or briefly discussed the man and poet as he developed. This approach in passing or in depth predominates because of the apparent fascination most critics experience when confronted by a poet who also happened to be an insurance executive. If this phenomenon inspires more frequent mention of the poet's real life, it also inspired in the poet a doggedness in segregating his real life of business and family from his imagination's life in poetry. In this irony one finds the flame that both attracts the critic and insures critical incompleteness. The poet who shuns examination as a man in the world lends himself more readily in his art to the exegesis of more easily discerned technique and theory.

Chronology Examined through Technique and Theory

Of those critics who devote more attention to the technique and theory as manifestations of the chronology, two provide the best book-length studies available on the poet. A study by Helen Hennessy Vendler and one by Joseph N. Riddel examine chronology as an internal development, inherently related to changes in the poet's theory and technique. This approach provides an interesting contrast to that found in Morse and Kermode who find the phases of chronological development more closely bound with biographical extensions.

Joseph N. Riddel's *The Clairvoyant Eye* (1967) examines the poet's work with a historical and chronological perspective that nonetheless discriminates between the quality of the poet's early and late techniques. As Riddel states, his study is intended as a compilation of readings that focus on both the individual poems and the chronological development of Stevens's verse. Riddel's approach is appropriate because of his thesis that Stevens's theory of imagination is inherently bound to the poet's changes in and development of style. While Riddel does occasionally provide a historical perspective on this development, he nonetheless devotes primary attention to the explication of individual poems. For Riddel then, Stevens's theory of poetry and continuity of development are interrelated in a way that requires attention to specific selections, but selections as they evolve and emerge in a chronological progression inherent in the changing and aging of any poet's sensibility.

Because this thesis demands attention to style, technique, and theme, it does not relegate the chronological perspective to a secondary role as background, but incorporates consideration of chronology in the analysis of theme and technique. And, this thesis forces Riddel to examine Stevens's changing theory and evolving style as inherently related aspects in the poet's phases of chronological development. Riddel uses Stevens's longer poems (which he terms the poet's greatest achievement) to elucidate Stevens's theory of the imagination and to explain how that changing theory parallels chronological changes in the poet's style. After initially examining Stevens's prose, Riddel treats the poetry in five phases with each phase discussed in a chapter which begins with a commentary on the history of the time and its informing ideas, then moves to a consideration of individual poems culminating in the examination of at least one long poem. Here, the study resembles Morse's in its basic assumption that poetry was for Stevens creating oneself and that living was figuratively and literally a part of poetry, but Riddel's study is far more tightly structured in its discussion of this theme.

Riddel suggests that Stevens's achievement must not be measured in individual poems but in the continuity of his work. That continuity is based on the theme "poetry as the subject of poetry" and the development of that theme as Stevens's thought became progressively more intensified and his style concomitantly more stripped. Although Riddel believes that to deny Stevens developed is also to deny his greatness, he nonetheless does not value the progression to the later poetry at the expense of the earlier. He finds in *Harmonium* the strengths of alternating gaiety and world-weariness, an extensive musical range, a sense of wit, and a masterful craftsmanship. The sensuous energy of this first volume is refined by the poet into the reflection and statement of later volumes, a process which, according to Riddel, is meaningful because, by evolving a style, Stevens created a sensibility and moved further in aesthetic adventure toward an ultimate form or wholeness. If such vague, general terms as "sensibility" and "aesthetic adventure" detract from the explicitness of Riddel's argument, he redeems himself with the astute description of development when he notes that images in Stevens's late poetry are "no longer the tenor of perception but the vehicle of mediation" (p. 10). Riddel's emphasis on the poetry as developing whole is further exemplified by his view of *Harmonium* in light of the entire canon rather than vice versa, and his opinion that *Harmonium* is not Imagist, Symbolist, or Hedonist poetry as most critics maintain, but an in- ward poetry juxtaposing delight and despair. Examined in these terms, *Harmonium* is described by the critic as a precursor to the later meditative mode.

Riddel completes his discussion of *Harmonium*'s position in the total poetic effort with explications of poems such as "Peter Quince at the Clavier," "Sunday Morning," and "Le Monocle de Mon Oncle." His isolation of the predominant themes in these selections provides a meaningful perspective for each of the poems: "Peter Quince" deals with the preservation of art in the world of flux; "Sunday Morning" manipulates Christian imagery in an antitraditional way to produce a Pater-like interviewing of Christian imagery and purely aesthetic form; and "Le Monocle" is a Prufrockian exercise in anxiety but with a non-Prufrockian affirmation in the presence of mortality. These themes—art's mod- ern role, the quest for meaning amid discarded traditionalism and myth, and pessimism coupled with acceptance of mortality—cul- minate in the longest poem of this early period, "The Comedian as the Letter C." Riddel is more enlightening than many critics in his discussion of themes in these individual poems, and he is also more aware of the seriousness inherent in these early themes He notes that though *Harmonium* communicates delight in living in the physical world, disillusionment is evident in "Anatomy of Monotony," a grievance is expressed in "Banal Sojourn," disquie- tude surfaces in "Lunar Paraphrase," and pessimism is transcended only with the occasional affirmation in poems such as "Le Mon- ocle" or with irony in poems such as "The Comedian."

Like Morse, Riddel suggests that the thirties threatened Ste- vens's poetry with ideology and caused a change in the poet's tone if not in his theme. Both critics describe Stevens's preoccupation with the artist in this world, but Riddel is more attentive than Morse to the changes in style that accompany this preoccupation. In *Ideas of Order*, Stevens's second volume, Riddel finds a signifi- cant reduction in irony and sensuous detail as well as a new em- phasis on metaphoric nuance rather than precise imagery. Riddel devotes more attention to *Ideas of Order* than Morse does, but views it only as traditional poetry naturally growing out of *Har- monium*. According to Riddel, the themes of the first volume are present in the second as Stevens reexamines the poet's responsibil- ity to reality, the formlessness of the modern world, man's need for order, the natural world in opposition to an artificial order, and death as an issue in any idea of order.

Owl's Clover is less successful than either earlier volume, but like *Ideas of Order* is judged important by Riddel because of its place in Stevens's total development. Although resorting to argument in *Owl's Clover*, Stevens begins to use a dialectical rather than a narrative or lyrical progression. Riddel contends that this dialectical structure coupled with a new intellectual emphasis in the lyric form foreshadow Stevens's late style. *Owl's Clover* ultimately fails, however, not because of the innovative combination of dialectic and lyric, but because those modes are combined in a loose, rambling fashion with no ordering principle other than Stevens's idea that the imagination is a faculty shared by all men; and because the dialectic functions not as intellectual emphasis within lyric form, but as political argument for the poet's right to create in a disordered world. Although *Owl's Clover* is one of Stevens's worst creations, the succeeding volume, *The Man with the Blue Guitar* is Stevens's poetry of the thirties at its best and worst. The disorder in *Owl's Clover* is forced into an improvisational structure, a manifestation of the poet's emerging mature style, while the *Owl's Clover* theme of creativity struggling to exist in the ruins of modern society, in *Blue Guitar* characterizes man as stripped of all but his being. In the latter Riddel also finds Stevens beginning his search for a myth to replace the myth of God. Here Riddel errs because the beginnings of such a search may be found in poems as early as "Sunday Morning" and "The Comedian as the Letter C." Yet, Riddel accurately notes that *Blue Guitar* succeeds where its predecessor failed because in it Stevens emphasizes the lyrical mode in combination with an improvisational dialectic, rather than utilizes argumentative dialectic at the expense of lyrical flow.

The most crucial period in the poet's development follows *The Man with the Blue Guitar*, according to Riddel. The years between 1937 and 1942 culminate in the publication of *Parts of a World* in which Stevens accomplishes his chronological transition from the early to the late style and in which he specifies the preoccupations of his last years. *Parts of a World*, Riddel contends, is characterized by short academic exercises in defining perception or by lengthy examinations of the hero figure, but it is also characterized by a craftsmanship unmatched in the earlier volumes. This craftsmanship is realized in a style based on assertion, formulation, and exposition aimed at creating a sense of the perceptual process. In the longer poems of this volume, Riddel finds the preparatory exercises necessary for the poetic climax, "Notes Toward a Supreme Fiction." According to this critic, all that pre-

cedes this poem is building toward its synthesis of intellectual
lyric and discursive statement, rational argument and improvisational anecdote, and all that succeeds this poem is simply a refinement of the mode it establishes.

Transport to Summer, the volume to follow Parts of a World,
is more specialized in its focus, Riddel asserts, because this volume
examines (by analyzing metaphors and the motive for metaphor)
the very devices poetry manipulates. The shorter poems of the
volume are examined by Riddel as mere footnotes to the longer
poems such as "Esthétique du Mal" and "Credences of Summer,"
but the importance of the volume is emphasized by the critic
when he notes it contains Stevens's first truly meditative exercise,
"Credences of Summer," and when he labels it the first major
volume after Harmonium. Riddel describes both Harmonium and
Transport as similar in theme, but qualifies his comparison by noting the muted quality of the themes in the earlier volume and their
more blatant expression in the later verse. In the meditative exercise from Transport, "Credences of Summer," the poet exhibits
a control of his tone coupled with a sensitivity to fine nuance
which recall Harmonium. By the time of "Credences" the perceptions are a part of the poet's inner world instead of a reporting of
the outer reality. The abstractions of such an inner world reach
their epitome in The Auroras of Autumn, a volume to follow
Transport and one more difficult to grasp or to defend. Riddel
characterizes Auroras as a natural answer to the question posed in
Transport: "What can man ultimately know?" According to
Riddel, Stevens answers "forms of his own conceiving." In
Auroras Stevens is trying to extend the boundaries of poetry to
encompass presentation of the mind in the act of creating and decreating. The strengths of such an attempt are also its weaknesses,
Riddel suggests. The lulling repetitions and deliberate abstractions
are coupled with less humor and wordplay as Stevens's tone becomes almost religious in promoting his secular belief in the
solipsistic power of the imagination.

Riddel extends this continuing analysis of changing theme and
style when he notes that the intellectual lyric form becomes a
"ruminative solemnity" in Stevens's final group of poems, The
Rock. Riddel's opinion of the poet's final attempt is mixed. Like
many critics, he finds in "To an Old Philosopher in Rome" the
supreme achievement of Stevens's latest work, but he describes
the longer, more ambitious "An Ordinary Evening in New
Haven" as loose in structure, aphoristic in execution, and platitu-
dinous in tone. His ultimate verdict, that Stevens's approach to

poetry is from start to finish the equation of a theory of poetry
and a theory of life, reaffirms the conclusion of Stevens's biographer, Morse. Yet, in general, Riddel's study is more enlightening
than Morse's, especially since it precedes the Morse study and
more thoroughly examines the troublesome Stevens of the thirties.
Riddel, at his best when he discusses the specific elements and
development of Stevens's style, includes many passing and perceptive comments on that style as it relates to the style of poets such
as Williams, Pound, Moore, Eliot, and Cummings. This critic's
ability to isolate the specific characteristics of the developing style
is helpful to the new and the seasoned reader of Stevens as are the
extensive footnotes summarizing various influences on Stevens's
poetry. As the critic most apparently well read in Stevens criticism, Riddel is also one of the most sensitive and perceptive in
defining poetic theme and style while confronting both weaknesses and strengths in the poet's chronological development.

Like Riddel, Helen Hennessy Vendler in her *On Extended
Wings: Wallace Stevens's Longer Poems* (1969) emphasizes the
importance of Stevens's longer poems to his overall development,
and in so doing, contributes one of the most perceptive analyses
of Stevens's internally developing chronology. Vendler views these
longer poems as characteristic pieces in each period of Stevens's
life and as his most successful verse. Asserting that Stevens's ultimate subject, the creation of an "authentic and fluent speech,"
evolves through a search for his personal poetic style, Vendler
resembles Riddel in her double approach to reading Stevens. She
examines the long poems as individual entities but also as steps
in an extended poetic progression of phases in which words are
"realized" as a personal and poetic sense of the world. She differs
with many critics in her opinion that Stevens is a poet of feeling
rather than of doctrine and in her preference for "The Snow
Man" over "Peter Quince at the Clavier" and for "The Auroras
of Autumn" over "Sunday Morning," but her extended evaluation of chronologically developing changes in Stevens's style and
subject as the key to his poetics is shared with critics such as
Riddel.

Throughout Stevens's longer poems Vendler finds three manners: an ecstatic idiom that proclaims joy in life; an apathetic idiom
that despairs of a withered life; and, the most characteristic of
Stevens, a tentative search for a route between ecstasy and despair. Vendler is most proficient in isolating the syntactic particulars of Stevens's manner as she notes his diction of uncertainty
that suggests the tentative nature of his conclusions, and as she

notes his tendency to deemphasize the conditional nature of his propositions by syntactically requiring that multiple phrases, clauses, and meaning depend on a propositional sequence. Vendler isolates his use of questions not as interrogations but as a qualified way to make a statement; his intermingling of conditional and present tense to integrate speculation and fact; and his achievement of a timeless state by utilization of a tenseless infinitive or by creation of a future tense in the combination of a present tense verb with "when" or "until." And she relates these stylistic idiosyncrasies to the poems themselves when she accurately assesses the interaction between constructional and thematic elements in, for example, "The Idea of Order at Key West."

> She sang beyond the genius of the sea.
> The water never formed to mind or voice,
> Like a body wholly body, fluttering
> Its empty sleeves; and yet its mimic motion
> Made constant cry, caused constantly a cry,
> That was not ours although we understood,
> Inhuman, of the veritable ocean.
>
> The sea was not a mask. No more was she.
> The song and water were not medleyed sound
> Even if what she sang was what she heard,
> Since what she sang was uttered word by word.
> It may be that in all her phrases stirred
> The grinding water and the gasping wind;
> But it was she and not the sea we heard.
>
> For she was the maker of the song she sang.
> The ever-hooded, tragic-gestured sea
> Was merely a place by which she walked to sing.
> Whose spirit is this? we said, because we knew
> It was the spirit that we sought and knew
> That we should ask this often as she sang.
>
> If it was only the dark voice of the sea
> That rose, or even colored by many waves;
> If it was only the outer voice of sky
> And cloud, of the sunken coral water-walled,
> However clear, it would have been deep air,
> The heaving speech of air, summer sound
> Repeated in a summer without end
> And sound alone. But it was more than that,

More even than her voice, and ours, among
The meaningless plungings of water and the wind,
Theatrical distances, bronze shadows heaped
On high horizons, mountainous atmospheres
Of sky and sea.

It was her voice that made
The sky acutest at its vanishing.
She measured to the hour its solitude.
She was the single artificer of the world
In which she sang. And when she sang, the sea,
Whatever self it had, became the self
That was her song, for she was the maker. Then we,
As we beheld her striding there alone,
Knew that there never was a world for her
Except the one she sang and, singing, made.

Ramon Fernandez, tell me, if you know,
Why, when the singing ended and we turned
Toward the town, tell why the glassy lights,
The lights in the fishing boats at anchor there,
As the night descended, tilting in the air,
Mastered the night and portioned out the sea,
Fixing emblazoned zones and fiery poles,
Arranging, deepening, enchanting night.

Oh! Blessed rage for order, pale Ramon,
The maker's rage to order words of the sea,
Words of the fragrant portals, dimly-starred,
And of ourselves and of our origins,
In ghostlier demarcations, keener sounds.

In this poem, according to the critic, a sequence of conditional terms—"even if . . . since . . . it . . . may be . . . if . . . or"—integrates the poetic images—sea, girl, water, song, wind, air, sky, cloud, voices—until they become indistinguishable from each other.

For Stevens's first phase, the *Harmonium* years, Vendler explicates "The Comedian as the Letter C," "Sunday Morning," and "Le Monocle de Mon Oncle" as exemplary of Stevens's early exercises exploiting a very physical, tropical world with two stylistic forms: an "artificial primitivism" evinced in a poem like "Earthy Anecdote" or "verbal mimetic reproduction" (p. 52) in a poem such as "The Comedian." She describes the poems of this period as resignation to the death of God in "Sunday Morning," as broad variations in mood when man confronts death in life or the aging process in "Le Monocle," and as an escape from the mournfulness of these two poems into the irony of "The Comedian."

As an example of Stevens's next volume, *Ideas of Order*, Vendler focuses her attention on "Like Decorations in a Nigger Cemetery," which she terms an experiment in epigram and a varied meditative form; but she finds the succeeding *Owl's Clover* a break from these experiments. According to Vendler, the emphasis on myth and the development of mythical entities in this volume are achieved through a reverential mythical style of luxuriant diction and unequivocal syntax. The myths are intermingled with social commentary in response to the Burnshaw review (to be discussed later in this chapter) and with reflections on the poem's primary image, the statue. Vendler, in her description of *Owl's Clover* as an experiment with satiric, social, and mythical modes that reveals to the poet the limits of rhetoric and topical allusion, is more kind to Stevens than Riddel is.

After this insight Stevens proceeded to write what Vendler terms his "declaration of independence" (p. 122), "The Man with the Blue Guitar." The poem is Stevens's return to the simple and basic in poetry: stripped vocabulary, syntax reduced to declarative sentence, and rhetoric reduced to simple indication. Even in the following volume, *Parts of a World*, Stevens's "disbelief in decoration" (p. 144) mars, for Vendler, poems such as "Study of Two Pears" and "Examination of the Hero in a Time of War" in which the poetic form combines mutually exclusive approaches to the imagery, factual recording, and eccentric fancy, and thereby confuses the tone.

> To grasp the hero, the eccentric
> On a horse, in a plane, at the piano—
> At the piano, scales, arpeggios
> And chords, the morning exercises,
> The afternoon's reading, the night's reflection,
> That's how to produce a virtuoso.
> The drill of a submarine. The voyage
> Beyond the oyster-beds, indigo
> Shadow, up the great sea and downward
> And darkly beside the vulcanic
> Sea-tower, sea pinnacles, sea-mountain.
> The signal . . . The sea-tower, shaken,
> Sways slightly and the pinnacles frisson.
> The mountain collapses. Chopiniana.

Other critics have pondered over the incongruity of image and emotion in Stevens' "Examination of the Hero," but only Vendler has stipulated the source of the disparity.

She also notes the importance of "Examination of the Hero" in establishing a rhetorical frame of multiple topic sentences which could be used as a model of composition in the later "Credences of Summer" and "Auroras of Autumn." Although these two later poems merit Vendler's discussion, she focuses her ultimate attention, like Riddel, on "Notes Toward a Supreme Fiction." In this example of Stevens's late genius, Vendler finds hints of the poet's earlier changes in tone, but she also finds his adoption of a new lyrical "I." The poem's strength she lodges in its allegorical personifications and in its juxtaposition of antithetical rhetoric; and the poem's importance she establishes by describing verses to follow as enumerations of old themes in old modes or mere jumbles of earlier style. In Vendler's estimation, the lyrical "I" adopted in "Notes" is further developed in "Credences of Summer" and "The Auroras of Autumn." She uniquely labels these two poems Stevens's "Allegro" and "Penseroso," but she values the latter poem more than the former. In Stevens's development of the aurora figure as correlative for change and for the poet's fear and fascination with the ongoing aging process, Vendler finds evidence of the poet at his most economical and most brilliant. The ambivalence toward the aging process so artfully communicated in "The Auroras" degenerates in "An Ordinary Evening in New Haven," the poet's last long poem, to examinations by an old man of the bareness in life. According to Vendler, the poem is sad in its unremitting minimalizations and weak in its redundancy coupled with randomness.

Indeed, the Vendler study is explicit in identifying Stevens's weaknesses as well as his strengths. But, because she confines her emphasis primarily to Stevens's long poems, she misses much that is valuable throughout the short poems. Her assessment of "Notes" as the climax of Stevens's career is valid, and her analysis of the struggle that characterizes this important poem is the most helpful of the poem's explications to date. Her attention to the short poems after "Notes" provides an accurate summary of a poet who turned from the withering in reality of life in the long poems to the transformations of such reality in the momentary meaning amid bleakness which short verse provides. In short, *On Extended Wings* is well written, well structured, perceptive, critical analysis that undoubtedly rivals Riddel's study as one of the best in Stevens criticism. Vendler combines the perspective of biography, mythic criticism, astute textual elucidation, unified construction, and critical objectivity to isolate and explain the difficulties of Stevens's poetics as they contribute to the individual poems and the chronological development. She is strongest in the explicit and precise communication of her approach to Wallace Stevens, and because his poetry seems clarified as a result of her clarity in approach, the book is one to be studied rather than quickly perused.

In comparison, other chronological studies of Stevens are far less satisfactory in design and execution. Merle Elliott Brown's book, *Wallace Stevens: The Poem as Act* (1970), like Vendler's and Riddel's, attempts to examine Stevens's poetry as it developed through the changing techniques and themes of the individual volumes. Similar to Vendler, Brown discusses the import of the longer poems, but unlike Vendler he is caught up in his own criticism rather than the actual poems. Brown deals with generalities of a philosophical nature, and when he moves in to examine an actual poetic line or phrase, he is so selective with the passages chosen and so unable to reintegrate poem selections with the whole critical argument, that his examinations of text are too few, too selective, and too isolated to clarify his argument or elucidate Stevens's poetics. The entire study might be characterized as a study in Brown's approach to criticism as it occasionally relates to his philosophical paraphrase of Stevens's general meaning in a chronological context. The structure of the volume itself lacks the cohesiveness of a Riddel or Vendler study: Brown's entire first chapter is devoted to his notes toward a supreme criticism and is followed by five chapters chronologically arranged as paraphrases of selected longer poems, a seventh chapter on social poetry in general, and a final chapter on Stevens's last poems of old age.

Brown's first chapter, "Criticism as the Animus of Poetry," because of its very subject, demands of the critic a discussion revealing the poet's ideas on the relation of criticism and poetry. Stevens's collected essays and adages in *The Necessary Angel* and *Opus Posthumous* as well as his *Collected Letters* provide extensive and complex if occasionally contradictory comments on this very relationship, yet Brown neglects even mentioning any of Stevens's comments on the subject. The critic briefly examines, in his discussion of *Harmonium*, "The Death of a Soldier," "Domination of Black," "On the Manner of Addressing Clouds," "Stars at Tallapoosa," "Le Monocle," and "The Comedian," but only mentions the "greatness" of "Sunday Morning" without including it in his discussion. Of "The Death of a Soldier" he notes, "One must, as critic, spin away and around and back to these stunning lines,

never wrapping them up in an anesthetizing formula, drawing
analogies which, in their very inadequacy, propel one back to the
sufficing act of the poem, which continues to turn and spin, even
if in crystal, in the permanence of infuriated words" (p. 41). The
reader is hardly enlightened by such descriptive passages or by the
analogies which Brown, as language contortionist, bends in his
metaphors.

After *Harmonium*, the poems written through *Transport to
Summer* are, according to Brown, poems of discovery. Poems of
this period like "The Idea of Order at Key West" or "Asides on
the Oboe" are Stevens at his most "revolutionary" or his most
"tragic." He judges "The Man with the Blue Guitar" Stevens's
first great long poem while he acknowledges the poem's lack of
narrative sequence; and he condemns "Notes Toward a Supreme
Fiction" for beginning and ending at the same point, the poet pro-
claiming that the world is seen in its purest form only by one who
responds to it with feeling. Like many critics floundering in the
complexity of Stevens, Brown resorts to paraphrase which in his
study lacks the clarity of the poem it is intended to expose. With
circular definitions part of his paraphrase, Brown uses Stevens's
terms to modify themselves when he says of "Notes," "This poet
sings monotony monotonously, or chaos chaotically" (p. 128). As
a result of such criticism the diction and meaning of the poem are
abstracted from their context and diluted.

After briefly comparing "Esthétique du Mal" to a poem by
Giacomo Leopardi, Brown abandons his chronological movement
for a discussion of Stevens's social poetry which he defines as
poetry with action, feeling, and thought of its own, autonomous
and therefore like "small societies." Here he discusses "Sunday
Morning," but moves quickly back into his chronology to examine Stevens's poems of old age characterized by the poet's awareness of withering, the estrangement of body and external objects,
and the oneness of opposites. Brown, in an attempt to meliorate
Stevens's confrontation of mortality, concludes his book with a
postscript claiming all is right in the world of poetry because of
Stevens's conclusions on the inevitability of aging and because
Stevens is not the end of a tradition but the beginning of a new
one. This postscript of simplistic resolution seems inappropriate for
a study which sought out the contradictions and paradoxes in the
poetry and refused, by its imprecise and paradoxical diction, to
resolve these incongruities in the poems.

To communicate the multiplicity and complexity of Stevens's
beliefs, Brown utilizes syntax and diction that are muddy in their

attempt to note all of the variations and nuances of apparent Stevens incongruities, rather than clear in an attempt to communicate ideas about basic meaning and technique in the poetry. One of Brown's comments on "Dutch Graves in Bucks County" provides an example: "These concluding lines of the poem make unmistakably clear the fact that this poem, though seeming only to affirm the discontinuity of American experience, is also affirming the continuity of this discontinuity" (p. 137). This style based on circular definition, juxtaposition of apparent mutually exclusive terms to qualify one another, paradox as elucidating opposites, and words with multiple denotations used in multiple ways in one sentence, becomes even more annoying in Brown's summary of "social poetry" in which Stevens "abandons his tradition of no tradition" allowing him to "turn his despair into a 'literate despair' and achieve a freedom of insight and awareness that goes beyond the servitude of his freedom" (p. 174). It is a style that intrudes often and communicates so little where so much is demanded. One might characterize Brown's study as he characterized Stevens's late poetry in which the mind "begins and ends with a oneness of a twoness" (p. 179). Such confusion exemplifies this study marred by repeated, distracting, self-conscious intrusions of Brown's own thought processes and wordplay.

This book-length study was preceded by a Brown article "Concordia Discors in the Poetry of Wallace Stevens" (*American Literature*, May 1962) which, although limited in scope, communicates some basic interpretive points in an undiluted manner. The essay deals only with three poems—"The Man with the Blue Guitar," "Notes," and "An Ordinary Evening in New Haven"— as examples of Stevens's middle, late, and final phases. Brown examines one theme common to the three poems—Stevens's concern with the ordinary man and the exceptional man living in harmony —in order to counteract the view that Stevens is "esoteric" and "obscure." In all three poems and periods, Brown suggests that Stevens uses "concordia discors," the identification of opposites, to reconcile the exceptional and the ordinary man. By limiting his scope and devoting more attention to poet and text rather than critical gymnastics, Brown is somewhat more successful in proposing a Stevens theme and supporting it with textual analysis. The article is hardly a "must" on any list of Stevens criticism, but it spares the reader the extended tedium of *Wallace Stevens: The Poem As Act*.

Like Brown, Lucy Beckett structures her *Wallace Stevens* (1974) along the chronological lines of Stevens's individually published volumes, and like many other chronologically-based critics she thereby divides the oeuvre into phases. Varying this order a bit, Beckett intermingles chapters devoted to specific volumes with chapters devoted to theoretical concerns of that volume's period. She prefaces her discussion on Stevens's first phase with an examination of what she terms the primary relationship in this first phase of development between George Santayana's philosophy and Stevens's poetry. According to Beckett, Santayana's vision of the poet's task is embedded throughout Stevens's poetry but is particularly evident in Stevens's essay "Imagination as Value" and his poetic tribute to Santayana, "To an Old Philosopher in Rome." Beckett denies any direct Santayana influence on Stevens's specific poems, noting only a brief relationship between the two men and failing to define its dimensions. Like Morse, she lodges Stevens's first phase of development in his pre-*Harmonium* years at Harvard, but unlike Morse, she unnecessarily speculates about Stevens's ambition, priggishness, and sensibleness when confronted with the necessity of earning a living, and finds evidence for what she terms his "religious sensibility" in the seriousness and sense of duty found in his early diary and letter comments.

In the context of this early sensibility Beckett discusses the later "Sunday Morning" as, contrary to the opinion of early Stevens critics, far from a celebration of Hedonism. For Beckett "Sunday Morning" expresses a sadness inherent in the poet's awareness that the ancient symbolic structures of Christianity would not suffice. This sense of loss, she suggests, forces the poet to search for what would suffice in the new symbolic structures of his poems. She extends this idea by proposing that one finds in the *Harmonium* poems a definition of the imagination as the "human ability to make from reality significance that will satisfy human need for significance" (p. 69), and one finds a sense of man's bereftness, as the poet describes a world without God in which the bleak reality of death is robbed of saving significance. Her emphasis on this volume's bleakness is not only contrary to the gaiety of language Stevens calls for in poetry and the artistic playfulness most critics find here, but to the tone of the poems themselves.

Beckett notes in the *Ideas of Order* poems a similar mood of bareness varied with a "new bleak courage" far removed from the atmosphere of *Harmonium*, but she also contends that Stevens made a crucial discovery in the *Ideas of Order* period, that an illusion may be a thing of consequence while remaining an illusion. Inaccurately defining the subject of these poems as man's self-reliance coupled with God's absence and death's reality, she introduces an Emersonian strain not clearly evident in this volume that presents man questing for order not within his soul or beyond his world but in his momentary perceptions. However, she acknowledges the search that characterizes the volume, and accurately comments that behind all of Stevens's work "lies neither a philosophical system nor a set of random states of mind, but a search" (p. 103). According to this interpretation, the poems not only record the progress of the search in which resolution and uncertainty occur, but are the object of the search. The point is well taken.

She disagrees with the conclusion that Stevens's real greatness is to be found only in his long poems and condemns the long poems of the middle phase, "The Man with the Blue Guitar" and *Owl's Clover*, as "dry exercise" and "aberration," respectively. Although she comments that "The Man with the Blue Guitar" provides a framework for the later poems, she, like many critics, is not sure how to explain this middle phase except to note that in it Stevens leans toward politics but is unequipped to handle the subject because of his concern with theoretical rather than social reality. Beckett excuses Stevens from the Burnshaw criticism (to be discussed later in this chapter) of this period by noting Stevens's compassion and honesty. Such acknowledgment of the poet's personal integrity adds little more to the understanding of Stevens than Burnshaw's misdirected Marxism. Beckett's other comments on this phase—that the short poems in *Parts of a World* provide the preliminary sketches for *Notes Toward a Supreme Fiction* which is concerned primarily with the interdependence of reality and imagination—are hardly innovative or original. After *Notes* Beckett finds no new themes, though she comments that after *Notes* Stevens wrote nearly half of his poetry. The volume in which Stevens placed "Notes," *Transport to Summer*, is, like that poem, concerned with the power of poetry and the power of words. After *Transport*, Beckett contends, the concern is not assaulted directly or discursively, and poems in the later *The Auroras of Autumn* suffer because of it. Although she finds admirable passages in the long poem of this volume, "An Ordinary Evening in New Haven," she also finds decreasing poetic vitality which she fails to define or relate to specific poetic techniques.

In Stevens's final phase she notes a resurgence of certainty when in poems such as "Final Soliloquy of the Interior Paramour" Stevens discovers that the imagination and god are one. Beckett's study is weakest in its analysis of this final period in which, she asserts, Stevens achieves meaning by a return to orthodox Chris-

tianity. Straining to find such orthodoxy, she attempts to explain
"The World as Meditation" by comparing Penelope's power to
what might be termed God's love. This specific reading is unfounded, as is her general conclusion that what in Stevens helps us
to live our lives is "an affirmation of the value of the individual
soul and of the meaning of its relation to the absolute" (p. 215).
Beckett thinks that one learns from Stevens's work an appreciation
of human virtues—faith, patience, honesty, and humility. This conclusion is neither supported by her comments and explications, nor
is it evident in Stevens's poetry. Although she argues otherwise,
Stevens's verse cannot be characterized as moralistic in tone, and
his discovery of meaning cannot be discerned in orthodox conceptions of man's soul. Such an imposition of Christian dogma or
aesthetic concern is precisely what Stevens avoided in all phases of
his poetry. Unfortunately the Beckett study achieves little more
than such an imposition.

Emphasis on the Early Verse

Other critics who approach Stevens as a poet of chronological
phases emphasize the early or late phase as the period of ultimate
poetic power. For those who take this approach, much if not all
that follows *Harmonium* is merely repetitive, or worse, a printed
testament to the poet's decline. The best study that emphasizes the
early published verse, A. Walton Litz's *Introspective Voyager:
The Poetic Development of Wallace Stevens* (1972) is most informative. As an in-depth analysis of chronological detail, the
book traces not just volume publication, but the progressive creation of individual poems as Stevens composed, revised, grouped,
published, then often regrouped for volume publication. The
study adheres to this purpose and structurally develops with strict
attention only to chronology. Unfortunately, Litz analyzes Stevens's development only from 1914–37. When he concludes his
explication of "The Man with the Blue Guitar" by describing all
poems that follow as variations of the same theme, one winces
at the critical rationalization. If the later poetry is similar to the
earlier as Litz notes, it could benefit from Litz's critical eye which
detects many useful similarities among earlier Stevens volumes.
Litz distinguishes the later poems from the earlier as more austere
and isolated, an assessment in contradiction to his earlier verdict
citing the close similarity of the two phases. Because of his cursory
treatment of these later poems, Litz not only fails to resolve this

apparent contradiction, but also must change, in his last fifty pages, the very format of his study: in *Introspective Voyager* all Stevens's work up to "The Man with the Blue Guitar" is examined n a chronological context with an emphasis on poetic development and continuity, but the study's final chapter only briefly summarizes the common themes in all volumes after *The Man with the Blue Guitar*. Any complete assessment of the relative merits in the early and late poetry requires a thorough analysis of both periods in the poet's life. By slighting the late verse, Litz evades the important critical issue of relative merit. The evasion is quite maddening because of the critic's obvious perception and thorough treatment of the poet's work between 1914 and 1937.

Beginning his chronology with *Harmonium*, Litz nonetheless identifies the individual poems published in groups before the volume itself appeared. The first poems to be published after Stevens's undergraduate work on the *Harvard Advocate*, the group "Carnet de Voyage," appeared in the September 1914 issue of *Trend*. Litz suggests that these poems resemble the mimetic "academic romanticism" of Stevens's undergraduate verse, but were followed by the far superior group "Phases." Two of Stevens's great early works were composed in this 1914–16 period in which, according to Litz, Stevens experimented with Imagist techniques. These two, "Peter Quince at the Clavier" and "Sunday Morning," were completed when Stevens still questioned traditional techniques and subject, and differ significantly from poems in a 1917 group, "Primordia," composed in Stevens's early days with the Hartford Accident and Indemnity Company. The relationship between Stevens's new job and his new poetics is established by Litz when the critic attempts to integrate aspects of the poet's life and poetics. Litz extends this integration into thought-provoking speculation when he suggests that Stevens's new business position and walks to work provided the opportunity for new perspectives on varying landscapes. As a result, experiments with landscape perception begin to appear in poems like "Thirteen Ways of Looking at a Blackbird," a poem of the "Primordia" group.

After the landscapes, Stevens turned, in Litz's view, to the war poems he based on *Lettres d'un soldat* by Eugene Emmanuel Lemercier and to the "Pecksniffiana" group collected in 1919. These 1919 poems and a few which appeared in 1918 such as "Earthy Anecdote" and "Metaphors of a Magnifico" are, according to Litz, lighter in tone than the war poems, more decorous and more crafty. However, in Stevens's poetic development of 1921-22, Litz identifies a growing preoccupation with the subject of poetry coupled with a confrontation of the less desirable in reality and a resulting ennui.

Although Litz acknowledges Stevens's barren period which followed *Harmonium*, he does not yield to convenience and use this period of inactivity as the unexplained end of Stevens's early phase. Instead, Litz suggests that Stevens's continuing interest in reworking "Academic Discourse at Havana" is an important bridge between *Harmonium* and *Ideas of Order*. Once over this inactive Stevens period which has caused several critics great pain, Litz attempts to dispel his critical colleagues' inaccurate assumption that Stevens bade farewell to the romantic effulgence of the *Harmonium* world when he wrote "Farewell to Florida" at the beginning of his second volume, *Ideas of Order*. Litz asserts that the poem was only placed first in the collection but was most likely written after the other poems in the volume were completed. Holly Stevens's suggested chronology in *Wallace Stevens: The Palm at the End of the Mind* (1967) supports this contention.

Litz judges the following volume, *Owl's Clover*, as most critics do, a failure, but approaches the years 1934–37 as the pivotal stage in Stevens's development. Because of the upheaval in this period of history, Stevens questioned his artistic assumptions, and moved toward an art of aesthetics climaxed by his artistic synthesis in "The Man with the Blue Guitar." According to Litz: "The poet of *Harmonium* was constantly reacting to the manners and styles of contemporary poetry, seeking for his own idiom; the poet of *Ideas of Order* and *Owl's Clover* was reacting to the external pressures and general disorder of the practical world around him. "The Man with the Blue Guitar" marked a point of consolidation. After its composition Stevens was a poet who reacted mainly to his own achievements and theories, building the self-referring world of the later poems" (p. 259). After this Litz characterizes *Parts of a World* as an exploration of elements in "Blue Guitar"; *Notes Toward a Supreme Fiction* as working out themes in "Blue Guitar"; and *The Rock* as a clarifying and purging of the world created in "Blue Guitar." He qualifies the unity of all that succeeded "Blue Guitar" only by noting the more austere and isolated quality in Stevens's last poems of the forties and fifties.

While many critics might differ with Litz's praise of and emphasis on "Blue Guitar," few would question his analytical method. He is not only exact in attempting to locate Stevens's development in time, but is also precise in his interpretive descriptions of individual poems, published groupings, and phases of development.

However, his primary failing must be seen in his emphasis on the early poetry, understandable because of the early poetry's vitality, but nonetheless limiting in its exclusion of the later verse.

Other critics who emphasize the early poetry usually do so because they evaluate it as more successful poetry than that which followed. Robert Lowell's review of *Transport to Summer*, "Imagination and Reality" (*Nation* Apr. 5, 1947), and Peter Viereck's review of the reissued *Harmonium* and *Transport to Summer*, "Stevens Revisited" (*Kenyon Review* Winter 1948), judge *Harmonium* to be a volume of more successful and exciting poetry than that contained in *Transport to Summer*. Both see the theme of imagination common but varied as Stevens progressed to what Lowell terms a more simple and mature late poetry that nonetheless lacks the intricate organization of a "Sunday Morning" or "Peter Quince at the Clavier." The point is in obvious agreement with Litz's study and with William Bevis's "The Arrangement of *Harmonium*" (*Journal of English Literary History* Sept. 1970) as well as Joseph Riddel's "Stevens' 'Peter Quince at the Clavier': Immortality as Form" (*College English* Jan. 1962). Bevis, like Litz, devotes attention to the early grouping of poems that preceded volume publication, but unlike Litz, he also notes that Stevens discarded the groupings when he prepared *Harmonium* because the poet attempted, in this volume, juxtaposition of contrasting approaches or themes. According to Bevis, the homogeneous and unified groups of poems published between 1914 and 1923 became the contrasting juxtapositions in *Harmonium* that led critics to label Stevens whimsical and dandyish, to disregard certain poems as discordant oddities, and to interpret the early Stevens verse as fragmented. The point is perceptive as is Joseph Riddel's agreement with Litz and Lowell that "Peter Quince at the Clavier" and "Sunday Morning" attest to Stevens's early mastery of his medium.

Robert W. Buttel extends this glance at early Stevens back farther by examining the poet's Harvard years. In "Wallace Stevens at Harvard: Some Origins of His Theme and Style" (*Journal of English Literary History* Mar. 1962), Buttel, like Morse, judges the Harvard poetry worthy of examination. According to Buttel, this immature verse exhibits the genesis of Stevens's conflicting but interdependent imagination and reality. Although evidence of Stevens's break with poetic conventions of the past is found in his short stories and sketches of this period, Buttel suggests that the poems of 1898 and 1900 are only fairly successful adherents to techniques and forms of the nineties, while the stories of this same period foreshadow Stevens's later comedy and irony. Even in the mediocre sonnet sequence of these years Buttel finds hints of Stevens's important budding interest in French language and art. Buttel's study is an essay someone had to write, but with its writing enough is said because more differences than similarities exist between the student Stevens and the later poet, and because the early sophomoric verse is meaningful only in terms of the later poetry.

Before moving to those who value the late poetry at the expense of the earlier, some classic studies on early Stevens must be reviewed. One of the more controversial of these, Yvor Winters's "Wallace Stevens or the Hedonist's Progress" (1947), appeared early in the Stevens criticism. Winters suggests that "Sunday Morning" is the "greatest American poem of the twentieth century" because it renders the "uncertainty . . . of modern mind" and the "consciousness of the imminence of death" (p. 433). However, after "Sunday Morning" presents the poet's primary themes, a rapid decay erodes the poet's style as a result of his Hedonist subject. In the poet's succeeding verse, Winters thinks that Stevens pursues emotion divorced from understanding in a search that is hopeless because the new always becomes old without understanding. This creates a futile exercise in which the poet's irony and wit are really self-ridicule of his own irrationality. According to Winters, Stevens is unable to think himself out of this *Harmonium* predicament. In attempting to break the impasse, the poet is forced to choose between renouncing his art, which Stevens considers but rejects in "The Comedian as the Letter C," and pursuing increasingly "elusive and incomprehensible" experience. In choosing this latter alternative Stevens selects a Hedonistic philosophy of art which results in the degradation of his style. Because of this, Stevens wrote, in Winters's view, no great poems after *Harmonium*.

Randall Jarrell agrees in "Reflections on Wallace Stevens" (1972) with Winters's assessment. Like Winters, Jarrell finds some of the "most beautiful poems an American has written" (p. 139) in *Harmonium*, but he also finds in Stevens a steadily increasing weakness "of thinking of particulars as primarily illustrations of general truths, or else as aesthetic, abstracted objects, simply there to be contemplated" (p. 140). If the two critics disagree on the reason for deterioration, they strike a note of harmonious accord in assessing Stevens's first volume as his most alive, immediate, and precise creation. According to Jarrell, after *Harmonium* the beauty and perfection of these early poems is lost in rhetoric and artifice.

A later essay by Graham Hough, "The Poetry of Wallace Stevens" (*Critical Quarterly*, Autumn 1960), reaffirms for the sixties what Winters and Jarrell suggested to the forties and fifties: "Sunday Morning" is Stevens's best poem, and after *Harmonium* Stevens pursued "certain kinds of badness." Hough's article is more questionable than the previous two studies cited because he voices more blatant misjudgments. He criticizes Stevens's early titles as tasteless and unrelated to the poems, his diction as tiresome and wantonly trivial, his imagery as exhibitionist, his use of foreign language as presumptuous, his essays as portentous, and his irony as undirected. According to Hough, Stevens published too much, but readers should not exalt either his early or late work at the expense of the other because the poet's excellence can reappear anywhere from *Harmonium* to *The Rock*. Perhaps here Hough tentatively redeems himself.

Some early critics were not so kind in their assessments of Stevens's budding genius. These, often among the earliest of Stevens reviewers, were unsure how to assess what they found to be extraordinary and strange. *Harmonium* fell under these rubrics for critics such as Gorham Munson and Llewelyn Powys. Munson ("The Dandyism of Wallace Stevens," *Dial*, Nov. 1925) and Powys ("The Thirteenth Way," *Dial*, July 1924) describe Stevens's early approach to poetry as bizarre and exotic, but, seemingly startled by the poet's newness, offer little real explanation of the why or how of that exoticism.

Emphasis on the Later Verse

Unlike those critics who emphasize early Stevens, the critics who emphasize the later poetry usually view the earlier work only as important preparation leading progressively to their particular favorite late volume or poem. Frank Doggett in "Wallace Stevens' Later Poetry" (*Journal of English Literary History*, June 1958) approaches this progressive development as a gradual change in style if not in subject. Doggett characterizes the late style as chastened and reduced, more sparse in imagery, more frequent in assertion, more subdued in lyricism, and more economical in composition. In reaching these conclusions he relies heavily on an analysis of that style's grammatical components: predicate nominatives, appositives, and metaphors. For Doggett, these components comprise the assertions of resemblance and statements of equalization that typify a late volume such as *The Auroras of Autumn*. He suggests the existence of a lyric mode in Stevens which he describes as a strategy of development, a structure based on identification, conjunction, then modification by appositives.

According to Doggett, this mode does not originate in *Harmonium*, a volume characterized by dramatically developing poems in sharp contrast to later lyric verse. Unfortunately, Doggett does not mention where he finds drama in *Harmonium*, a disappointing omission since dramatic development is hardly obvious in much of Stevens's poetry.

According to Doggett, the subjects of the later poetry in *The Auroras of Autumn* and *The Rock*, the transformation of external reality into experience and the confrontation of formlessness and death, are based in the poet's late ambivalence toward the interaction of internal and external world. In these subjects Doggett finds evidence that Stevens's focus shifts from a concern with the duality of imagination and reality to an examination of imagined and perceived reality in combination. The critic further asserts that these late poems, like earlier ones, maintain a human at the center of a universe which is inanimate and unfriendly. Doggett is least convincing in this assertion because in it he ignores the benevolent universe and the self's integral part in that universe of poems such as "The World as Meditation" and "Of Mere Being."

In a second study by Doggett, "The Transition From *Harmonium*: Factors in the Development of Stevens' Later Poetry" (*PMLA*, Jan. 1973), the critic more exactly defines his focus on the later verse when he asserts that the aging Stevens became more committed to a poetry of abstraction and thought. Doggett places in the 1930s and 1940s the development of a late style appropriate to this mode, and cites evidence for Stevens's changing habits of thinking in the *Letters of Wallace Stevens*. According to Doggett, the change in the poet's style parallels a change, noticeable in the letters, in his conception of art and his growing tendency toward abstraction. The critic supports this idea by relating comments in the letters to changes in the verse. In this view, after *Harmonium* Stevens becomes more committed to a poetry of thought as a result of his correspondence with Hi Simons in the early forties. Simons's questions forced Stevens to examine his intent and to clarify his meaning. As a result, the style of the middle and later periods includes subtle modifications of the early manner while attempting to retain the gaiety of language and imagery and yet move toward explicit theorizing. Although this study is informative because it directs attention to the letters as pertinent to the composition of the poems, an inconsistency exists in Doggett's approach to the late poems: he notes that Stevens's thought progresses inductively from image to abstraction, but he also notes that Stevens turns more and more in the late poems to pure thought and abstraction. The ambiguity is not a serious flaw and is certainly outweighed by Doggett's analysis of Stevens's late personae as personifications that, like elements in poetic synecdoche, serve as part of, not symbols for, universals.

Like Doggett, Louis L. Martz in "Wallace Stevens: The Word as Meditation" (*Yale Review*, June 1958) and Jay M. Semel in "Pennsylvania Dutch Country: Stevens' World as Meditation" (*Contemporary Literature*, Summer 1973) place the period of Stevens's most important development in the forties. Martz's classic essay, first delivered as a paper at the English Institute in September 1957, explores Stevens's late poetry as an answer to the question "what is the nature of poetry in a time of disbelief?" Martz finds the answer in Stevens's "The World as Meditation" where meditation is an exercise of the imagination releasing creative energy and enabling the artist to compose a self. Martz praises the meditative poetry as equal in excellence to the Hedonist poetry of the earlier *Harmonium*, and traces the development of the meditative mode, or Stevens's mind in the act of finding what will suffice, through poems in *Ideas of Order, The Man with the Blue Guitar,* and *Transport to Summer* to is most artistic realization, "The World as Meditation" in *The Rock*. According to Martz, the meditative structure mirrors for Stevens the mind concentrating thoroughly on an object and creating resemblance through metaphor, but it enables Stevens, as it enabled Donne, to counteract the dissolution in the early poetic self. Martz divides the meditative structure into three phases: deliberate creation of setting and intrusion of self in that setting, intellectual analysis of a problem pertaining to the self, and emotional resolution when projected self and mind of meditator merge in a spirit of devotion. Tracing the development of this meditative structure while all the time supporting his contentions with references to the text and apt critical analysis, Martz provides one of the more readable studies on Stevens, and certainly one of the more enlightening perspectives on the verse in general and the later poetry in particular.

Jay Semel does not question Martz's approach but extends Martz's thesis by stipulating that Stevens's development in the forties and the continuity of his meditative style are functions of Stevens's family problems. Semel cites personal disappointments and poems of the early forties to account for Stevens's mastery of the meditative mode, and he proposes that the poetic elements of this style reflect Stevens's Pennsylvania Dutch origins. Names of specific places in Pennsylvania associated with Stevens's family history recur throughout the poetry as he incorporates people and places from his personal past in a meditative approach to his own art. Semels goes so far as to assert that Stevens's ties with his past contribute significantly to his successful development of meditative poetry. The assertion is hardly tenable when one acknowledges the impersonal nature of most Stevens poetry and the poet's tendency to use abstract names and places not as personal allusions but as general connotative figures. By emphasizing the past as a crucial aspect of the meditative mode and by emphasizing pioneer heritage, Semels misses the emphasis of the poet who above all else explored the perceptual experience and momentary creation of the present's interaction between imagination and reality. If Stevens's poetic glance ever strayed from the present or from the present as a continuation of past and contemporary perceptions, he looked to an inevitable future inherent in the mortality of every man.

Agreeing with these more extended studies, many brief comments about the poems and short reviews of his later volumes also voice a general approval of Stevens's late verse. Poets themselves, William Carlos Williams and Randall Jarrell, have viewed Stevens's later poetry in retrospect as a calm and contemplative poetry. Jarrell's "Fifty Years of American Poetry" (*Prairie Schooner*, Spring 1963) asserts that Stevens, like no other American poet, wrote his best poems in the last years of his life. Jarrell not only differs from many critics in this assertion but differs in his conclusion that these poems are more exact than earlier ones. Indeed, Jarrell even differs with his own earlier opinion cited in this chapter as an example of critics who found Stevens deteriorating as he aged. Williams, on the other hand, in "Wallace Stevens" (*Poetry*, Jan. 1956) also differs from most when he finds the mood of the early as well as the late poems characterized by restraint. Jarrell's and Williams's comments are brief and unsupported statements in articles with other concerns: Jarrell's more general summary of recent American poetry, and Williams's more emotional comment on the poet's life, written shortly after Stevens's death.

A third poet, John Ciardi ("Wallace Stevens' 'Absolute Music'," *Nation*, Oct. 16, 1954) differs with both when he finds hints of the master Stevens as late as *The Auroras of Autumn* and *The Rock*, but hints evident only in verse that repeats earlier subjects. Taking the more popular view, that early Stevens is the better Stevens, Ciardi, however, extends the poet's golden period beyond *Harmonium* to include all volumes through *Transport to Summer*. Joseph Bennett is more benevolent toward *The Auroras of Autumn* in his review "Five Books, Four Poets" (*Hudson Review*, Spring 1951). More specific than Ciardi and more complimentary in his adjectives, Bennett judges the volume masterful in its play with syllables and rhetorical flourishes as well as in its use of the pause.

Similar positive comments about the merits of Stevens's late verse may also be found in reviews of the *Collected Poems*. Hayden Carruth's "Without the Inventions of Sorrow" (*Poetry*, Feb. 1955) and Gerard P. Meyer's review of the same volume, "Actuary Among the Spondees" (*Saturday Review*, Dec. 4, 1954), praise the volume as a cumulative gathering of masterful smaller volumes. Both are completely honorific in the terms they apply to the early poetry, but both see the later poems as improvements and indications of Stevens's poetic power that increased with advancing years. Neither review is particularly enlightening in supporting these claims, and Meyer's uncontrolled praise approaches the foolish when he flippantly admires "Anecdote of the Jar," then compares Stevens's physical appearance to his jar in Tennessee.

Before the appearance of the *Collected Poems*, F. O. Matthiessen in *The Responsibilities of the Critic: Essays and Reviews* (1952) early declares that Stevens ripened as he matured. Like Carruth and Meyer, Matthiessen lauds the later poetry while also praising the early gaiety of language which manipulates the nonsensical and grotesque to defy the restrictions of rational discourse. In general comments that preceded Matthiessen's, Lloyd Frankenberg (*Pleasure Dome*, 1949, pp. 197–267) distinguished himself as one of the first critics to note the cumulative effect of Stevens's work. Frankenberg notes that each Stevens poem is a preparatory exercise for later work; that all of the early verse leads toward "Notes Toward a Supreme Fiction"; and that *Ideas of Order* formed a transition between the harlequin gaiety of *Harmonium* and the intellectual seriousness of the later verse. His discussion of this progressive development is, however, marred by his inaccurate assumption that "The Man with the Blue Guitar" preceded "Owl's Clover." The error is glaring.

While an emphasis on early or late poetry is not uncommon in the reviews and articles of the Stevens criticism, an emphasis on and accompanying examination of the middle years is noticeably absent. Certainly, this middle phase with its *Owl's Clover, The Man with the Blue Guitar,* and possibly including *Parts of a World* is troublesome in the unevenness of the verse. But, it is also crucial as a transition phase in the chronological development of Stevens's poetics. The most critically sound studies such as Vendler's and Riddel's confront the difficulties in this phase and relate it to preceding and succeeding verse. Yet, much work remains to be done on this middle period, not as we are about to approach it as a function of the age, but as a phase in the development of Stevens's themes and techniques.

Emphasis on Pressures of the Age

Although critics who approach Stevens's chronology as an external manifestation of internal poetic change (for the better or worse) predominate and several critics exist who extend this approach into biography, a few critics turn their attention to the more easily described external phenomena which accompanied, if not caused, the phases of poetic development. These are the critics who approach Stevens's chronology as a series of poems influenced by the social and aesthetic milieu of the times.

Stevens and the pressures of the modern age were very early thrown together by a relatively obscure reviewer, Stanley Burnshaw, who scathingly criticized Stevens's second volume, *Ideas of Order*. A Marxist critic by bent, Burnshaw damned Stevens for ignoring the social and political issues of a world in collapse. In this volume Stevens exemplified a belief that all order flowed from within man as a result of the imagination's quest for order, while the Marxist implicitly called for an external order based in ideology. In the absence of such an ordering ideology Burnshaw found a world flawed by poverty, social unrest, and political upheaval. For a Marxist critic, such mundane matters in a world perceived to be chaotic, of necessity, had to be the cause championed by poetry. In contrast, before Stevens was attacked by Burnshaw, he as poet was oblivious to ideology. The order he proposed in the verse collected in *Ideas of Order* focused not on ameliorating social injustice or political unrest, but on aesthetic creation as an activity of the imagination interacting with poetic reality. Only later in his rebuttal to Burnshaw voiced in the verse of "Mr. Burnshaw and the Statue" did Stevens confront the interrelationship the critic suggested between order and ideology. In *Ideas of Order* Stevens examined the role of the creative imagination as the cause and focus he believed to be legitimate domains for poetry. And in this stance by Stevens, Burnshaw detected a bourgeois complacency that illustrated simply a lack of social consciousness. An indictment of this stance Burnshaw formulated in his review.

Most book-length studies mention the review, many respond to it attempting to save the poet from adjectives such as "insensitive," and the poet himself judged it worthy of a verbal reaction, the "Mr. Burnshaw and the Statue," originally for publication in *The*

New American Caravan, later included as part two of *Owl's Clover*, and finally reprinted in *Opus Posthumous*. The impact of this review on budding Stevens criticism cannot be overemphasized, not because of any cogency or acuity in the critic's comments, but because of the profound effect those comments had on the poet himself and on those who then and now study Stevens. The review, "Turmoil in the Middle Ground" (*New Masses*, Oct. 1935), labels Stevens a "middle-ground" poet with a troubled mind and ambiguous ideas. If Burnshaw backhandedly praises *Harmonium* as a sense poetry voicing powerful emotions, he turns on himself with the conclusion that it is poetry hard to stomach in troubled times. *Ideas of Order* fairs worse in Burnshaw's judgment when he condemns the volume as a work characterized by confusion, speculations, questionings, and contradictions. Describing Stevens as a writer burdened by class-conscious clashes between capitalism and labor, Burnshaw writes more for his own Marxist audience than for any general following of Stevens.

The furor created by Burnshaw's review continued for years and even included a retrospective reassessment by the critic himself. In "Wallace Stevens and the Statue" (*Sewanee Review*, Summer 1961), Burnshaw reexamines Stevens's art as it is manifested in the poem about Burnshaw and maintains that the verse must be interpreted within the context of its period. Of his own review and Stevens's response to it, Burnshaw suggests they were nothing more than "actions of their time" (p. 356). He defends his own earlier statements against critics who he contends falsely describe his argument as an indictment of Stevens's indifference to the world, then seeks to explain how he came to write the review. These comments, resembling confessional "how the times demanded I write Marxist criticism," flow gradually into a more distanced analysis of Marxist critical terms, and finally into a reprint of the original review. Burnshaw's attempt to evaluate his own earlier critical type is admirable if somewhat defensive, while his reprint of the earlier comments is valuable because of the inaccessibility of the 1935 review.

Compared to Burnshaw's attempts, critics who approach the pressures of the age do so with far less conviction and zeal. Several of these studies purport to analyze the forces of the eras in which the poet wrote, but few are able to sustain this emphasis. In a fiction, poetry, and drama series edited by Warren French, studies examining the Stevens of a particular era are included. Donald Sheehan's article "Wallace Stevens in the 30s: Gaudy Bosh and the Gesture's Whim" (1967) in the first of the French vol-

umes is, of the three articles on Stevens (one in each volume), most
to the point. According to Sheehan, the Stevens of the thirties
who, unlike any other poet in the period, affirmed art and his
ability to create in the face of world chaos, must be seen in the
context of the twenties Stevens. The esthete and dandy who
wrote pure poetry in *Harmonium* became the bitter complainer
who wrote a poetry of loss in *Ideas of Order*. Sheehan agrees with
Burnshaw's assessment, but questions the critic's Marxist rhetoric
while agreeing with the Marxist's conclusion, that Stevens failed
to account for worldly chaos. Sheehan further indicts Stevens for
the poet's response, *Owl's Clover*, to the Burnshaw review, because
that response was a poetic failure; then proceeds to praise Stevens
for his next volume, *The Man with the Blue Guitar*. Despite his
pejorative comments on Stevens in the thirties, Sheehan acknowledges this decade as the time when Stevens was first considered a
serious artist and the time which forced the poet to be supremely
confident in his art. The first conclusion is valid but the last one is
unsupportable when one reads the poet's reexamination of his art
and his own mortality in later poems such as "Notes Toward a
Supreme Fiction" and "The Auroras of Autumn."

In the French collection on the forties, Sheehan devotes more
attention to an explication of "Notes Toward a Supreme Fiction"
than to the relationship of the poetry to the era. Sheehan accurately defines the emphasis of "Notes" as on the speaker and his
responses rather than on the content of the speaker's ideas, but
he goes astray in his analysis of the poem's structure. He suggests
that the poem is unified not by any causal or progressive relationship but by simple juxtaposition of stanzas. In this view the very
sequence itself acts as the cohering agent, with each section not
determined by other sections but functioning as a probable antecedent for preceding sections. According to Sheehan, this prob-
ability results when a section is related in any way to a preceding
section. If one takes Sheehan's comments to their logical conclusion *any* juxtaposed elements would be related, a combination
which hardly could be called an order. Aside from this examination of structure, Sheehan's comments are helpful in identifying
the Platonic aspects and the importance of the imagination's role
in the poem. Yet only in his final paragraph does the critic begin
to relate the poet and poem to the decade, and this he pursues only
briefly by noting that the poem's epilogue ties the war and world
of 1942 to the dynamics of imaginative argument.

Sheehan thinks that the epilogue of "Notes" is one of Stevens's "boldest strokes" because in this section the poet briefly describes the 1940s world of war.

> Soldier, there is a war between the mind
> And sky, between thought and day and night. It is
> For that the poet is always in the sun,
>
> Patches the moon together in his room
> To his Virgilian cadences, up down,
> Up down. It is a war that never ends.
>
> Yet it depends on yours. The two are one.
> They are plural, a right and left, a pair,
> Two parallels that meet if only in
>
> The meeting of their shadows or that meet
> In a book in a barrack, a letter from Malay.
> But your war ends. And after it you return
>
> With six meats and twelve wines or else without
> To walk another room . . . Monsieur and comrade,
> The soldier is poor without the poet's lines,
>
> His petty syllabi, the sounds that stick,
> Inevitably modulating, in the blood.
> And war for war, each has its gallant kind.
>
> How simply the fictive hero becomes the real;
> How gladly with proper words the soldier dies,
> If he must, or lives on the bread of faithful speech.

According to Sheehan the allusion to a moment in history yokes Stevens's theory of imagination and external events of the era, and is crucial to an understanding of the poem in which the task of the imagination cannot be understood apart from the pressures of external reality. Sheehan praises the "cool elegance and urbane wittiness" (p. 176) of "Notes" because he finds in it Stevens's solution to the world's and the mind's dissolution. For the Stevens of the forties the answer could be found in the spirit of the Supreme Fiction that could bring peace to both internal and external chaos.

The third Sheehan article in the French series acknowledges the overdue acclaim Stevens's poetry received with the National Book Award of 1951 for *The Auroras of Autumn* and of 1955 for the *Collected Poems*. This article, unlike the other two, does not discuss the interrelatedness of poet and era, but provides an era perspective on the emerging Stevens criticism of the fifties. Sheehan notes that the critical labels of Stevens as "aesthete" in the twenties, "snob" in the thirties, and "hermit" in the forties seemed wrong by the fifties when critics discovered he had been creating a continuous oeuvre. For Sheehan, this discovery was the turning point in Stevens criticism. Sheehan contends that the attention such recognition of greatness brought to Stevens not only encouraged a proliferation of critical analysis, but also diverted attention from the poems to the poet's philosophy. To correct this, Sheehan focuses attention on the expertness of Stevens's poetic techniques, and on the constancy of those techniques throughout the verse. However general, Sheehan's most perceptive comments emphasize these poetic techniques but ignore period forces. Although this is inconsistent with the purpose of French's series, it is nonetheless tangentially related to era assessments of the poet because Sheehan's discussion is a reaction against omissions in the approach fifties critics took toward Stevens. Sheehan's statement, that Stevens's poems are not unified by traditional techniques of prosody or by unifying philosophy but by the poetic utterance of the determining personality or poetic persona who unifies by his or her very presence, is interesting if somewhat confounded by Stevens's erratic use of the persona and frequent lack of development in the persona figure. But the critic's statement, that a determining personality recurs in a pattern throughout the oeuvre to function not as narrator or philosopher but singer of songs and teller of tales, is worth further critical exploration. Sheehan examines Stevens's rhythm, syntax, and mode of structure in order to prove the poet a master on grounds not established, according to this critic, by his colleagues in the fifties.

More specifically related to decade influences on the poet are studies by Joseph Riddel and William Rose Benet. In " 'Poets' Politics' — Wallace Stevens' *Owl's Clover*" (*Modern Philology*, Nov. 1958), Riddel labels Stevens's *Ideas of Order* a plea for poetry "in a decade which would subordinate art to ideology" (p. 118). In comments from this article later incorporated into his book-length study, Riddel places *Owl's Clover* in the mode of Stevens's late style and views its concern with man's will to order as indicative of Stevens's poetry from beginning to end. While it is certainly not Stevens's best poem, Riddel values it for its conception of art which evolved into Stevens's later concept of the supreme fiction. Accepting the poem's shortcomings, Riddel provides a valuable analysis of the poem as a work of literature beyond the social issues introduced by the Burnshaw controversy.

He establishes the work firmly in the domain of poetry while skirting Stevens's intrusion into the world of social concerns by calling these concerns a pervasive reality that threatened the poet's artistic concern with the balance between reality and the imagination.

In a later article, "*Ideas of Order:* The Rhetoric of Politics and the Rhetoric of Poetry" (*New England Quarterly*, Sept. 1951), Riddel again prefigures comments in his *The Clairvoyant Eye* (1967) when he notes the change of tone in Stevens's poetry of the thirties. In this article Riddel examines the "leftist" qualities of Stevens's "militant romanticism" which describes the imagination-reality dichotomy as a manifestation of man's struggle with nature and of the mutual determinism in the self and the world. But Riddel also emphasizes the relationship of the thirties Stevens to the poet of the twenties; to Riddel, the social upheaval of the 1930s did not force Stevens to abandon his poetic convictions voiced in *Harmonium.* Instead, in *Ideas of Order* the poet becomes more attuned to external, universal realities which are coercive and threatening to the spirit as well as the body because they threaten to strip man of his power to order. Riddel's argument is based on the assumption that the new aspect of reality required a change in Stevens's rhetoric. Although that rhetoric might be termed "leftist," Riddel reminds that it communicates a leftist approach to personal, aesthetic order rather than social, political ideology. Riddel bases his argument on the assumption that the American social and economic collapse at the end of the 1920s demanded of Stevens an "urgency" of statement that changed the poet's style. According to Riddel, the qualitative differences in the Stevens poems of the thirties must be attributed to the external world from which that poetry came, and to Stevens's "sense that the conditions of one's environment and the temper of one's age determine to a degree the reaction of the poetic self" (p. 330). In "Owl's Clover" Stevens reacted "sincerely and conscientiously to his time," because as Riddel views this poem, it communicates Stevens's theory of poetry in the political and social terminology of the period. While order had always been an important concept in Stevens's theory, it surfaced even more in the thirties and was voiced in a new style because the concept of order itself had become associated with political and social institutions that demanded a more active rhetoric.

This new style Riddel describes as characterized by statement rather than suggestion, which predominates in *Harmonium.* Yet, the new style in its discursiveness and theme with variation pattern also foreshadows the style of late Stevens verse. In this changed style, Riddel does not, however, find evidence of Stevens giving way to the leftist attitudes of the period. On the contrary, Riddel views this change as Stevens's adaptation to the realities of the period that demanded the personal search of *Harmonium* be forged into some relationship with the impending social crisis. Stevens achieves this relationship in *Ideas of Order* when he confronts ideological pressures by reasserting the strength of the poet's personal power to order.

William Rose Benet's much earlier review of *Owl's Clover* ("Contemporary Poetry," *Saturday Review*, Jan. 16, 1937) precedes Riddel's argument that in the thirties Stevens said something about art as well as about his own place and time. Riddel reasserts Benet's early claim that when confronted with Wallace Stevens's language in *Owl's Clover* one is in the presence of poetry and nothing else. Leon Howard (*Literature and the American Tradition*, 1960, pp. 315–18) also examines Stevens's poetry in light of the tumultuous thirties. According to Howard, the upheaval of this decade forced Stevens to turn from the hedonism of *Harmonium* to a more serious substitute, poetry as a retreat. This critic differs here from Riddel and Benet, both of whom found Stevens confronting the problems of his time rather than retreating from them. And, unlike Riddel who specifically lodges the turning point of Stevens's style in the volume *Ideas of Order*, Howard lodges the change later in "The Man with the Blue Guitar," Stevens's first major project after *Owl's Clover*.

Unified Grand Poem: The Poet without Change

In contrast to most critics examining change throughout the poet's chronology, there are those who, in examining both early and late poems, find little or no substantive change in the poet's verse.

An Oeuvre with Minimal Change

Richard Blessing's study, *Wallace Stevens' "Whole Harmonium"* (1970), provides an interesting transition between the critics who find change and those who don't. In short, Blessing tries to straddle both of these worlds by arguing that a unified oeuvre exists while also suggesting that change occurs in this grand poem. Blessing might have been more convincing had he thoroughly defined that change or described how it contributes to the unified whole—but he does neither. Defining the *Collected Poems* as one grand poem with *The Rock* naturally growing out of the poems in *Harmonium*, Blessing detects changes in technique, subject matter, imagery, and tone that grow out of a dynamic view of life and poetry. This approach is similar to Riddel's in *The Clairvoyant Eye* and Morse's in *Wallace Stevens: Poetry as Life*, but is not developed as thoroughly as either of these two earlier discussed studies. Blessing's limitations are primarily noticeable in his sketchy explications and superficial examinations of theme or technique. When explicating a poem, he usually cites a few major critical approaches then expands the cumulative approach with perhaps one minor point. When he does add an original interpretation to an element in the poem he is most often inaccurate and imprecise because he is too simplistic in his associations to the symbols he attempts to explain. This inadequacy is evident in Blessing's explication of "The World as Meditation," a poem in which this critic misses the subtle, intricate interplay of reality and imagination intended by the poet.

> Is it Ulysses that approaches from the east,
> The interminable adventurer? The trees are mended.
> That winter is washed away. Someone is moving
>
> On the horizon and lifting himself up above it.
> A form of fire approaches the cretonnes of Penelope,
> Whose mere savage presence awakens the world in which
>   she dwells.
>
> She has composed, so long, a self with which to welcome
>   him,
> Companion to his self for her, which she imagined,
> Two in a deep-founded sheltering, friend and dear friend.
>
> The trees had been mended, as an essential exercise
> In an inhuman meditation, larger than her own.
> No winds like dogs watched over her at night.
>
> She wanted nothing he could not bring her by coming
>   alone.
> She wanted no fetchings, His arms would be her necklace
> And her belt, the final fortune of their desire.
>
> But was it Ulysses? Or was it only the warmth of the sun
> On her pillow? The thought kept beating in her like her
>   heart.
> The two kept beating together. It was only day.

It was Ulysses and it was not. Yet they had met,
Friend and dear friend and a planet's encouragement.
The barbarous strength within her would never fail.

She would talk a little to herself as she combed her hair,
Repeating his name with its patient syllables.
Never forgetting him that kept coming constantly so near.

By reducing Penelope to a mere symbol of the imaginative, passive, and feminine with Ulysses as physical, active, and masculine,
Blessing betrays the verse in his inattention to the complexity of
the Penelope figure and to the poet's emphasis, through the Ulysses
figure, on the ambiguity of interacting imagination and reality.

The book is further weakened by Blessing's false assumption
that the poems were written in the order in which they appeared
in the "grand poem," but the study is occasionally punctuated by
a refreshing humorous comment such as the critic's note that the
Collected Letters might be subtitled "why new critics grow old."
Blessing characterizes the poetry of *Harmonium* as external in
outlook, sensory in emphasis, and rejoicing in tone, then moves to
Ideas of Order which he describes as Stevens's volume of transition from the poetry of sensory experience to a poetry of reflection and meditation. But, he fails to see that in a poem as early as
"Sunday Morning" the poet had combined sensory and reflective
perception. This seems to be a recurring problem in Blessing's
study: by attempting to discuss briefly the *whole* of *Harmonium*,
he must ignore or exclude the exceptions to the dominant themes
or the adaptations in slight nuance that occur throughout Stevens.

Following *Ideas of Order* he chooses to discuss *Owl's Clover*
which is not printed in the *Collected Poems*, Blessing's stipulated
subject. Why he selects this and no other poem from *Opus Posthumous* is never mentioned. He does use the poem as an example
of Stevens's newly found intellectual lyric mode evident in *The
Man with the Blue Guitar*, but other examples from *Collected
Poems* would have served the same purpose. According to Blessing, the conscious, logical order of *Harmonium* and *Ideas of Order*
is replaced in *Blue Guitar* by an order of free association, and the
external emphasis of the first two volumes is abandoned for the
"inward" subject, poetry, in *Blue Guitar*. *Parts of a World* which
followed, is, in Blessing's view, a more intellectual volume artfully
constructed to exhibit a sense of the mind in the process of creating; the intellectual character of poetic exercise; and a tone of
"reasonableness" beneath the poetics. Differing from most critics

such as Riddel, Vendler, and Morse who see these poems of the middle years as artistically weaker and less successful than Stevens's early or late attempts, Blessing is also very positive in the terms he uses to describe the poems in *Transport to Summer*. He isolates "Chocorua to Its Neighbor," "Esthétique du Mal," and "Notes Toward a Supreme Fiction" as the most ambitious and important poems in this volume, then briefly explicates the first two, but leaves the third, the most successful and important poem of the three, by referring the reader to other critics.

Finally moving into the late poems of *The Auroras of Autumn*, Blessing marks the end of Stevens's inward journey. Contending that the basis of Stevens's poetic theory is still the imagination and reality, Blessing thinks the poet displays more interest in the relationship between those two elements than in the two as polarities. Although the critic accurately identifies the appropriateness of the auroras image for conveying the increasingly swift movement of polarities Stevens found in the perceptions flickering between mind and objective world, and although he agrees with Martz that this volume and *The Rock* consist of meditative poems of introspection and retrospection, he nonetheless fails to add much to existing criticism. This and the limitations noted earlier severely weaken the study.

An Oeuvre with No Change

Reading Stevens's work as an entire oeuvre, other critics have decided that Stevens exhibited no growth or change. Richard Eberhart voices this thought in his review of *Transport to Summer* (*Accent*, Summer 1947) as does A. Alvarez in *Stewards of Excellence* (1958). Alvarez notes a slight change in the developing Stevens but no signs of increasing maturity. John J. Enck bases his book, *Wallace Stevens' Images and Judgments* (1964), on the unchangeable qualities throughout Stevens's technique and theme, qualities Enck defines as "imagistic exercises." Enck does not ignore all variations in the Stevens canon, but his superficial approach to the oneness of all Stevens's verse forces many individual poems into a superimposed critical mold. The book is structured as an accumulation of ideas, sometimes related, sometimes not; and as a result, at times suffers from the lack of a unifying thesis or clear emphasis. Enck moves from one idea about Stevens's poetry to another without developing either, then rationalizes his preliminary judgments and tentative remarks by noting Stevens's own lack of a unifying, rigid philosophy.

The topics discussed by Enck are presented as "images" because they are not fully "documented." These ten images include Stevens as part-time businessman, part-time poet; Stevens as modern; Stevens's idiom as combination of archaic, colloquial, and foreign; Stevens's unconcern with stanzaic unity; his indifference to academic matters; his focus on the present; his use of place as figure for attitude; the ambiguity of his personae; his refusal to separate life and art; and his tendency to examine subjects only in their context. Attempting neither to unify nor develop, Enck finds in the poems these disparate "images" presented in a poetic style that did not change. Because Stevens's style is unchanging and because "unnecessary complications" might result, Enck does not "worry about" more precise dates than the years in which Stevens's volumes were published. He discusses *Harmonium* as Imagist in precept, and disregards the individual poems by unexplained generalizations: "Domination of Black," according to Enck, communicates that "an awareness of personal inadequacy causes fear" (p. 72). His reading of "Sunday Morning" is even more puzzling because in it he finds the poet engaged in a "meditative argument" with the female persona. The inaccuracy of such a comment rivals the critic's misperceptions. He cites "The Comedian as the Letter C" as important in the volume because it is Stevens's turning point away from the clown style. At this point one wonders how a style that "exploits a nearly identical range for forty years" can have a turning point. In summarizing *Harmonium* he notes, but does not explain, five predominant themes: the poet creates a persona who believes in things he cannot champion but who rejects superstition; uses reality as the basis for finding solace in a "disembodied imagination"; lives by poetry, recognizing its inability to alter physical qualities; considers religion meaningless; and utilizes a clown's mask to protect a defenseless sensibility.

Combining his discussion of *Ideas of Order* and *The Man with the Blue Guitar*, Enck suggests that Stevens maintains in *Blue Guitar* the "freedom" of *Harmonium* and the examination of worldly problems presented in *Ideas of Order*. The critic's judgment, that "A Postcard from the Volcano" in this period is better than any poem Stevens published before it, is indeed questionable. He further weakens his premise by praising it for prophetically joining the themes of the later philosophic verse. Yet, he correctly notes some "confused premises" in *Owl's Clover* and *Blue Guitar*, but blames the statue as allegorical cypher amid social comment for the failure of *Owl's Clover*. Enck's critical focus is blurred: the weakness of the poem resides not in the unifying image itself but in its burdensome topical surroundings. In summary, he superficially notes that these two volumes fail "because the vocabulary cannot resist its accustomed wayward impudence" (p. 129). Enck's diction hardly elucidates this vocabulary.

Like many critics, Enck criticizes *Part of a World* as Stevens's most uneven volume, but unlike many he praises *Transport to Summer* as Stevens's most successful because of its controlled satiric tone and refined use of imagistic exercise. Certainly in the critical minority, he proposes that "Esthétique du Mal" will come to be known as Stevens's finest single achievement because of its unity and completeness. He argues that in *The Auroras of Autumn* Stevens turned to "darker topics" and created a difficult title poem that explores the area between separate images and undefined mythology. The point is an interesting one and might have been fruitful had Enck explored it.

After devoting four chapters to the "images" in Stevens, he turns for a final analysis of particular poems as "standards," but bases the entire chapter almost exclusively on paraphrase. A double "movement" in these poems explains to Enck why they seem to echo one another. In the first aspect of movement, the verse and prose move toward exactitude, while in the second they function together to define concepts in their own terms. In all poems Stevens moves, according to Enck, between the two extremes of the very specific and the very rarefied. His poetry therefore "mediates between its own transcendency and this world and by its very nature shows how it infuses, without altering, the physical" (p. 224).

In this final chapter Enck also negatively reviews selected Stevens critics and casts stones at those who force rather than detect parallels in the poet's work. He then draws a parallel between Stevens's verse and the *I Ching* but, like those he reviews, fails to use even one poem to support his thesis. Pursuing himself what he labels bad in others, he also notes the danger in comparing Stevens's work to other modern art forms, then obliquely compares Stevens to Klee without noting common techniques or subjects in the two artists.

William Burney's book *Wallace Stevens* (1968) is similar to Enck's in emphasis and inadequacy. Admitting his study relies on paraphrase, Burney does not refer to specific poetic passages as the basis for his conclusions, and he arrives at no logical unified interpretation as an outgrowth of his paraphrase. And, like Enck, Burney contends that Wallace Stevens's themes remain the same. In *Harmonium*, and even more explicitly in its longest poem, "The

Comedian as the Letter C," Burney isolates the three themes that
for him characterize all Stevens's verse: life, death, and the vulgar.
Such simplistic generalizations intrude into his paraphrases when
he notes "birds, in Stevens' poetry, tend to speak for insensate
reality" (p. 18). He describes Stevens as "cynical" without
explaining his reasons with more than the casual aside, "Being a
poet and a successful lawyer-businessman might tend to make any-
one cynical" (p. 27). Contrary to William Bevis's earlier discussed
description of the *Harmonium* volume as intentionally structured
on contrast, Burney thinks the poems were thrown together by
chance. He misses the poet's wit and punning in poems of this
volume such as "Peter Quince at the Clavier" and "To the One
of Fictive Music," and reads far too concretely "The Emperor of
Ice-Cream," which he explicates as a poem about a brothel in
which a woman died or was murdered. This reading as well as
his assessment of Stevens's emphasis on the vulgar in *Harmonium*
epitomize the weaknesses in the Burney study. He defines the
vulgar in Stevens as "an automatic assembling of fixed, dead pieces
of common experience," but never acknowledges that this is ap-
proximately Stevens's definition of reality, a reality in no way
judged dead by the poet. And he symbol hunts among the images
and metaphors to find easily specified literal correspondences
where none in fact exist. As an example, one need only consider
his reading of "The Idea of Order at Key West" in which the
sea, for Burney, is an "economic and spiritual problem and re-
source forged into a comprehensive metaphor by Stevens in order
to alleviate the burden of the Depression" (p. 68).

Moving from *Harmonium* to Stevens's poetry of the thirties,
Burney claims to approach Stevens's work by examining the poems
in their chronological order, but he then divides *Ideas of Order*
into three divisions, falsely assuming that the poems were written
in the order in which they appear in the volume. Burney is more
exact in his examination of *Transport to Summer* in which he
notes the poems were arranged roughly in their order of publication (except for "Notes Toward a Supreme Fiction" published at
the beginning of this period, but placed at the end of the volume).
In analyzing poems of this period such as "Jouga" and "Debris of
Life and Mind" Burney suddenly metamorphoses into a psychoanalytic critic finding Oedipal conflicts and Jungian psychic drama
lurking between the lines. If the approach is valid for Stevens's
verse (a considerable if), one wonders why Burney utilizes it only
on these two isloated poems.

Approaching Stevens's succeeding volume, *The Auroras of*

Autumn, as he approaches *Ideas of Order*, Burney divides the volume into sections of development, but fails to justify his divisions with the use of biographical fact, chronological publication, or thematic evolution. When he progresses to *The Rock*, described by most critics as Stevens's volume of the hard, definitive, certain and constant in life, Burney finds a symbol and period of nothingness to which the poet responds as an unborn or sleeping child. Unlike other critics who explore Stevens's chronology, Burney goes beyond *The Rock* to a discussion of *Opus Posthumous*, the volume of Stevens's previously uncollected works compiled and edited after the poet's death by Samuel French Morse; and he claims to identify Stevens's criterion for excluding poems from the *Collected Poems*. According to Burney, only those poems which Stevens thought allowed metaphor to create its own metamorphosis were included. Stevens was hardly so rigid or objective in defining and applying any one criterion to his work.

Perhaps the most irritating flaw of the Burney study exists, however, not in his capricious volume divisions, simplistic interpretations, or even in his unfounded conclusions, but in the tidy answers he formulates for often thorny questions. Literally, when Stevens poses a question as he does at the end of "The Man on the Dump" ("Where was it one first heard the truth?"), Burney tries to answer it with "there is no such thing as the truth." In short, one would do well to explore the questions in the actual poems rather than the answers in Burney's study.

William York Tindall agrees in his *Wallace Stevens* (1961) with Enck and Burney: although he acknowledges a chronology of publication, he finds no signs of development in theme or technique. Tindall thinks Stevens was at the end of his career what he was at the beginning, an insurance executive who wrote poetry. As a poet constantly concerned with "The the," Stevens wrote two kinds of poetry, according to Tindall, "the one strange and imagistic, the other lean and discursive" (p. 12). From start to finish, Tindall finds in Stevens's poetry analogy and interaction as the structuring principles and a manner issuing from a persona or mask. Although Tindall himself begins with what appears to be a chronological structure, he spends most of his time discussing the early poems with only brief attention to the later ones. The booklet is indeed quite difficult to characterize because Tindall randomly mixes biography, historical perspective, explication, structural analysis, and thematic examination with no discernible emphasis on any one approach. His coherence is therefore oblique, but unlike Enck or Burney, his comments are often concise, as when he notes that "by his [Wallace Stevens's] prose you can prove anything you like" (p. 17), and that "Stevens gets his particular effects by surprising conjunctions of discourse and image, of the bare and the bizarre" (p. 33). Tindall's comments on the poems are also insightful; he classifies "The Bouquet" as a poem that is "at once a still life, a commentary on it, and a comment on the commentary" (p. 36). He also discusses "Sunday Morning," "Peter Quince at the Clavier," "Anecdote of the Jar," "Sea Surface Full of Clouds," "The Man with the Blue Guitar," and "An Ordinary Evening in New Haven" but ends his booklet with a brief examination of "Transport to Summer" as if Stevens's career ended here.

Perhaps this random selection concentrating on the early work can be accepted if one also accepts Tindall's thesis that Stevens's techniques and themes never changed. Unfortunately, this premise is not so easy to accept. The critic's intermingling of poetry, biography, modern art, and philosophy as perspectives on Stevens's ideas is at times a refreshing critical concoction, but tends at times to disturb because of the study's lack of a beginning, middle, end, or emphasis other than simply "Wallace Stevens." For this weakness but also for its strength of comment in confronting the poetry itself, Tindall's study might have been titled "Notes *Toward* the Poetry of Wallace Stevens." Of the studies that contend Stevens did not change, Tindall's is by far the most readable though the earliest and the briefest.

Collected Criticism: Critics' Attitudes in Change

The numerous studies devoted to Stevens's chronology coupled with an apparent academic compulsion to categorize and order rapidly proliferating verbiage have inspired several volumes of collected criticism designed to survey changing critical attitudes toward this poet. In short, with this poet so burdened by chronological second-guessing, editors have removed themselves one step further from the melee in an attempt to assess the chronology of the criticism as a barometer of the poet's literary milieu. These collections that claim to present samples of the developing Stevens criticism are not without merit and do indeed include readable though often selective passages. Because these studies are seldom reprinted in their entirety owing to space limitations, such collections should be used only as broad, general introductions and sources directing further investigation.

The best of these collections, *The Achievement of Wallace Stevens* (1962), is edited by Ashley Brown and Robert S. Haller. Beginning with the earliest Stevens criticism of the 1920s, Brown and Haller reprint essays and excerpts of essays that are often difficult to find in any but the most long-standing, well-funded library. Harriet Monroe, Marianne Moore, Llewelyn Powers, Gorham Munson, Morton Zabel, and R. P. Blackmur are among the groundbreakers cited. Although the collection claims to use such samples as a chronicle of Stevens's emergence from the Imagist school, it is far more successful in simply presenting a limited history of Stevens's reputation. It does not, however, as the preface purports, adequately survey the changing critical attitudes toward the poet. Several classic assessments such as the infamous Burnshaw review and Yvor Winters's honorific pronouncements are omitted. If the collection is to be commended for its combination of early critics, a combination which accurately exemplifies the poet's early reception, it is to be criticized for its too-lofty, unfulfilled goals such as the introduction's claim, not only to chronicle Stevens's emergence from Imagism and to survey changing critical attitudes, but also to reflect the poetic climates of four decades. Such a task is admirable if impossible in a volume of selected, even excerpted, criticism about one poet. Brown and Haller, however, do identify a primary trend in the Stevens criticism when they note a change in concern from Stevens's principle theme, the relation of the imagination and reality, to a consideration of the later poetry itself. Yet, even this trend is not thoroughly represented by reprinted studies because the collection stops in the early 1960s.

Far less successful in the breadth of critical samples selected for collection are Irvin Ehrenpreis's *Wallace Stevens: A Critical Anthology* (1972) and Peter L. McNamara's *Critics on Wallace Stevens* (1972). McNamara varies the chronological approach to Stevens critics by emphasizing recent criticism as a "truer guide" to Stevens's poetry. Toward this end he neglects important early responses as well as developing exegesis by Stevens critics such as Benamou and Riddel. Introducing his chosen few with "Stevens on Poetry," four pages of out-of-context quotes from *The Necessary Angel* and *Opus Posthumous*, McNamara strives to characterize Stevens's "act of the mind," but fails because of the brevity of such quotes. Although the selection of studies included is, for "recent" criticism, adequate, it does not reflect, as McNamara would have us believe, an invalidation of earlier criticism. On the contrary, many of the more perceptive studies included here, such

as James Baird's "Transvaluation in Stevens' Poetics," Samuel
French Morse's "Some Ideas About the Thing Itself," and Marjorie Perloff's "Irony in *The Rock*," are continuations of or responses to earlier studies.

Ehrenpreis's collection, on the other hand, avoids favoring early
or late criticism and thereby attempts to avoid any value judgment
of the poet and his critics. *Wallace Stevens: A Critical Anthology*
is composed of fragments from Stevens's journal, letters, and
essays, as well as of sections from critical essays and books, all
interspersed in a chronological order. Many of the "Selections"
have bracketed titles invented by the editor, which, like the
selections themselves, seem to have been chosen as thumbnail
sketches of the poet's views on everything and his critics' views
on all aspects of his poetics. As such, they are superficial at best.
The lack of coherence makes reading difficult for the Stevens
student with minimal interest in the poet, and the incompleteness
of the selections makes the collection undesirable for any more
experienced Stevens reader. The criticism is frequently reprinted
in such brief excerpts that even a limited understanding of the
critic's position is impossible unless the reader is familiar with the
original source. And, needless to say, such familiarity precludes the
need for a collection of abridged miscellany. Ehrenpreis, however,
in comments preceding each of his book's three sections ("Early
Character and Opinions," "Early Criticism," and "The Developing
Debate") voices a few very general conclusions about Stevens
criticism. According to this editor, an obvious inadequacy is evident in the criticism that attempts to explain the changes which
took place in Stevens's poems; and according to Ehrenpreis,
Stevens's influence on poets to follow has yet to be defined. Both assessments are accurate, but are unfortunately lost amid vaguely suggestive and qualitatively uneven conclusions in these introductions.

Despite the relative inadequacy of studies that attempt to bring
edited order out of critical chaos, and in spite of the abundant
sometimes redundant responses to the issue of Stevens's chronological development, one rather certain conclusion is possible:
Stevens's chronological development is so much a part of the
changing twentieth century that his poems as well as the changing
critical approach to them reveal much about this century's approach to art and literature; about its uneasy juxtaposition of the
traditional and atraditional; about its need to create relationships
where none are immediately apparent; and about its tendency to
place in some historical context that which defies established order.
The attempts to find such a historical perspective take the form in

criticism not only of chronological studies, but also of literary heritage examinations. While this chapter focuses on those who attempt to interpret that chronology as a poet's development, chapter 2 turns its attention to those who attempt to review the poet's development in its relationship to literary history.

References

Alvarez, A.
  1958. *Stewards of Excellence.* New York: Scribner.
Beckett, Lucy
  1974. *Wallace Stevens.* New York: Cambridge Univ. Pr.
Benet, William Rose
  1937. "Contemporary Poetry." *Saturday Review* Jan. 16, p. 18.
Bennett, Joseph
  1951. "Five Books, Four Poets." *Hudson Review* Spring, pp. 133–43.
Bevis, William
  1970. "The Arrangement of *Harmonium.*" *Journal of English Literary History* Sept., pp. 456–73.
Blessing, Richard Allen
  1970. *Wallace Stevens' "Whole Harmonium."* New York: Syracuse Univ. Pr.
Brown, Ashley, and Robert S. Haller
  1962. (editors) *The Achievement of Wallace Stevens.* New York: Lippincott.
Brown, Merle Elliott
  1962. "Concordia Discors in the Poetry of Wallace Stevens." *American Literature* May, pp. 246–69.
  1970. *Wallace Stevens: The Poem as Act.* Detroit: Wayne State Univ. Pr.
Burney, William
  1968. *Wallace Stevens.* New York: Twayne.
Burnshaw, Stanley
  1935. "Turmoil in the Middle Ground." *New Masses* Oct. 1, pp. 41–42.
  1961. "Wallace Stevens and the Statue." *Sewanee Review* Summer, pp. 355–66.
Buttel, Robert W.
  1962. "Wallace Stevens at Harvard: Some Origins of His Theme and Style." *Journal of English Literary History* Mar., pp. 90–119; reprinted in *The Act of the Mind,* ed. Roy Harvey Pearce and J. Hillis Miller. Baltimore: Johns Hopkins Pr., 1965.
Carruth, Hayden
  1955. "Without the Inventions of Sorrow." *Poetry* Feb., pp. 288–93.
Ciardi, John
  1954. "Wallace Stevens' 'Absolute Music'." *Nation* Oct. 16, pp. 346–47.

Doggett, Frank
1958. "Wallace Stevens' Later Poetry." *Journal of English Literary History* June, pp. 137–54.
1973. "The Transition from *Harmonium:* Factors in the Development of Stevens' Later Poetry." *PMLA* Jan., pp. 122–31.
Eberhart, Richard
1947. [Untitled Review]. *Accent* Summer, pp. 251–53.
Ehrenpreis, Irvin
1972. (editor) *Wallace Stevens: A Critical Anthology.* Middlesex, England: Penguin.
Enck, John J.
1964. *Wallace Stevens' Images and Judgments.* Carbondale: Southern Illinois Univ. Pr.
Frankenberg, Lloyd
1949. *Pleasure Dome.* New York: Doubleday.
Hough, Graham
1960. "The Poetry of Wallace Stevens." *Critical Quarterly* Autumn, pp. 201–18.
Howard, Leon
1960. *Literature and the American Tradition.* New York: Doubleday.
Jarrell, Randall
1963. "Fifty Years of American Poetry." *Prairie Schooner* Spring, pp. 1–27.
1972. "Reflections on Wallace Stevens." In *Poetry and the Age,* pp. 133–48. Rev. ed. New York: Noonday.
Kermode, Frank
1960. *Wallace Stevens.* New York: Grove.
1968. *Continuities.* New York: Random House.
Litz, A. Walton
1972. *Introspective Voyager: The Poetic Development of Wallace Stevens.* New York: Oxford Univ. Pr.
Lowell, Robert
1947. "Imagination and Reality." *Nation* Apr. 5, pp. 400–2.
Martz, Louis L.
1958. "Wallace Stevens: The World as Meditation." *Yale Review* June, pp. 517–36.
Matthiessen, F. O.
1952. *The Responsibilities of the Critic: Essays and Reviews by F. O. Matthiessen.* Selected by John Rackliffe, pp. 71–4. New York: Oxford Univ. Pr.
McNamara, Peter L.
1972. *Critics on Wallace Stevens.* Coral Gables, Fla.: Univ. of Miami Pr.
Meyer, Gerard Previn
1954. "Actuary Among the Spondees." *Saturday Review* Dec. 4, pp. 26–27.

Morse, Samuel French
  1970. *Wallace Stevens: Poetry As Life*. New York: Pegasus.
Munson, Gorham
  1925. "The Dandyism of Wallace Stevens." *Dial* Nov., pp. 413–17.
Powys, Llewelyn
  1924. "The Thirteenth Way." *Dial* July, pp. 45–50.
Riddel, Joseph N.
  1958. " 'Poets' Politics'—Wallace Stevens' *Owl's Clover*." *Modern Philology* Nov., pp. 118–31.
  1961. "Wallace Stevens' *Ideas of Order*: The Rhetoric of Politics and the Rhetoric of Poetry." *New England Quarterly* Sept., pp. 328–51.
  1962. "Stevens' 'Peter Quince at the Clavier': Immortality as Form." *College English* Jan., pp. 307–9.
  1967. *The Clairvoyant Eye*. Baton Rouge: Louisiana State Univ. Pr.
Semel, Jay M.
  1973. "Pennsylvania Dutch Country: Stevens' World As Meditation." *Contemporary Literature* Summer, pp. 310–19.
Sheehan, Donald
  1967. "Wallace Stevens in the 30s: Gaudy Bosh and the Gesture's Whim." In *The Thirties: Fiction, Poetry, Drama*, ed. Warren French, pp. 149–57. Deland, Fla.: Everett Edwards.
  1969. "The Ultimate Plato: A Reading of Wallace Stevens' 'Notes Toward a Supreme Fiction'." In *The Forties: Fiction, Poetry, Drama*, ed. Warren French, pp. 165–77. Deland, Fla.: Everett Edwards.
  1970. "The Whole of *Harmonium*: Poetic Technique in Wallace Stevens." In *The Fifties: Fiction, Poetry, Drama*, ed. Warren French, pp. 175–86. Deland, Fla.: Everett Edwards.
Stevens, Holly
  1967. *The Palm at the End of the Mind*. New York: Random House.
Tindall, William York
  1961. *Wallace Stevens*. Minneapolis: Univ. of Minnesota Pr.
Vance, Will
  1964. "Wallace Stevens: Man Off the Street." *Saturday Review* Mar. 23, p. 8.
Vendler, Helen Hennessy
  1969. *On Extended Wings: Wallace Stevens' Longer Poems*. Cambridge: Harvard Univ. Pr.
Viereck, Peter
  1948. "Stevens Revisited." *Kenyon Review* Winter, pp. 154–57.
Williams, William Carlos
  1956. "Wallace Stevens." *Poetry* Jan., pp. 234–39.
Winters, Yvor
  1947. "Wallace Stevens or the Hedonist's Progress." In *Defense of Reason*, pp. 431–59. Denver, Colo.: Swallow.

CHAPTER 2

Literary Heritage

> One cannot spend one's time in
> being modern when there are so
> many more important things to be.
>
> WALLACE STEVENS "ADAGIA"

The debate about Wallace Stevens's place in twentieth-century
poetry and the school of poetic thought to which he belongs
began early in controversy. On May 10, 1919, Conrad Aiken published in the *New Republic* a review of Louis Untermeyer's book
The New Era in American Poetry. Aiken's review, "The Ivory
Tower I," was followed in the same issue by Untermeyer's rebuttal of that review, "The Ivory Tower II." In reviewing *The
New Era in American Poetry*, Aiken criticizes Untermeyer's animosity toward Stevens and other poets. At the heart of the critical
disagreement and the animosity is the issue of Stevens's literary
heritage: is he part of the "lustihood" and "democracy" of Americanism or to be associated with the magical and elaborated art for
art's sake of French Impressionism? Although these two critics
exchange verbal snipes rather than resolve issues surrounding
Stevens's literary heritage, they began a debate that continues
today. At issue is not only Stevens's Americanism or French Impressionism, but his romantic, modern, and traditional strains as
well.

The American Tradition

One of the most cogent definitions of what constitutes the
"America tradition" may be found in Roy Harvey Pearce's *The
Continuity of American Poetry* (1961, pp. 376-419). In this study
Pearce differentiates between two antithetical tendencies in American poetry, the mythic poem which depends on greater meaning
and authority beyond man or his work, and the Adamic poem
based on the processes of the creative imagination as acts of self-
definition. In this Adamic mode the poem, regardless of its superficial subject, will ultimately be concerned with its own existence

and the role of the poet who created it. It allows the poet the freedom to create, but in this freedom the poet distinguishes himself from the common man and the American community, both of which require his self-definition. According to Pearce, in Wallace Stevens this Adamic phase reaches a climax because in his poetry the opposition of self and world typical of American poets can be seen at its most extreme. This opposition between the poetic and antipoetic and between the self or imagination and reality is not resolved in Stevens's poetry, but on the contrary is sharply defined as a means toward the ultimate poem. This ultimate poem depends upon the self's acknowledgment of its own limitations and its desire not to transcend but to contain these. According to Pearce, transcendence in the American continuity is replaced entirely in Stevens by containment. Yet, like other American poets, Stevens deals with "Sunday, not workaday, matters: aspiration, understanding, belief, commitment in the North American portion of the modern world" (p. 376); and through this containment, Pearce thinks Stevens approaches the problems of an American poet in the modern world more clearly than any of his contemporaries.

In focusing on Stevens's climactic role, Pearce does not slight his relationship to earlier Americans. The critic does note that Stevens, like Emerson and Poe, looked to other cultures and languages not for ideas but for an innovative means to express them, and he notes Stevens's debt to Emerson's concept of Representative Men exemplified in Stevens's representative everyman, Crispin. Stevens associated himself with Walt Whitman by his chant and his subject in "Like Decorations in a Nigger Cemetery," a poem in which Stevens overtly alludes to the nineteenth-century poet.

Pearce reviews the Stevens canon chronologically with an emphasis on the philosophical issues in the poems as they relate to this Adamic tradition. As early as *Ideas of Order* Stevens appears to repeat himself and evade the general implications of his adopted view of man as a being caught between imagination and reality. But Pearce thinks Stevens approaches this issue more directly in *Parts of a World* and *Transport to Summer* when he abandons a lyric or dramatic situation as the context for philosophical musings and turns to an "explicitly dialectical mode" (p. 391) based on discursive analysis. Yet in *Parts of a World* Pearce also finds poems that in their hortatory character exemplify the problem of an egocentric poet who sees himself as the self-creating Adam and as the community-oriented humanist. By asking in a poem of this volume, "Asides on the Oboe," how can a central man be made real, Wallace Stevens culminates a major American poetry tradition, because in asking such a question he, like Emerson and Whitman, searches for the basis of the American self's identity. He finds that identity in "collective egocentrism" and "universal humanism," both forces that negate a limited American identity and thereby create a larger identity.

In the philosophical examinations of belief in the later poems of *Transport to Summer* and *The Auroras of Autumn*, Stevens provides for the twentieth century what Emerson provided for the nineteenth—a "self-imposed demand to *think* things through, all the while calling the processes of thought itself into doubt" (p. 404). And in "Notes" and "Esthétique du Mal" he explores in the tradition of Whitman a song of myself without the transcendental rationale available to the earlier poet. Like Emerson and Whitman he is the American poet wanting to become Adam, but for Stevens this wish leads to a discovery possible only in the twentieth century: wanting to become Adam is no longer wanting to be man but god.

The opposing traditions in American poetry, mythic and Adamic, culminate in twentieth-century dichotomous strains represented by T. S. Eliot and Stevens. For Pearce, Eliot embodies the theocentric, orthodox emphasis on culture and history without man but associated with the mythic mode and contrasted to Stevens who embodies the egocentric, antinomian emphasis on personality and man without history associated with the Adamic mode. Pearce goes so far as to examine Stevens's "The Comedian as the Letter C" published in 1923 as an answer to Eliot's *The Waste Land* published in 1922. To the journey that leads to a transcendence of reality found in *The Waste Land*, Stevens proposes a journey that leads to a return to reality in the "Comedian." Pearce buttresses his case by citing Stevens's admissions that he and Eliot are opposites and that the "Comedian" is an antimythological poem. Although speculative, the point is interesting and exemplary of Pearce's attempt to cite meaningful relationships that may be interpreted as a continuity throughout most American verse. In this attempt Pearce is masterful and his study a classic one, not for any elucidating comments on particulars in Stevens's work, but for his ability to relate Stevens's idiosyncratic poetic approach to American poetry in general.

In a later article, "Wallace Stevens: America the Primordial" (*Modern Language Quarterly*, Mar. 1971), Dwight Eddins varies the Pearce approach and focuses not on Stevens's position in the

American literary tradition, but on the poet's awareness of America as the particular place where the poet as Adam may view reality with a subjective vision and create rather than perceive order. For Eddins, "the result of this awareness is that America becomes within the scope of Stevens' work both subject and symbol" p. 73). In poems such as "Farewell to Florida" and "A Mythology Reflects Its Region" the content not only illuminates the American experience but also makes that experience a metaphoric vehicle for a tenor with much broader implications, the human response to disordered reality. Eddins's definition of this American experience varies significantly from Pearce's. Pearce focuses on a continuous theoretical antithesis spanning the development of American poetry as it pertains to the poetic theory of Stevens, while Eddins defines the American experience by examining Stevens's use of geography as an index to the poet's theoretical progression. Yet from two directions, the critics arrive at a point of agreement: Eddins, like Pearce, finds in Stevens a concern with "existential challenges" characteristic of American literature and defined by the poet as a personal search for order rather than for institutional ceremonies that impose order. Eddins extends this point by asserting that these "existential challenges" are inherent in the geography of North America, cut off from Eastern culture and the Christian culture of Europe. This isolation creates an island landscape of symbols "unburdened by predetermined meanings and old accretions of emotional associations" (p. 76). Eddins's contention ignores the effect on Stevens of his Zeller family heritage and its concomitant Christian values, the very values which inspired repeated Stevens poetic refutations of Christian dogma.

According to Eddins, the island, wilderness, landscape symbolism becomes more obvious in Stevens's poems set in Florida, because in this environment the wilderness is a life source evident in tropical vegetation, sea, flora, and fauna. The raw forces of nature challenge the imagination, but eventually this same abundance becomes stagnating and oppressive. To support this, Eddins refers to "Farewell to Florida" as an example of Stevens's modifications of his wilderness aesthetic: the poet turned from the individual amid disordered lushness of the South to societal contact in the North. Stevens's poetic movement from South to New England exemplifies a change of focus from one aspect of the American wilderness to another, from the individual establishing order in primeval abundance to the individual in the stark, rocky landscapes which remind that order has issued from the physical world. This critical observation is a helpful qualification on the

Pearce thesis as is Eddins's conclusion that Stevens's use of American geography in the later poems is "an attempt to symbolize man's integration in physicality" (p. 87). This latter comment is particularly relevant to poems such as "An Ordinary Evening in New Haven" and "A Mythology Reflects Its Own Region," but one wishes Eddins would have included analyses of such poems in order to develop this point.

Stevens's version of the American Adam is also discussed by Edward Guereschi in " 'The Comedian as the Letter C': Wallace Stevens' Anti-Mythological Poem" (*Centennial Review*, Fall 1964). According to Guereschi, Stevens's "Comedian" is a "mock-heroic satire on the archetypal symbol of American self-confidence and assertiveness—the figure of Adam" (p. 465). Stevens directs his satire against the "naive folklore" and "transcendental optimism" that form the basis of the American Adam myth, but he also examines the unreality of the myth by confronting the clown Crispin's unheroic behavior. To expose Crispin and myth, Stevens manipulates the various stereotypes associated with the myth into mock-heroic reversals that parody Crispin's aspirations. Guereschi contends that the poem's structure is based on Stevens's denial of heroic destiny, earthly paradisal Eden, and mythopoeic imagination associated with the American Adam. The manifest destiny one finds in earlier American poems such as Whitman's "Passage to India" is rejected by Stevens's characterization of Crispin as aimless man wandering amid hostile nature. Rather than finding Eden, Crispin finds constant fluctuation between the imagination and reality, and rather than encountering a masculine mythic world of infinite possibilities, Crispin yields to domesticity. Unlike Pearce and Eddins, Guereschi thinks Stevens has replaced the nineteenth-century archetype with a young man whose journey reveals only the failure of the old myth and the difficulties of facing an antiheroic world without illusions.

In a 1958 lecture presented at the American Embassy in London and later published as "Wallace Stevens: A Hero of Our Time" (1962), Geoffrey Moore provides a pejorative and somewhat unenlightened English opinion of Stevens's place in the American tradition. Similar to other critics who examine this place, Moore looks closely at the "Comedian," at Stevens's relationship with the Whitmanian tradition of organic order, and at Stevens's inquiry into spiritual beliefs. But unlike other critics, Moore contends that Stevens questions and deviates from the "American socio-cultural pattern." Although Moore criticizes the poet for his inherent American lack of the "blood-beat" one finds in an English "Lycidas" or "The Ode to Melancholy," he rationalizes this fault as traceable to the American split between the intellectual and the unread masses. The article is useful only in that it exposes the unread masses of Stevens's poetry who populated England earlier in this century. Yet, to the American Adam theme, Moore provides an interesting variation; without mention or apparent knowledge of the Adamic tradition, he labels Stevens a hero of our time because of the poet's ability to confront the problems of the modern age. These problems, such as the craving for order, the nature of reality and transfiguring imagination, and the potential wholeness of life, are all associated with the American Adam by critics such as Pearce and Eddins.

The Transcendentalists and Stevens

More specific is the criticism that lodges Stevens not only in the American Adamic tradition but in the Transcendental movement as well. The most notable example of this view is presented by Marius Bewley in "The Poetry of Wallace Stevens" (*Commonweal*, Sept. 23, 1955). Unfortunately Bewley attempts to provide a complete definition of Transcendentalism's complexities, and instead quickly translates apotheosis in the physical world into modern terms that reduce Transcendentalism to "an intenser apprehension of life" (p. 618) in which physical boundaries disappear. Immediately after proposing that Stevens is an American Transcendentalist, Bewley admits the difficulties this presents without specifying them, and feebly suggests this approach will make Wallace Stevens "an explicable phenomenon"—without specifying how. Such lack of thorough definition and analysis characterizes Bewley's article. He cites Stevens's "Prologues to What Is Possible" as an example of the poet's attempt to metamorphose nature and art into a higher state by allowing the creative mind to climb toward some insight. This process approaches mysticism, according to Bewley, but he never explains how, why, or to what end it becomes mystical. Based on such undefined mysticism, Bewley compares Stevens with Emerson because both poets insist on the power of thought; are attracted to the physical world; examine a process of the world interacting with the creative mind and undergoing metamorphosis; and hold similar conceptions of the poet's role and language's power. Even such a harmless comparison is seriously damaged by Bewley's mistaken conclusion that in Stevens's work as in Emerson's one finds a soul with creative power. If Stevens spent a lifetime analyzing that power as creative imagination, he would rise from his grave at the hint of an orthodox, traditionally religious soul as its base.

Agreeing with Bewley's conclusion that Stevens is a Transcendentalist, Richard Eberhart differs from Bewley in his progress toward this conclusion. According to Eberhart in "Emerson and Wallace Stevens" (*Literary Review*, Autumn 1963), Stevens is a Transcendentalist in spite of himself because his spirit transcends this world and mortality by constructing an artistic realm for the soul. Although Eberhart thinks that Stevens produces a poetic world of an Emersonian "over-soul" in which man is one with other things through unity of being, Eberhart also notes the differences in Stevens and Emerson. Emerson believed in another world, the soul, and in the dominance of an intellectual power, reason, whereas Stevens believes in this world, the flesh, and the dominance of the senses. That Transcendentalism meant for Stevens as it did for Emerson in a lighter moment "a little beyond" is more revealing when Eberhart defines that "beyond" for Stevens as an artistic realm. This clarification of the transcendence in a twentieth-century poet is a more precise specification of Stevens's relationship to the nineteenth-century movement. Eberhart's discussion is also more helpful than Bewley's because Eberhart notes the crucial difference in Stevens's Transcendentalism: never embracing orthodox Christian spirituality, Stevens always returns from the spiritual to the worldly.

In *American Poets from the Puritans to the Present* (1968, pp. 428–42), Hyatt H. Waggoner also notes the differences between Stevens and Emerson when Stevens in *Harmonium* calls for a modern poet who is a realist creating art not as the Transcendentalist Emerson did on the aeolian harp, but as a man playing on an old-fashioned reed organ which a mortal rather than nature must play. However, in Stevens's late poetry such as "Forms of the Rock in a Night-Hymn," he approaches Emersonian Transcendentalism in the rock symbol as a twentieth-century version of Emerson's fate; and in his celebrations, Stevens provides a twentieth-century chorus to Whitman's songs of being. According to Waggoner the "new knowledge of reality" achieved in Steven's last collected poems is a function of an Emersonian imagination, emanating naturally from the world rather than imposing order on it. Waggoner's comments on the two poets, though brief, are among the most insightful on this subject.

Written on the occasion of Stevens's seventy-fifth birthday and publication of the *Collected Poems*, Delmore Schwartz's "In the Orchards of the Imagination" (*New Republic*, Nov. 1, 1954) places Stevens firmly in the tradition of New England poets like Robinson, Frost, Emerson, Thoreau, and Dickinson. Schwartz sees in Stevens the solitude, exoticism, and Puritanism of this regional school and the poetic techniques of Whitman. In judging Stevens purely American and profoundly modern, Schwartz also notes the poet's debt to Baudelaire and vers libre (a subject to be discussed later in this chapter), but fails to reconcile this French debt with the seemingly contradictory pure American Puritanism he notes in Stevens.

Many critics place Stevens more specifically in the Whitman tradition of American poetry. The most thorough treatment of the two poets' relationship to one another may be found in *Walt Whitman and Wallace Stevens* (1974) by Diane Wood Middlebrook. Middlebrook bases her comparison on what she terms the poets' "analogous contributions to American literature and to modern poetry" (p. 16), and the resemblance of the two issuing from their shared theory of poetry deriving ultimately from Coleridge's theory of the imagination and translated into the American idiom by Emerson. This theory assumes two mental conditions exist—the ordinary, workaday state of mind and a creative state of mind; and it also assumes that when the mind ascends to the creative mode, man transcends his own ego and, because he utters universal truths, becomes a poet. On the basis of this "potential" poet Whitman and Stevens formulate what Stevens terms supreme fictions. According to Middlebrook these are myths personifying the human imagination and giving this human faculty epic importance in the American culture. Her point is well taken; and her definition of a supreme fiction is one of the most lucid in the Stevens criticism and most revealing of Whitman's and Stevens's common theoretical approach to poetry. She extends this comparison of mythic approaches by noting in Whitman's *Leaves of Grass* and Stevens's *Collected Poems* a mythology in which the heroic "I," a fictive being, transcends the "malady of the quotidian." The very design of this fictive self is a mythology of imagination because it evolves from the Coleridgean idea of the mind and because it characterizes the self as a participant in discontinuous imaginative acts.

Middlebrook is quick to add that though analogous, Whitman's and Stevens's myths are not identical, and that though mutual ideas exist, Stevens was not necessarily influenced by Whitman. In allowing Stevens a similar conception of art but not demanding that such similarity be based in a direct inheritance, Middlebrook examines both poets as adherents to a belief in the unfailing sufficiency of the mind's creative relation to reality. This approach based on mutual theory and shared ideas broadens Middlebrook's scope and allows her to examine an interchange of ideas between the two poets rather than limiting her to a one-directional un-proved influence.

Middlebrook strengthens her analogies between the two poets by comparing specific poems. To Whitman's "Song of Myself" she appropriately juxtaposes Stevens's "Notes Toward a Supreme Fiction" because both poems establish the identification of "my-self" as a fiction but personification of an act of the imagination; both narrative lines are presented by personae lounging and there-by allowing perceptual receptivity and contact; and both express the sensual, sensuous, and sexual nature in the imagination's pro-cess. Although she analyzes "Song" in much detail, she depends on the reader's familiarity with "Notes" and does not provide much detail or overt comparison with the Stevens poem. Yet, her direct analogies between large sections in each of the poems, such as comparisons of Whitman's sections I-V with Stevens's "It Must Be Abstract," are invaluable to the reader interested in concrete examples of similarities in the two poets. Similar comparisons be-tween "The Auroras of Autumn" and "As I Ebb'd with the Ocean of Life" as dejection odes or "The Bouquet" with "Crossing Brooklyn Ferry" as examinations of the poet in the poem are original and perceptive readings.

In *Leaves of Grass* Whitman established his elusively autobiogra-phical persona, "the real me," who developed, as the poem pro-gressed, into a rapt perceiver and self-created identity. According to Middlebrook, Stevens's most pervasive concern in his poetry after 1942 is how to give twentieth-century form to the Whit-manian "real me." This figure becomes for Stevens the hero who reappears frequently in the poems from *Transport to Summer* through *The Rock*. In Stevens's late heroic poetry this figure be-comes the noble, affirmative, solitary, central man metaphorically identified with the sun, but a figure who takes two forms, the first-person narrator in poems such as "Notes" or a mere image such as the giant in poems concerned with defining a heroic image. Middlebrook correctly notes that the "real me" hero of Stevens's verse differs from the earlier Whitman version because the two poets and their eras possessed different perspectives on man: for Whitman imperfection was an illusion, but for Stevens such a ro-mantic notion itself was an illusion that needed revision (Stevens saw man as fallen but redeemable through the self and imagina-tion). A second important distinction correctly noted by Middle-brook resides in Whitman's autobiographical strain: Whitman's "real me" is himself personally as well as a hero, but Stevens's hero is never so personal. A third difference is noted by Middlebrook in the mythic cycles each poet's hero must undergo. Whitman's myth is based on the natural cycle from birth to death, ending in death objectively treated, while Stevens's myth is based on the natural cycle of the seasons from winter to winter with no end because the poet finds recurring hope in the returning spring.

Middlebrook borrows terms such as "ego identity" and "ego integrity" from Erik Erikson's psychoanalytic study *Childhood and Society* to explain the stages of the maturing psyche in these poems. She lapses into such external props infrequently, but when she does, such concepts seem superfluous to her thesis, distracting, and critically questionable. In general, her study is an excellent examination of the two poets with the comparisons and contrasts between them often only implied by juxtapositions of their poetic theory and practice. She leaves to the reader the final transition and thereby both strengthens and weakens her analysis: strengthens by not forcing analogies or decreating poems with too close imposition of her approach; but weakens by never specifying many common strains in the two men. The strengths obviously outweigh the weaknesses in this study which is perceptive in content and astute in structure.

Joseph N. Riddel's earlier essay "Walt Whitman and Wallace Stevens: Functions of a 'Literatus' " (1963) also firmly places Stevens in the Whitmanian tradition by isolating some elementary and general similarities in the two poets. According to Riddel, the basic common ground for Stevens and Whitman is their "indifference to traditional disciplines and an unqualified faith in poetry" (p. 31). Riddel describes Stevens's poetry as the naturalistic end of Whitman's vision of "cosmic consciousness" which climaxed in Stevens as an "existential consciousness," nonetheless grounded in a faith in poetry. For each poet, the poet himself is myth-maker. Each is fascinated by poetry as process; for Whitman a process of seeing nature's organic order as dramatization of divine law, but for Stevens a process of seeing change as primal law in man's search for permanence. Each rejects the faculty of reason for the imagination, but for Whitman this leads to spiritual flights, while for Stevens it means finding spiritual order using a secular imagination. Each accepts evil and death as realities for poetry, but for Whitman death is a union of the many and one, while for Stevens the tension between death and life leads a human to skepticism that is above immortality. Each finds poetry motivated by a feeling of alienation from nature and god but capable of functioning as a reintegration of man and his environment, and both share the "American experience" which, according to Riddel as well as Roy Harvey Pearce, includes "a search outside of tradition for some kind of personal order: moral, spiritual, even aesthetic" (p. 40).

Ultimately Riddel recognizes that Stevens rejects the Whitmanian transcendental answers found in that search. And Riddel acknowledges that the cosmic oneness Whitman establishes between poet and nature is not possible for Stevens who identifies himself with the world by sensing his separation from it. Riddel's article is as valuable as Middlebrook's book because he early detected not only similarities but rather specific and qualifying differences between the two poets.

Critics have also noted similarities in the two poets' use of language. Among these, William York Tindall in *Wallace Stevens* (1961), a study discussed in chapter one, is most laudatory in comparing the poets' celebrations of freedom, space, and landscape through an incantatory mode. Hayden Carruth's review of Stevens's *Collected Poems*, "Without the Inventions of Sorrow" (*Poetry*, Feb. 1955), is less kind to Whitman. Carruth compares both poets' use of odd, archaic, and foreign words but judges Stevens in better control of language than Whitman. In opposition to Carruth, Frank Kermode in "The Gaiety of Language" (*Spectator*, Oct. 3, 1958), a review of Robert Pack's book on Stevens, takes a back-handed slap at Stevens's Whitmanian diction. According to Kermode, Stevens exemplifies an American gaiety of language in his mixture of formal diction and "vulgar eloquence." These three comparisons devote only passing attention to the two poets and therefore lack the specificity of more exhaustive studies.

A more thorough study may certainly be found in Harold Bloom's *Wallace Stevens: The Poems of Our Climate* (1977). In this book Bloom emphasizes the longer poems and their relation to "Stevens' unacknowledged precursers: Wordsworth, Shelley, Keats, Emerson, and most crucially, Whitman" (p. vii). Bloom bases his study on a common apothegm for all post-Emersonian American poetry: "Everything that can be broken should be broken." But, he notes that this apothegm follows a triple rhythm: "It must be broken; It must not bear having been broken; It must seem to have been mended" (p. 1). To explain the common bond between these poets, Bloom proposes, in his own terms, a theory of poetic crossing. According to this theory, three types of crossings (defined as crises of poetic vision) may occur: the poet may move from ironic to synecdochal thinking; from metonymic to hyperbolic thinking; and from metaphoric to transumptive thinking.

While Stevens wrote Romantic crisis poems in the Wordsworthian-Whitmanian vein throughout his career, he experienced, according to Bloom, three periods of crisis: the Crossing of Election in 1915; Crossing of Solipsism that continued from 1921–22 through 1934–36; and the Crossing of Identification in 1942. These poetic formulations in Stevens are traceable back to Emerson's translation of ethos, logos, and pathos a la British Romanticism, into the American dialectic terms, Fate, Freedom, and Power, respectively. These same terms Bloom applies to Stevens, who, like his transcendental ancestor, wanted Freedom, reconciled himself to Fate, but loved only Power. Even more specifically, Bloom compares early Emerson to the Stevens of *Harmonium*, the skeptic Emerson who wrote *The Conduct of Life* to the Stevens who also revered Fate in *The Auroras of Autumn* and *The Rock*.

Bloom admits that though Stevens read Emerson, his "Emersonianism" was filtered through an even more pervasive influence on Stevens's work, Whitman. Like Wordsworth, Whitman wrote crisis odes of "passion and suffering rather than of act and incident." In such poems Whitman adopts an ancient heuristic device, metalepsis, defined about 150 B.C. by Hermagoras as the rhetorical stance "which translates the orator's own belatedness into a perpetual earliness" (p. 11). Although Bloom acknowledges Stevens's insistence that he never read Whitman, this critic maintains that Stevens adopts this stance in poems that, like Whitman's, deal with the ethos of man's condition. In Stevens's poems, however, the crossing in the text of the poem can not be easily detected because of the antithetical images that lead to rhetorical disjunctiveness.

After such an introduction, Bloom moves into a thorough discussion of Stevens's major volumes, confronted by the critic in the chronological order of their publication. These discussions are firmly grounded in detailed, original, and insightful explications of poems such as "Sunday Morning," examined by Bloom because of his stated dissatisfaction with the many earlier interpretations. According to Bloom, "Sunday Morning" is Tennysonian in its elegiac intensity, but Emersonian in the female persona's need for ethos and the poet's response that praises the American pathos of passion, pleasure, and pain. She is Stevens's Emersonian seeker of the First Idea, but the development of the poem in which she resides is, to Bloom, a revision of Wordsworth's *Intimations* ode, the model Romantic crisis poem. Stevens's "Peter Quince at the Clavier" in this same volume Bloom describes as an epilogue to the greater "Sunday Morning," but nonetheless an important footnote releasing "the repressed eroticism of Stevens' meditation upon his muse, death, and the death of God and the gods" (p. 36). While overburdened with Freudian connotations, this pithy characterization of "Peter Quince" provides a new and interesting interpretation that relates seemingly disjoint samples of Stevens's early style. Here, as in later comments about Stevens's Oedipal tendency to domesticate his muse as his mother, Bloom betrays his perceptivity and momentarily relies on the unnecessary crutch of Freudian criticism.

In far more appropriate and explicit critical terms, Bloom applies comments from Ruskin's *Modern Painters* III (1856) to Stevens's "The Snow Man." Stevens, like Ruskin, Bloom cogently notes, condemns the pathetic fallacy of "imagistic homogeneities." Drawing poetic and prose comments from Emerson, Whitman, and Nietzsche, Bloom explicates "The Snow Man" as a poem which is reductionistic in that it strips man of his mythologies and divinity. Continuing his analysis of the *Harmonium* years, Bloom describes "The Comedian as the Letter C" as a parody that culminates and almost destroys the Romantic quest poem tradition. Bloom agrees with Helen Hennessy Vendler (see chapter 1) that, though the poem is hardly comic, it participates in the quest mode that it ostensibly mocks. Labeling this poem as "the most outrageous in modern poetry," Bloom also finds evidence in its absurd heterogeneity of the Romantic crisis poem which sinks to even greater depths of disorder in "Sea Surface Full of Clouds." In a strongly negative but well-founded conclusion about this era of Stevens's development, Bloom compares Stevens's sea scenes to those in Whitman, but finds "the Whitmanian ocean has been evaporated, and what remains is a beholding that is replete with signification yet quite devoid of meaning" (p. 85). The visionary capacity for response in the early "Sunday Morning" could not be sustained by Stevens as it had not been sustained by Wordsworth, Coleridge, Emerson, and Whitman. The result, for Bloom, is the common crisis of a Romantic poet.

While Bloom sustains this approach throughout by utilizing chronological development as a means of tracing, through detailed explications, Stevens's adaptation of the Romantic crisis poem, he is at his best when he withdraws from the individual poems and their development in order to deduce a statement of general meaning in the Stevens canon. In a discussion of "Thirteen Ways of Looking at a Blackbird" Bloom masterfully asserts, having logically progressed through several chapters to his conclusion, that this and other Stevens poems are studies in disjunction. Yet, he continues, while disjunction is a part of the Romantic crisis poem, Stevens's use of the technique is distinguished by this poet's emphasis on his own disjunctiveness and the crossing itself as an overt rather than hidden source of meaning. For Bloom "Stevens writes a poetry centered on the *aporia* between rhetoric as persuasion and rhetoric as a system of tropes, and in a curious way this centering became a guarantee of his poetic importance" (p. 105).

Bloom values "The Man with the Blue Guitar" as pivotal in the poet's development and examines its "intertextual relationships" with other poets' verse. Specifically, Bloom discusses this poem as a variant of Whitman's "Song of Myself" model and as a characteristic crisis poem in which the crossings may be easily isolated. This poem's order progresses in sections I-IV from "dialectic irony of presence and absence" to the "synecdochal reversal" in V-VI and the "metonymic isolation" of VII-XVII. The "Crossing of Election" becomes the "Crossing of Solipsism" in the "hyperbolical Sublime" of sections XVII–XXVII; and moves into the "Crossing of Identification" in the "transumptive balance between projection and introjection" (p. 120) of sections XXVIII–XXXIII. Bloom's analysis of the poet's techniques that reflect crisis resolution is, however, firmly grounded in comparisons with theory and technique combinations found in Emerson's American Sublime, Coleridge's imagination, and Shelley's transformations.

Bloom proceeds through *Parts of a World* as a model American Romantic volume replete with images of transcendental despair and a poet as central man; through *Notes Toward a Supreme Fiction* as the *Song of Myself* for our time; through *Transport to Summer* with its poems representative of an Emersonian dialectic between Fate and Power and its images that recall Shelley, Keats, and Whitman; through *The Auroras of Autumn* with its title poem as a culmination of the Wordsworthian crisis tradition and origin traceable to Wordsworth's "Prelude," Emerson's "The Poet," Dickinson's lyrics, and Shelley's "Ode to the West Wind" and "Mont Blanc"; through *An Ordinary Evening in New Haven,* Stevens's Whitmanian affirmation of the eye's plain version of reality; to *The Rock* and Stevens's final phase in which Bloom finds the poet mastering a shorter, more intense and original lyric form. In these late poems, Stevens exemplifies a Whitmanian acceptance of his own mortality, and a mastery of the American elegiac mode evident in "To an Old Philosopher in Rome." But, he also typifies the final assertion of poetic power in the poem's creator, a version of the heightening American Sublime, that for Bloom issued to Stevens through the American mythology of Emerson and Whitman.

Bloom's final chapter, "Coda: Poetic Crossing," examines the philosophical predecessors of this critics approach to poetry. He briefly summarizes elements of theory from studies such as Owen Barfield's *Saving the Appearances*, Paul de Man's *Intentional Structure of the Romantic Image*, C. G. Clarke's *Romantic Paradox*, and Geoffrey Hartman's *The Fate of Reading;* and reviews contentions made by John Hollander, Walter J. Ong, Richard McKeon, and W. J. Bates. Yet, Bloom's theory of crossings, though evolved from problems and needs isolated by other theoreticians, is, in its approach to the process of interaction between linguistics and meaning, original in its emphasis on the psychology of rhetoric.

> A crisis is a crucial point or turning point, going back to the Greek *krisis*, which derived from *krinein*, "to separate" or "to decide," from which came also the Greek *kritos*, "separated" or "chosen," and so *Kritikos*, "able to discern," and so to be a critic. The Indo-European root is *skeri*, "to cut, separate, sift," from which stem such allied words as scribble, script, and hypocrisy, as well as crisis and critic. "Crossing" comes from a different root, a hypothetical one, *ger*, for "curving" or "crooked," but the accidents of linguistic history make it natural for us to associate "crossing" with the groups that include crisis, criticism, and script. I use "crossing" arbitrarily but precisely for the negative moments that collect meaning in the post-Romantic crisis-poem, insofar as meaning ever is present within a single text rather than wandering about between texts. But meaning also wanders about within a text, and its location by crossings ought to provide a perspective for interpretation that we haven't had before, a more certain link between rhetoric and psychology than my own ventures into identifying tropes and defenses have thus far been able to establish (400–1).

For Bloom, a crossing "intervenes" at a crisis point in which the poet questions his own creative ability (Crossing of Solipsism), or confronts mortality through identifying with another object or individual (Crossing of Identification). In describing these, Bloom unnecessarily relies on psychoanalytic terms, sublimation, introjection, repression, regression and reaction formation, in order to explain poetic techniques such as synecdoche, metonymy, and metalepsis. When Bloom as critic moves away from the constructs of the analyst's couch and back into the scholar's vernacular, he is admirably explicit in noting that these crossings represent negative moments and places in which the poet's rhetoric is most disjunctive but paradoxically the meaning most intense.

With the efficacy of psychoanalysis itself a matter of considerable debate between psychologists and psychiatrists, its transplanted validity in a separate domain, theory of literary criticism, is even more questionable. Bloom's penetrating comments on specific poems as well as his apt discussion of the poetic process are too precise to rely on the imprecision of an approach borrowed from another time, place, and discipline. In short, his own approach to poetry is too meaningful in its own terms, to borrow from the subjective constructs of the Freudian critic.

Wallace Stevens: The Poems of Our Climate attests to the fact that Stevens criticism has improved with age. Bloom, divested of his Freudian lapses more than any critic before him is able to astutely explicate the poems; provide a unifying theory of Stevens's development within the British-American Romantic tradition; deduce from poems and theory Stevens's importance in literary history; judge the good and the bad in the poet's verse as separate from his contribution as a major poet; and propose a viable approach to poetry in general. So much is seldom asked of one critic, and is almost never given. Bloom's study is important because of this contribution to a theory of poetics and because of its integral place in the development of Stevens criticism. What most critics praise as the abstract unpracticed right and just analysis of their critical predecessors and peers, Bloom incorporates in his method. He responds to other critical ideas not as correct answers or inaccurate assertions but as springboards that allow his own dive into the complex issues of poetic meaning and historical continuity.

Yet one crucial distinction is never made by this otherwise readable critic: Bloom neglects to differentiate the English Romanticism of Wordsworth, Shelley, and Keats from the American Transcendentalism of Emerson and Whitman. Instead of specifying any variance between the two schools, Bloom subsumes under the general rubric of "romanticism" all in Stevens that resembles any of these poets' work. Left to the reader's determination then is any definition of the term "romantic."

The Modern American Landscape and Stevens

Delmore Schwartz in "Wallace Stevens—An Appreciation" (*New Republic*, Aug. 22, 1955) links Stevens not only to Whit-

man, but to Poe, Melville, and Dickinson because of similarities he
finds in style, reticence, and "depth of feeling." Beyond Stevens's
relationship with these earlier poets, Schwartz notes in Stevens's
poems a pure twentieth-century American tone. Other critics
have been more exact though hardly more precise in defining the
modern aspects of Stevens's Americanism. F. O. Matthiessen in
The Responsibilities of the Critic: Essays and Reviews (1952)
notes Stevens's use of the modern nonsensical and grotesque in
language to defy rationality, but he finds in Stevens's concern with
observed things, the imagination's power over the observable, and
in the recurrence of sunlight and moonlight symbols, an echo of
Nathaniel Hawthorne.

Examinations of Stevens's American and modern symbols have
not always been as brief as Matthiessen's comment, but they have
frequently focused on the nineteenth-century heritage behind
those images and symbols. In "Wallace Stevens in the Tropics: A
Conservative Protest" (*Yale Review*, Dec. 1970), Jan Pinkerton
suggests that Stevens's early attraction to images of the tropics and
jungle vegetation places him firmly in the American tradition,
while his poetic longing for an exotic and forbidden land as an
alternative to America labels him a participant in the "nineteenth-
century American tradition of conservative protest" (p. 215) associated with Hawthorne and Melville. Pinkerton is inaccurate
and misleading in suggesting all of these men feared the "renova-
tive tendencies of Northern man" (p. 218). Such a statement
exemplifies the critic's misunderstanding of Stevens's concept of
North in poems like "The Snow Man" and "The Auroras of
Autumn." Pinkerton misses entirely the poet's ambivalence toward
nothingness and purity coupled with sterility and beauty in such
poems. That these men "embrace" the tropics is Pinkerton's evidence for their "conservative protest against destructive activity
and spurious progress" (p. 220). Pinkerton's comparison of Stevens and Hawthorne on the basis of mutual objections to change,
improvement, and nonacquiescence to the status quo, as well as
their evocation of ease and indolence to counter such change, is
misleading to say the least. Such a contention is contrary to the
emphasis of Stevens's "Sunday Morning" in which indolence and
ease are a form of passive rebellion against the status quo, and to
Stevens's "Disillusionment of Ten O'Clock" in which acquiescence
to the status quo is reflected in boring and complacent sleep.

Pinkerton further asserts that Stevens embraced the South as an
"indictment of his countrymen" (p. 221) and a protest against
"impoverished sensibility." Although the critic is correct in noting

the refreshment and inspiration the poet obtains from the southern landscape, Pinkerton seriously weakens the contention by interpreting Stevens's preference for Florida as conservatism and racism. This and Pinkerton's unfounded opinion that Stevens ultimately rejected Florida for the "life of an austere New Englander" (p. 220) are hardly defensible when one examines the scope and focus of Stevens's tropical images.

Louise Bogan in "*Harmonium* and the American Scene" (*Trinity Review*, May 1954), briefly praises Stevens for the "American background" he establishes in his first volume's geography. Contrary to Pinkerton, Bogan finds wit, elegance, and charm in Stevens's use of the South's geography, but she finds that geography devoid of the romanticism and sentimentalism most critics note in Stevens's creations of American landscape.

The romanticism associated with Stevens's natural scenes has led critics such as David Kalstone in "Conjuring with Nature" (1971) to place Stevens in the pastoral tradition. According to Kalstone, in Stevens's pastoral the poet is not only an intruder into natural scenes, he is merely an isolated spectator as well. In this, Stevens is representative of a modern sensibility that defines the spectator as an intense viewer of nature who detects some relationship between his mind and that nature. Although Stevens repeatedly suggests the rich and changeable character of the natural world, he achieves a sense of "the traditional feeling of pastoral" by noting the poet's limited vision and by affirming nature only in conditional or guarded terms. Kalstone extends his examination by comparing Stevens with Robert Frost because both attempt to convince the reader that the hostility and changeability of nature are subjects for the imagination. This modern version of the pastoral in the two poets is based, according to Kalstone, on the perceptions of the eye and ear rather than on the traditional "companionable song" (p. 263). Graham Hough in "The Poetry of Wallace Stevens" (*Critical Quarterly*, Autumn 1960b), also briefly relates Stevens and Frost as examples of a characteristic American feeling that nature is independent of man and indifferent to him.

Arthur C. McGill (*The Celebration of Flesh: Poetry in Christian Life*, 1964, pp. 126–86) is more thorough than Kalstone or Hough in specifying what characterizes nature for the modern sensibility. McGill thinks Stevens's attempt to dispel the modern attitude toward nature contributes to the trivial and difficult in his poetry. Unlike the typical modern poet, Stevens does not find nature accessible only through precise measurement, appearance by way of the senses untrustworthy, and nature's behavior fixed through constant and predictable repetition. And, according to McGill, Stevens not only rejects accepted modern tenets about nature, but traditional techniques for describing nature as well. Because the poet discards accepted modes of description, his style is obscure as he avoids familiar scenic arrangements, distant scenes, and rural places. Instead, he places his people and objects not in space and landscape but in time and the moment of impact.

Although McGill's focus on Stevens's Christianity or lack of it is tangential to the poetry at best, in spite of that bias and McGill's judgment that Stevens's world view must be rejected by Christians, the critic does offer a few momentary illuminations. He examines Stevens's "Late Hymn from the Myrrh-Mountain" as a poem that does not "tell" anything but simply in its obscure style creates and communicates relations between the mind and surrounding world. And, he acknowledges that the reader of Stevens, though finding the poet's redemptive significance in the secular world and therefore judging it unpalatable, may enjoy the poet's "glory in nature."

Cleanth Brooks agrees with this judgment in "Poetry Since *The Waste Land*" (*Southern Review*, July 1965). For Brooks, poetry since Eliot's "Waste Land" is based on the juxtaposition of and confrontation with interconnections in the reader's imagination. But the land bequeathed to Stevens after Eliot's poem is one of benevolent, post-Christian nature. One finds in Stevens, then, reassuring green pastures and comforting waters. Robert Langbaum (*The Modern Spirit*, 1970, pp. 101–26) comes to the same conclusions as Brooks and McGill but for different reasons. According to Langbaum, Stevens's use of nature is very modern in the extreme distance it creates between man and the natural world. Like Wordsworth, Stevens manipulates nature to communicate a sense of the age in which he lives; and like Marianne Moore he is concerned with the relationship of nature and civilization's styles. Langbaum finds in Stevens and Moore a direct proportion between the poet's sense of the wildness in nature and an artistic appreciation of the artificial in art and civilization. Langbaum's comments would have been more accurate had he not found nature and art in Stevens as mutually exclusive elements. In an earlier published article, "The New Nature Poetry" (*American Scholar*, Summer 1959), Langbaum examines Stevens's "The Snow Man" as the juxtaposition of a human apprehending a winter landscape with a mindless "mind" of a snow man apprehending that same landscape. The poem is used by Langbaum as an example of Stevens's nature poetry based on nature's mindless and nonhuman otherness as well as its inaccessibility to human knowledge.

In direct opposition to these critics who place Stevens in the tradition of American nature poetry and modernism, or in the tradition of nineteenth-century Transcendentalism, one critic finds Stevens unlike any other American poet. John Tryford in "Wallace Stevens" (*Trace*, Fall 1967) praises Stevens for his calm, unperturbed, and cerebral characteristics amidst the emotional outbursts the critic notes in other American poets. Seeming to disregard the entire Transcendental strain, Tryford thinks Stevens differs in that he focused his sensibilities on himself. Little more can or should be said about Tryford's undeveloped remarks except that they disagree with most if not all of the well-founded criticism on the subject.

The French Tradition

Perhaps the most frequently discussed and frequently agreed upon issue in criticism about Stevens is the poet's debt to the French Symboliste movement. The critics seem to naturally fall into two roughly chronological camps: those who early established similarities between the poet and his French predecessors; and those who followed early critics' leads by acknowledging similarities but also proposing differences. This latter group also contains those who recently have found more variance than similarity.

Similarities between Stevens and the French

The classic essay on the subject, "Wallace Stevens and Mallarmé" published by Hi Simons in *Modern Philology* (May 1946), is acknowledged, if not quoted, by most critics who examine the question of French influence. Because the Simons essay appears so early in the criticism, it is amazingly astute in its groundbreaking task. As one of the first critics to systematically examine Stevens's relationship to the French Symbolists, Simons reviews previous passing comparisons of Stevens and Mallarmé made by critics such as John Gould Fletcher, Horace Gregory, Yvor Winters, and Morton Zabel. To support his analogy, Simons cites seven specific textual parallels between the two poets and seven more general likenesses only some of which he labels as "due to derivation." The textual parallels range from similar poet attitudes toward mortality in "Quand l'ombre menaca . . ." and "Of Heaven Considered as a Tomb" to similar images of women's feet lying cold in bed in "Don du poeme" and "The Emperor of Ice-Cream."

According to Simons, the most pervasive likeness resides in the poets' use of color symbolism. In Mallarmé, white and blue are the most important colors and may be used literally, metonymically for the sky but without any metaphoric tenor, or symbolically. Stevens uses colors more "variously" and "audaciously," according to Simons, but his "blue" is used symbolically as Mallarmé's "azur" is used, and in both cases, the symbol evolves from associations with the sky's color. The second similarity Simon cites in both poets is use of "figures of the negative order" (p. 244). This figure in Mallarmé is usually a paradox in which a negative is treated as a positive and an intangible is made tangible. Stevens uses the concept of "nothingness" in this way according to Simons. To both poets the negative order, or concepts emptied of ordinary sensuous content, exemplified "the mind turning to its own figurations as more valid than the figurations of brute reality" (p. 249).

In Stevens and Mallarmé, Simons finds a concern with the problems of poetics and the role of the poet in society, as well as an obsession with the theme of poetry issuing from a sense of the world of things impinging on the world of the imagination. The poets also resemble in their use of conceits, a poetic technique defined by Simons as "a figure in which two terms of a comparison meet on limited ground but are otherwise incongruous" (p. 251). Both poets use condensed conceits, but only Stevens is master of the expanded conceit, a characteristic which places the twentieth-century American in the metaphysical tradition of poets such as Donne. Mallarmé is not quite as successful with this technique because, according to Simons, he lacks the intellectual wit of Stevens. Yet both are masters of word play and word music, and both employ implication in their communication. In their metaphors the tenor is left to implication, a method which, at the base of both poets' rhetoric, changes ideas into images.

More specifically, Simons attempts to account for the overt French influence detectable in the Stevens of 1915–19. Although Simons interprets Stevens's second play, "Carlos Among the Candles" (published December 1917 in *Poetry*) as an attempt at Symbolist drama, he rationalizes such seeming signs of general influence as "Francophile tendencies of the American intelligentsia" (p. 257), resulting from a general air of the time. However, he notes a direct connection between Stevens and Mallarmé through a Harvard friend of Stevens, Walter Arensberg. While Stevens was writing his early postcollege verse, Arensberg was translating "L'Apres-midi d'un faune," a coincidence which, according to Simons, inspired or renewed the Stevens interest in Mallarmé. Although Simons notes that Stevens emulated Mallarmé's virtuosity in tone, image, and verbal effect, he is quick to add that Stevens did not imitate the French poet. Simons's focus on Mallarmé as provider of exemplary methods and style is an apt one as is his conclusion that Stevens's style is itself one of the most distinctive and individual in twentieth-century poetry.

A second early critic of Stevens, William Van O'Connor, agrees with Simons's analysis of the poet's metaphysical and Symbolist tendencies. In *Sense and Sensibility in Modern Poetry* (1948; pp. 76–167, 233, 259), O'Connor finds hints of the French in Stevens's "rapid movement . . . exclamatory and quizzical temper . . . sudden oscillations between joy and anger" (p. 76). Unlike Simons, O'Connor traces the poet's elegance and exoticism not to one French figure, but to many: Mallarmé, Gautier, Gourmont, Villiers de L'Isle-Adam, and the Comte de Lautreamont. In his later *The Shaping Spirit* (1950), the first book-length study of Stevens, O'Connor isolates many Stevens characteristics still accepted by critics today. Among these, O'Connor generally discusses many Symbolist tendencies without articulating Stevens's particular Symbolist habits, but for many others he notes the direct comparison between Stevens and his French antecedents. Acknowledging Stevens's indebtedness to the Symbolists in general, O'Connor lodges Stevens's antecedents specifically in the ambiguity of Mallarmé, the Correspondences of Baudelaire, and the ironic detachment of Laforgue. O'Connor is wisely unwilling to call these influences but is willing to label Stevens a twentieth-century representative of nineteenth-century estheticism. Stevens's "symbolist esthetic" includes his translations of one sense impression into another, similar to Baudelaire's correspondences and most obviously evident in "Peter Quince at the Clavier." In this poem, Stevens's correspondences take the form of synesthesia, intermingling art forms, and mergings of the artistic and the idealistic. Other poetic techniques O'Connor attributes to Stevens's French resemblance include his use of metaphor, expanding symbolism, irony, and language; but the repeated Symbolist theme that O'Connor returns to again and again is Stevens's examination of the human imagination's role in poetry.

Alfred Kreymborg's early assessment (*Our Singing Strength: An Outline of American Poetry*, 1929, pp. 500–4) of Stevens as an "American reared on French Symbolism" agrees with Simons's and O'Connor's longer analyses. In an extremely honorific glance at Stevens, Kreymborg notes the poet's perfection in his use of sensation, color, sound, versification, and language; and Kreymborg proposes that, although fantastic and grotesque on the surface, Stevens's poems are immersed in the imagination. Warren Ramsey merely reiterates much from these early critics when in "Uses of the Visible: American Imagism, French Symbolism" (*Comparative Literature Studies*, 1967) he notes French verse provided a rich and varied language model for Stevens as an alternative to the "don'ts" of Imagism. Like Simons, Ramsey isolates Mallarmé's influence on specific Stevens poems, and like O'Connor he examines Stevens's symbolic order as an effect of French Symbolism. According to Ramsey, Stevens's passion for symbolic order can best be seen in "The Idea of Order at Key West," an opinion shared by most Stevens critics.

An earlier article by Ramsey, "Wallace Stevens and Some French Poets" (*Trinity Review*, May 1954) is more cautious in its comparisons of Stevens and the French. Acknowledging the resemblances between Stevens's and Mallarmé's attitudes toward an examination of problems in cognition, Ramsey concludes that Stevens did not directly resemble any one French poet in particular but assimilated their manipulations of language in general. Citing the Simons article as adequate coverage of the Stevens–Mallarmé comparison, Ramsey suggests a discussion of their dissimilarities would be helpful. Yet Ramsey follows his own suggestion only by noting "azur" is a "more stable" term for Mallarmé than "blue" is for Stevens. The most obvious French influence, according to Ramsey, is evident in the themes of *Harmonium:* "mediocrity of the quotidian, the boundlessness of ennui, the limitations of the bourgeois, . . . the relentlessness and ungovernableness of the life force, the possibility of redemption in art" (p. 37). Ramsey concludes that thought in Stevens's poetry proceeds like the thought of several French writers. He cites Verlaine's influence in the stylized landscapes of *Harmonium;* Laforgue's influence in the artist as clown figure, inflated language, ambiguous titles, and equation of imagination with moon imagery; and Baudelaire's influence in the development of repeated images and a belief in means of apprehension as similar for all of the arts.

Simons's classic essay on Stevens and Mallarmé was preceded by an article devoted to Laforgue and Stevens. H. R. Hays's "Laforgue and Wallace Stevens" (*Romantic Review*, July-Sept. 1934) lacks the clarity of focus and reference to specific similar techniques and poems found in the Simons counterpart. Hays foolishly judges Stevens's poems before 1934 as definitive examples of his work, regardless of poems to follow, but also notes that from the beginning of Stevens's career, he assumed a Laforgian "ironic, technically brilliant, method" (p. 245). According to Hays, Stevens and Laforgue examine the same problems as well as use the same method to confront them. In both poets the problem of decay in religion and the resulting disillusionment are juxtaposed with fading traditional idealism and a sharpened perception of reality.

Although Hays emphasizes such similarities, he does, however, cite minor differences in the two poets. Faced with a lack of traditional idealism, Laforgue moves toward metaphysical horror and experiences maudlin emotion. Stevens, faced with the same lack, is willing to abandon traditional forms of thought, "apparently feeling that the spiritual side of life will automatically come out right" (p. 245). Wallace Stevens is not so passively optimistic as Hays would have us believe. Despite these differences, Hays finds in the two poets analogous artistic poses, but he fails to define or describe any such poses. The definitive Laforgian influence he isolates in Stevens's work includes the use of realistic detail, utilization of technical terms and foreign words, manipulation of dry humor and grotesque juxtaposition for irony, and choice of words for the associations produced by their sound and musical effects. Although Hays praises both poets as masters, he clearly emphasizes Stevens's debt to Laforgian influence. Critics since Hays have been wise in cautiously avoiding such speculative conclusions and unqualified terms like "debt" and "influence." Hays is quick to add that from Laforgue, Stevens borrowed technical devices and an elegant, precise attitude toward art but refined these techniques by adapting them to his own language. This point is accurate and the article generally useful, if sketchy, as an example of the earliest attempt to examine a subject—Stevens and the French—that is still bearing critical fruit.

In *Poetry of This Age 1908–1958* (1960, pp. 215–18), J. M. Cohen also labels Stevens a disciple of Laforgue but fails to find any virtue in the Frenchman's American follower. According to Cohen, Stevens's fault is "too great tranquility . . . a failure . . . to state any belief stronger than the wish to live by aestheticism if only aestheticism were a viable attitude" (p. 215). Judging Stevens's *Collected Poems* a failure, Cohen further characterizes Stevens as a "baffled metaphysician" and a self-deprecatory American typical of his generation. The source of this inferiority issues, according to Cohen, from Stevens's confrontation with European culture—a culture he could not absorb, reject, imitate, or rival. Although typical of the British critical mentality that condescendingly reviewed Stevens as some inferior imitator of English or Continental verse, Cohen's article needs to be acknowledged only for its passing reference to the Stevens–Laforgue relationship.

The Stevens–Baudelaire relationship is briefly discussed by William York Tindall in *The Literary Symbol* (1955, pp. 214–17, 258–61). The resemblance between the two poets, according to Tindall, is most noticeable in their shared dandy figure. For both poets this persona is characterized by ironic reservations, a sense of apartness from the world, a willingness to comment on that apartness, and a fondness for artifice. Unlike Hays and Cohen, Tindall does not pass judgment on the relative merits of either poet, but instead includes his comments on Stevens and Baudelaire within his more extended discussion of the discursive and non-discursive modes in poetry.

Oscar Cargill in *Intellectual America: Ideas on the March* (1941, pp. 255–58) extends comparisons with the French to include Rimbaud. In "Peter Quince at the Clavier" Cargill finds a mixture of Poe and Mallarmé, while in "The Weeping Burgher" he finds an imitation of Laforgue and in "The Paltry Nude Starts on a Spring Voyage" echoes of Rimbaud. Beyond these simplistic, undeveloped comments, Cargill's approach resembles Cohen's in its negativism. According to Cargill, Stevens belongs in the tradition of French Decadents, yet he falls short of their mark: "His eccentricities are parodies of their inventiveness; his verbalism, an effort to mimic their curious juxtaposition of words" (p. 255). Stevens adopted the Symbolist aesthetic that equates poetry to music and requires a pure art divorced from the political scene. This, according to Cargill, is what one finds in *Harmonium*. Cargill further damns Stevens as a good, not great, poet, confined by decadence and limited originality, who functions intelligently within such narrow confines. One wishes Cargill had functioned so.

Differences between Stevens and the French

Although many critics have placed Stevens firmly in the Symbolist tradition and either praised or chastised him for that place, other more moderate critics, building on evidence and analogies established by their more headstrong colleagues, have attempted to present the Stevens–French relationship as a more ambiguous topic. The most thorough and well known of those who emphasize differences as well as similarities, Michel Benamou, collected his published essays on the subject in one volume, *Wallace Stevens and the Symbolist Imagination* (1972). Benamou stresses that he is concerned not with proving any direct influence but with noting affinities between Stevens and the French. Benamou distinguishes between those poets such as Yeats who are interested in *symbolic* art, those such as Swinburne who are *Symbolist* in design, and those descended from the French *Symboliste* movement. He labels Stevens a combination of French and American Symboliste and symbolist heritage: "Stevens and the Symbolist imagination are one, if by symbolist we mean central, and by imagination a horizon of basic images the center of which has shifted, since ancient times, from god to man" (p. xiii).

Like other critics before him, Benamou develops his argument by comparing Stevens with individual French artists. He devotes separate chapters to Stevens and Laforgue; Stevens, Mallarmé, and Baudelaire; and to Stevens and Apollinaire. According to Benamou, Stevens and Laforgue share an Impressionist sensibility. Both use hyphenated colors for color mixing; both use color as symbolic rather than picturesque; both use mystical rhetoric ironically; both use foreign words to refresh their poetic lines; and both use nonsense words in a meaningful way. Despite these similarities, Benamou focuses on the more important differences. He disagrees with Paul Rosenfeld in "Wallace Stevens" (1925) and René Taupin (*L'Influence du Symbolisme Francais sur la Poésie Américaine*, 1929, pp. 276–77), both of whom view Stevens as a Laforgian Pierrot figure. Instead, Benamou finds Stevens akin to Laforgue's conception of the artist rather than his characterization of the clown. Stevens like Laforgue saw himself as a misfit in the "quotidian" of life, but Laforgue could never escape the negation and boredom of self, while Stevens found affirmation and a type of remedy in the imagination. In the Pierrot figure Laforgue manifests his attitude toward art: clownish and self-ironist. In Stevens this same figure seems to provide the basis for personae such as Carlos in Stevens's play "Carlos Among the Candles," Crispin in "The Comedian as the Letter C," and Hoon in "Tea at the Palaz of Hoon." Yet in Laforgue, Pierrot is allied with the symbol of moon and theme of death, while in Stevens, the moon is not associated with mortality and negativism. The emphasis of the two is, according to Benamou, quite different: Stevens is a poet of light and imagination while Laforgue is a poet of the dark and negation. Finding no textual evidence that Laforgue influenced Stevens and noting no direct Stevens allusions to the French artist, Benamou conservatively finds only an indication of affinity in their art.

In his chapter on Baudelaire, Mallarmé, and Stevens, Benamou compares Stevens's *Harmonium* with Baudelaire's *Les Fleurs du Mal* in both poets' use of metaphor and metamorphosis. Both manipulate the imaginative faculty into creating a poetic world in which a beautiful surface and superficial unity hide the darkness beneath. In other words, for both poetry is a means for overcoming the terrors of reality. Stevens was familiar with Baudelaire's work and alluded to it in several poems and essays including "Dutch Graves in Bucks County" and "Sea Surface Full of Clouds." In *Opus Posthumous* one finds Stevens's analysis of "La Vie Antérieure" and in *The Necessary Angel*, Stevens's pronouncement on the aesthetics of decreation, an obvious Baudelairian statement. According to Benamou, both confront "gnawing worms and icy hells" (p. 101), and both follow an exoticism that moves inward, but Stevens achieves a more positive attitude after his inward glimpses: the rapport between man and nature in Stevens's fecund images is not possible in Baudelaire nor is the Adamic hopefulness of Stevens. And, although both poets employ images of a dandy's clothes, Baudelaire manipulates them as spiritual symbols of a self-purification through petrification process, while for Stevens such clothing is usually mere self-protection.

In contrast, Sevens and Mallarmé share images of nakedness in which "divestment and naked sight" lead to some awareness of the supreme fiction. The poetic notion that links these two poets is the theme of purity which, according to Benamou, also distinguishes them. For Stevens purity is achieved in the real world but for the French it can only be found beyond this world. Both share the Symbolist's self-conscious attitude toward the fictive nature of poetry and the Impressionist's enthusiasm for purity in the artist's eye, but the two achieve such purity by different manipulations of vocabulary: "Mallarmé purified by sterilizing, Stevens freshened by renewing" (p. 110). Examples of Mallarmé's cutting away associations and Stevens's nondivisive technique would have been helpful but are not provided by Benamou. On the whole these, like all Benamou comments, are critically sound, thorough in documentation, and explicit in reference.

The last French artist to whom Benamou compares Stevens is surprisingly Apollinaire. The critic acknowledges no massive evidence exists to link the two, but he proposes that they shared parallel poetic development in the 1910–12 stylistic transformations of Apollinaire's poetry and the 1930–37 transformations of Stevens's. The major changes in both artists were inspired by individual crises in their symbolist values and by their consideration of cubist painting. Because of this latter emphasis, the chapter will be more thoroughly discussed as an example of the criticism linking Stevens to other art forms. Although Benamou excels most when he compares the roles of poetry and painting for Stevens (to be discussed in chapter 3), the objectivity of his total critical inquiry is admirable. He is able to focus on the similarities and differences in Stevens and the French without sacrificing either one to the other. More attention to specific poetic techniques would have strengthened these chapters by augmenting Benamou's lucid assessment of comparable poetic theories.

A summary of the Stevens–French criticism, Haskell M. Block's "The Impact of French Symbolism on Modern American Poetry" (1970), preceded Benamou's collection of his own previously published esays on the subject. Block's comments lack the specificity of analogy and adept comparisons found in Benamou's written articles' attention to individual French artists, but do provide a good general introduction and summary on the subject as well as some attention to poetic technique missing in Benamou. Describing Stevens as the "most complex of all American poets in his symbolist affinities" (p. 198), Block acknowledges that the American poet transcends any antecedent group or movement, and differs from as well as resembles his French predecessors. According to Block, Stevens's awareness of the French Symbolists may be traced back to Stevens's Harvard years, 1897–1900, in which the poet might have heard Henri de Regnier's Harvard lectures describing new French poetry. Block agrees with Robert Buttel's comment in *Wallace Stevens: The Making of Harmonium* (1967) that Verlaine was the earliest French poet to influence Stevens; but Block also finds evidence of broader French influence in Stevens's post-Harvard verse that appeared as early as 1914. Noting similarities with Mallarmé in Stevens's poems as early as "Carnet de Voyage" which appeared in the September 1914 issue of *Trend*, Block is also quick to quote Stevens's reply of July 8, 1941, to Hi Simons's question about French influence. In this letter Stevens disclaims any but an unconscious borrowing from the French.

Like Benamou, Block contends that such a disclaimer and lack of direct evidence or allusion lead a critic to examine "affinity" rather than "influence" when dealing with Stevens and the French. And, like Benamou, he finds Stevens most like the Symbolists in his theory of aesthetics. Unlike Benamou, Block extends his analysis of theory by also reviewing Stevens's Symbolist techniques. He associates Stevens's "Peter Quince at the Clavier," "a hymn to the music of poetry" (p. 203), with Symbolist synesthesia; the suggestiveness of "Sea Surface Full of Clouds" with Symbolist *pay-*

sage; and "Blanch McCarthy" with Symbolist "intimations of invisible powers" (p. 204). And, unlike most other critics on the subject, Block finds the most striking evidence of Stevens's Symbolist affinities not in *Harmonium* but in the later mature verse. According to Block, only in this late verse do the "conscious musicality," "misty evocations of landscape," "elaborate color symbolism," and "movement toward a poetry of ambiguity and abstraction" (p. 204) really become characteristic of Stevens's art. Other specific Symbolist tendencies which Block notes in Stevens include the poet's examination of the relationship between imagination and reality, "the identity of the self, the nature of consciousness, and the processes of inner transformation" (p. 205). These examinations coupled with Stevens's need for order, combination of abstraction and emotion, manipulations of language as meditative mode, fusion of thing and idea, and rejection of traditional supernatural belief, are typical of the French Symbolists and of Stevens's late poetry.

An even more general summary, Doris L. Eder's "Wallace Stevens: Heritage and Influences" (*Mosaic*, Fall 1970) appeared the same year as Block's study. Eder's article attempts to note briefly all of the literary strains present in Stevens's verse, ·including Elizabethan lyricists and dramatists, Shakespeare, Milton, Spenser, the Metaphysical poets, Romantic poets in general, and especially Wordsworth, Keats, Coleridge, Shelley followed by Tennyson, Browning, and Swinburne. She agrees with Hi Simons's comments in his 1946 article on Stevens and Mallarmé, but qualifies his comments by noting that Stevens, at times, differs radically from the French. The similarities she cites between Stevens and the Symbolists include their shared reliance on musicality, blending of clear imagery and suggestive meaning, and manipulation of synesthesia by creating mood pieces in which sound, color, and fragrance are intermingled for effect. Yet the crucial difference in Stevens and the Symbolists is the American poet's correspondences: his are confined to this world while theirs are not. In short, Stevens differs from the English Romantics and American Transcendentalists as well as the French Symbolists in that he does not posit existence on some transcendental plane.

Eder agrees with Benamou's conclusion that Stevens was attracted to the irony and elegance of the Laforgian dandy, but disagrees with Simons when she sees no affinities between Stevens and Valéry. Her comments on the Stevens–Verlaine relationship are brief and cautious, noting only Verlaine's and Stevens's shared use of sound to create mood. Like Benamou she differentiates between the exoticism and view of death in Stevens and Baudelaire, but she notes similarities in the two poets' use of metaphor. In Stevens and Baudelaire Eder finds tropes in which the vehicle is sharp and clear but the tenor left to implication. And, like many critics before her, she finds the greatest affinity between Stevens and Mallarmé because both postulate a supreme fiction, see poetry as that supreme world, exalt the role of the imagination, see their own individual poems as part of a greater *oeuvre*, and examine an uneasy relationship between the general and the particular. The two differ, according to Eder, in Stevens's naturalism and Mallarmé's idealism. Like Block she returns to Stevens's Americanism as the inspiration for transcending his French mentors. The combination of American and French strains allows him to illuminate an American way of life in a time and place alien to poetry. This final emphasis on the American-Whitmanian-poetry-as-process, Stevens's way of going beyond his French heritage, is the most original point in Eder's article.

In a similar vein other critics find in Stevens a merging of influences that are combinations of and improvements over the pure symbolist method. According to Yvor Winters in "Poetic Styles, Old and New" collected in Don Cameron Allen's *Four Poets on Poetry* (1959), Stevens's method is "post-symbolist" and "potentially the greatest achievement in occidental poetry" (p. 75). What Winters praises so highly as postsymbolist is Stevens's manipulation of the romantic image which, according to Frank Kermode, does not mean but be, and Stevens's use of structure which, unlike the rational progression in Renaissance verse, moves and coheres only by associations.

Even more specifically, Raymond P. Poggenburg in "Baudelaire and Stevens: 'L' Esthetique du Mal" (*South Atlantic Bulletin*, Nov. 1968) contends that as an individual poet Stevens surpassed Baudelaire and Symbolism in his attitude toward poetry. Poggenburg cites several of Stevens's poetic lines that appear to have been directly influenced by Baudelaire, and notes that both poets shared an acknowledgment of life's transitory qualities, a wish to involve the reader in the poem, a reluctance to judge, a faith in the imagination, and an interest in poetry's visual aspects. Yet Stevens moves beyond Baudelaire's traditional view of religion in his sharply antitraditional approach to religion. Baudelaire's influence on Stevens, according to Poggenburg, is most obvious in Stevens's "Esthétique du Mal" which resembles in structure Baudelaire's *Les Fleurs du Mal*. Both works are arranged mosaically with a central theme, evil, examined from a variety of angles. But for

Stevens, the beginnings of the modern in Baudelaire were only beginnings "towards the real" which, according to Poggenburg, Stevens pursued further.

In an examination of Stevens's notebooks, primarily his "Adagia" reprinted in *Opus Posthumous*, Samuel French Morse, the editor of that posthumous collection, notes some Stevens similarities with and improvements over the French. In "A Note on the Adagia" (*Poetry*, Mar. 1957) Morse compares the "Adagia" to Paul Valéry's "Littérature" and Georges Braque's *Notebook*, but judges the Stevens work more spontaneous than the former and more direct than the latter. He concludes that the "Adagia" suggest a literary affinity not only with the French and poets such as Mallarmé, but also with eighteenth-century literature, Thoreau, and Santayana. Like the "Adagia" themselves, Morse's comments are brief and diverse in focus, and thereby less than exhaustive on any one theme.

In Stevens criticism of the late 1960s, critics looked beyond combinations of similar and dissimilar qualities in Stevens and the French and began denying affinity or influence between the two. The most notable of these, Helen Hennessy Vendler (*On Extended Wings*, 1969), disagrees with those who compare Stevens to Whitman, Wordsworth, Keats, and Tennyson and even more specifically disagrees with critics who compare Stevens's "sense of the world" (p. 3) to that of French poets. According to Vendler, Stevens's manner evolved "through his sense of himself and through a search for his own style" (p. 3), rather than through affinity with or influence from other poets. Joseph N. Riddel (*The Clairvoyant Eye*, 1967) acknowledges a minimal Stevens debt to Symbolism, but quickly adds that Stevens varied the themes and ultimately resisted the transcendent elements at the heart of Symbolism. According to Riddel, Stevens rejected these elements when he adopted the philosophies of Santayana and Bergson revealing the "primacy of immediate experience, the dangers of conceptualism, and the duration of the self in consciousness" (p. 38).

In an article published in the same year, "*Symbolisme* and Modern Poetry in the United States" (*Comparative Literature Studies*, 1967), Frederick J. Hoffman concedes that Stevens may have sporadically been influenced by the Symbolists, but that examinations of Stevens's references to these poets are not profitable because Stevens is basically a nonsymbolic poet. Hoffman bases this conclusion on a tendency Vendler also notes: Stevens is more likely to explore and lodge meaning in the self than to look beyond. The earliest proponent of this idea, Anthony Hartley, acknowledged in "The Minimum Myth" (*Twentieth Century*, June 1960) the problem Stevens confronted in a world devoid of the possibility for transcendence. According to Hartley, in contrast to the tradition of French poetry from Baudelaire, Rimbaud, Mallarmé, Valéry, and Claudel, Stevens is concerned with the gap between mythical systematization and things as they are. Unlike his French predecessors, Stevens refuses to establish a poetry based on mythical cosmology and turns instead to the world of experience. Poetry then for Stevens functions as "not so much a transformation as an equivalence" (p. 548). And, unlike the French, Stevens found poetry to be functional in that it helps people to live their lives. In this, Stevens turns poetry away from the mythopoeic concerns of the nineteenth century and men such as Baudelaire or Rimbaud, and turns it toward a twentieth-century humanism.

Comments such as those by Vendler, Riddel, Hoffman, and Hartley are interesting because of the new perspective they provide on the rather worn topic of Stevens's French heritage. Yet, because such comments are made only as passing asides in the Vendler and Riddel studies, or fail to account for or refute the often discussed Symbolist strains of Stevens, as in the Hoffman and Hartley articles, this particular perspective, as Stevens himself might add, needs the attention of more imaginations.

The British Romantic Tradition

A third approach to the literary heritage of Stevens attempts to place him amid the English Romantic poets. According to Rosemary F. Deen in "Wonder and Mystery of Art" (*Commonweal*, Sept. 20, 1957), this is the "other" poetic tradition from that represented in modern times by T. S. Eliot. She places Stevens in such a tradition because of his focus on the artist's role, examination of perception as a function of the artist's imagination, belief in reality as the source of perception, and definition of poetry as a replacement for religion in an age of disbelief.

Romantic Ideas in Stevens's Poetry

Like Dean, many critics focus on attitudes toward art and the world associated with the rubric "Romanticism." While most critics fail to define their use of this general term, they nonetheless seem to think Stevens, in some vague way, was a benefactor of this artistic movement as it was found in nineteenth-century England. The lack of a specific definition for Romanticism is a common flaw in much of the criticism which chooses this elusive theme for its focus. As an example, the July 1971 issue of the *Southern Review, Wallace Stevens and the Romantic Heritage*, is an extremely varied combination of essays which are themselves similar only in their testimony to journal editors' eclectic, often undefined, interpretation of *Romantic*.

The collection begins with a short note "Bits of Remembered Time" by Holly Stevens, the poet's daughter. The note is precisely what its title indicates, scattered recollections and childhood perceptions of her father. Although brief and scanty in the illumination such bits cast on the poet, they are useful primarily as Holly's speculations. Questioning why her father seldom if ever travelled to or beyond the places about which he wrote, Holly Stevens suggests that her father's lack of tourist adventure may be attributed to her mother's predisposition for air, sea, and car sickness coupled with her father's refusal to travel without his wife; and to what Holly supposes was Stevens's post–World War II fear that Europe might have differed from his imagination's conception of it.

The second article in the collection, "*Harmonium* and William James" by Margaret Peterson, does not even tangentially relate to the theme of Stevens and the Romantic heritage, and therefore will be examined in the next chapter's discussion of Stevens and philosophy, a topic more congruent with Peterson's focus. The article that follows Peterson's, Helen Vendler's "Wallace Stevens: The False and True Sublime," examines Stevens's attitude toward the sublime, her term for the nobility in life and grandeur in language. According to Vendler, "the preeminent question life asked of Stevens was whether the sublime was livable" (p. 683). The American environment in which Stevens worked was hostile toward the achievement of the sublime because of that environment's pragmatic characteristic. To counter this, Stevens proposed an heretical American sublime, "the empty spirit in vacant space," but his search for this twentieth-century American sublime differs from that of poets in this century such as Eliot, Auden, or Crane who searched for it in ideological, political, or religious realms. Because Stevens's poetic search is atypical, the poetry that evolves in his later years is difficult and mysterious. But throughout Stevens's poems the sublime provides a constant source of tension between itself and the nonsublime or between its forms. The real dilemma throughout his poetry is "whether one reaches the sublime by fleeing the real or by seeking it" (p. 690). This problem leads Stevens to alternations of style between the terse and ironic, elegiac and philosophical, aspirational and incantatory. The dilemma also leads to a definition of sublime that contains inherent suffering, an inheritance from his romantic predecessors. But, unlike romantics such as Wordsworth and Shelley who foresee nobility in suffering, Stevens retrospects about the nobility with a tragic, comic, or ironic attitude.

In the early poems of *Harmonium* the sublimity achieved is uneasy because it suppresses the "grand style" Stevens uses to seek the false sublimity of private emotions and mortal beauties. As Stevens moves in later poetry toward discovering the sublime in the imperfect and the tragic, he achieves his truest sublimity in his elegiac and celebratory treatment of heroic effort and in his aphoristic treatment of liberating effort manifested in his birth metaphor. According to Vendler, both efforts include the conferring of some "new knowledge of reality" (p. 694), and eventually in his last poems Stevens recognizes the "perfect sublime as an inhuman thing" (p. 698). Vendler analyzes "The Sail of Ulysses" as an example of such late poetry in which that perfect sublime is less than human instead of more than human.

The romantic theme in James McMichael's essay, "The Wallace Stevens Vulgates," which follows Vendler's study, is exemplified in McMichael's concern with Stevens's supreme fiction as it relates to the interplay of reality and imagination. According to McMichaels, Stevens's poetry is itself a supreme fiction because the language of its composition is fictive by nature and the focus of its purpose is man's fulfillment. In support of this, McMichael discusses five of what he considers Stevens's best poems, all from *Harmonium*, in which the dialectic between imagination and reality is operative and in which the characteristics of the supreme fiction are explored. McMichael examines "The Death of a Soldier," "Of Heaven Considered as a Tomb," and "Domination of Black" as three poems in which the fiction offered, according to McMichael, suggests that regardless of the terrors of the real world, it has its beauties to celebrate that will ultimately bring fulfillment. Essential to such fictions is the contention throughout *Harmonium* that death is the mother of beauty. McMichael contends that Stevens's "The Snow Man" proposes that all that can be known is that nothing can be known; and that "Sunday Morning" extends the examination of fictions concerned with the acknowledgment of death and inability to know. McMichael's specific analysis of this last poem's focus is perceptive: "Sunday Morning" "invokes the rhetorical appeal of older imaginative orders, substituting as the object of that appeal the less ordered world in which we are inescapably, unsponsored, free" (p. 718). His analysis of Stevens's use of simile and repetition in "Domination of Black" is also revealing, as is his summary of the supreme fiction's role in later poetry. According to McMichael, in the late poetry the articulation of Stevens's theory itself became the supreme fiction, and as the poet began to describe rather than realize, stasis set in and caused the poetry to fail in meeting its own requirement—that the supreme fiction change. In all, McMichael's essay is one of the more lucid in the collection.

Grosvenor E. Powell's essay "Of Heroes and Nobility: The Personae of Wallace Stevens" is more confined in approach than McMichael's study. Powell glances briefly at Stevens's preoccupation with statues, gods, and heroes as representatives of nobility and definitions of man's limitations. To Stevens, the imagination's task is one of finding a persona capable of redeeming modern man. Poetry then functions as a means for transcending the human. The static and inhuman characters Stevens uses in this poetry represent fixed ways in which reality can be perceived, because "they are personifications in an epistemological sense, of various subject-object relationships" (p. 733). According to Powell this is a new, unique, economical, and subtle figurative procedure, but what Powell fails to detect is Stevens's inconsistent use of persona-like figures with varying degrees of development.

Like many of the articles in this issue of the *Southern Review*, Powell's study does not overtly pertain to the interrelationship of Stevens's poetry and romanticism. Doris L. Eder's "Wallace Stevens: The War Between Mind and Eye" more directly compares Stevens's prose with Coleridge's pronouncements on the distinction between fancy and imagination. In a short study she attempts to examine all of Stevens's prose writing, the role of philosophy in his work, and critical as well as interpretive problems faced by the critic confronting Stevens. Any of the above mentioned topics, with thorough analysis, would provide subject enough for a book-length study. Needless to say, Eder's brief comments suffer from incomplete development and scanty reference to her source, Stevens. She notes the chronologically increasing meditative character of the poet's verse, Stevens's dualist approach to perception coupled with a phenomenalist's approach to experience, and critics' problems of paraphrase: using poems as cross-references, deciphering Stevens's hermetic system of symbology, and accepting Stevens's overreadings of his own poetry. She also criticizes Stevens for his inability to celebrate objects for their own sake, then scathingly attacks one of the most obvious poetic examples of Stevens examining an object solely in its multiplicity of reality, "Metaphors of a Magnifico."

> Twenty men crossing a bridge,
> Into a village,
> Are twenty men crossing twenty bridges,
> Into twenty villages,
> Or one man
> Crossing a single bridge into a village.
>
> This is old song
> That will not declare itself . . .
>
> Twenty men crossing a bridge
> Into a village,
> Are
> Twenty men crossing a bridge
> Into a village.
>
> That will not declare itself
> Yet is certain as meaning . . .
>
> The boots of the men clump
> On the boards of the bridge.
> The first white wall of the village
> Rises through fruit-trees.
>
> Of what was it I was thinking?
>
> So the meaning escapes.
>
> The first white wall of the village . . .
> The fruit-trees. . . .

According to Eder this poem fails because "concrete details fail to support an abstract theme" (p. 756). She fails to see the importance of the concrete details and the perception of those details—in and of themselves. The oversight is puzzling because earlier in the essay Eder accurately describes Stevens's verse as poetry about the act of perceiving or thinking rather than about pure experience or thought. In general, her attitude toward Stevens is negative. She notes problems in interpreting his work as if they are always examples of poor poetics instead of inaccuracies and oversights by inadequate critics. And she finds much in Stevens that is "ill-considered, unfinished, inaccessible, and unintegrated," but fails to finish or integrate this thought by explaining what in the poet inspires such pejorative description.

George Lensing's "Wallace Stevens and the State of Winter Simplicity" in the same issue refuses to make any value judgments about Stevens's poems and avoids any hint of diffuse or multiple theses about the poet's work. Instead, Lensing uses one poem, "The Snow Man," as a starting point for his examination of Stevens's approach to human perception. According to Lensing the act of human perception is the source of all Stevens's poetry but also includes an inherent problem: in the act of perception an imbalance in imagination or reality may occur because the process is itself obviously human and therefore unreliable. The duality of imagination and reality is inescapable, but Stevens's poems of "winter simplicity" explore the possibility of a unity in this dualism. Lensing defines winter simplicity as a poet-created state in which the division between the self and world is bridged and reality thereby stripped of subjective imposition. The metaphor of winter is used by Stevens to communicate this state and is appropriate for the cold, inhuman vacancy of a world without intrusion by the subjective self. Lensing adds that Stevens is aware that such an absolute possession of reality is impossible, yet the poet employs a constant reorientation toward winter simplicity in the hopes of increasing the reliability of the unreliable interaction between self and world. Lensing's approach to Stevens's winter imagery is unique, but it is less tenable because it fails to account for the prevalence of the repeated Stevens image cluster which exploits positive and creative associations with summer and warmth.

The final study in this collection is by far the article most directly related to Wallace Stevens and romantic heritage. In "Postures of the Nerves: Reflections of the Nineteenth Century in the Poems of Wallace Stevens" Kenneth Fields compares themes in the early Stevens of *Harmonium* to Pre-Raphaelite themes of the previous century. According to Fields, the nineteenth century viewed literature as a refuge from the vulgarity of the real world or as a prison precluding access to actual reality. Stevens rephrases the imprisonment motif in some of his *Harmonium* poems when he characterizes the mind as separate from ordinary reality. Stevens, like his nineteenth-century philosophical predecessor Hegel, attempts to overcome the limitations of the intellect by viewing experience in antithetical terms. He confronts the nineteenth-century problem of the mind's and world's relationship; believes in thought and the mind as the last refuge from reality; and reflects nineteenth-century values in his "poetry of nostalgia" which expresses a desire for what he cannot have. Fields accurately notes that in Stevens this nostalgia creates a tension with his celebration of momentary beauties in a world of transition.

The element of Stevens's poetry most similar to nineteenth-century ideas is, according to Fields, Stevens's use of female figures. His women personae may be divided into two types: the "stunner," an elusive, detached, dreamlike female such as Dante Gabriel Rossetti's wife Elizabeth Siddal, admired by the Pre-Raphaelites; and the "princess," an isolated, elaborately adorned, regal figure such as Mallarmé's Herodiade or Pater's account of Leonardo da Vinci's Beatrice d'Este. Fields does not claim that these nineteenth-century artists directly influenced Stevens, but he does contend that their stereotypes inhabited the artistic air of the times, and as female types characterized by isolation, self-absorption, and disembodiment, might have affected Stevens's conception of his own muse. Field's comments on the female personae in Stevens certainly could bear expansion, but his remarks on the nineteenth-century influence in a journal volume purportedly devoted to the subject, but lacking in direct analysis of the theme, are refreshing.

Kathleen McGrory approaches Stevens's Romantic heritage even more directly in "Wallace Stevens as Romantic Rebel" (*Connecticut Review*, Oct. 1970). According to McGrory, in *Opus Posthumous* Stevens defines the modern Romantic rebel, including himself in the definition, as one who dwells in the ivory tower which nonetheless affords him an excellent view of the public dump. She characterizes Stevens's Romanticism as deriving from the American strain influenced by twentieth-century realists and Marx; as pertaining to religion not in establishing a link between man and god but between man and world; and as constructive in its recreation of an orderly world amid modern chaos. In short, Stevens establishes a new religion of aesthetics through a non-Transcendental form of Romanticism. While yet abjuring Transcendentalism, Stevens still resembles Whitman and Emerson and admires Wordsworth. Support for Stevens's Wordsworthian connection, McGrory finds in the twentieth-century poet's comments about Wordsworth in "The Noble Rider and the Sound of Words," and support for his basic Romanticism in general, McGrory finds in Stevens's preoccupation with the imagination in poetry. She concludes by praising Stevens because "his romanticism is not a detached idealism; his rebellion, not a sterile rejec-

tion" (p. 64). Her analysis is weakened because she never speculates on what he proposed as an alternative to detached idealism or
what he rebelled against.

Romantic Predecessors to Stevens's Verse

Critics like McGrory have turned their focus from Romanticism as a general artistic movement to Romantic poets themselves
as ancestral artists for Stevens. Helen Regueiro (*The Limits of
Imagination: Wordsworth, Yeats, and Stevens*, 1976) also emphasizes Stevens's romantic conception of the imagination. Her study
explores "the dangers implicit in any unqualified affirmation of the
imagination" (p. 10) which neglects the basis of poetry, a dialectic
between self and word, mind and nature, imagination and reality.
She chooses to discuss three poets, Wordsworth, Yeats, and Stevens,
because the work of all three is grounded in what she terms "the
dialectical relationship of imagination and reality" (p. 10). This
dialectic begins with the poet's attempt to balance reality and
imagination, then progresses through the poet's withdrawal into
self-consciousness and ultimately to the poet's final return to a
natural reality as the only realm in which the imagination can
exist. For Regueiro, Wordsworth balances imagination and nature,
while Yeats accepts the dialectical relationship of the two, but
nonetheless opts for an imaginatively constructed world. In contrast, Stevens's early verse defines the imagination as a power
that can transform chaotic reality, but he as poet also comes to
realize that the imagination can, through transformation, destroy
the real. What yokes the three is their mutual assertion of reality's
"ontological primacy" against the imagination and their mutual
search for the "poetic act that will suffice" but also transport them
beyond the limits of the finite world.

Beyond these general comments, Regueiro narrows her glance
and devotes each of three sections to one of these poets. In the
portion of her study devoted to Stevens she emphasizes Stevens's
rejection of the imaginative power that changes reality, and his
concomitant need to write a poetry in which imagination turns
on itself while the poet maintains the validity of a particular
moment, object, or place. This emphasis requires of Stevens a
poetry that must communicate the moment or object as it is experienced or perceived. Because such perception is momentary,
passing suddenly away, Stevens's verse describes moments or
objects perceived as an absence, and is firmly based in its own
inability to instantaneously transform or recreate. Yet, according to

Regueiro, the triumph of this verse issues in its very acknowledged failure, "because in its rejection of itself it ceases being an end, and becomes an instrument of experience, reaching the 'being' of the object in a transforming moment of awareness" (p. 149).

Regueiro, at her best in individual interpretations of specific poems, provides a detailed analysis of Stevens's "Domination of Black." She suggests that a tension exists in this poem between the interiorization of reality and the self-consciousness of the imagination's creative force which totally transcends reality. The poem wavers between the blackness of the open window with its outer darkness of leaves, planets, hemlocks, and the blackness of images associated with the creative imagination of the first stanza.

> At night, by the fire,
> The colors of the bushes
> And of the fallen leaves,
> Repeating themselves,
> Turned in the room,
> Like the leaves themselves
> Turning in the wind.
> Yes: but the color of the heavy hemlocks
> Came striding.
> And I remembered the cry of the peacocks.
>
> The colors of their tails
> Were like the leaves themselves
> Turning in the wind,
> In the twilight wind.
> They swept over the room,
> Just as they flew from the boughs of the hemlocks
> Down to the ground.
> I heard them cry—the peacocks.
> Was it a cry against the twilight
> Or against the leaves themselves
> Turning in the wind,
> Turning as the flames
> Turned in the fire,
> Turning as the tails of the peacocks
> Turned in the loud fire,
> Loud as the hemlocks
> Full of the cry of the peacocks?
> Or was it a cry against the hemlocks?
>
> Out of the window,

> I saw how the planets gathered
> Like the leaves themselves
> Turning in the wind.
> I saw how the night came,
> Came striding like the color of the heavy hemlocks
> I felt afraid.
> And I remembered the cry of the peacocks.

Regueiro's reading of this poem is helpful, while her critical self-assurance is admirable. After presenting one plausible, well-developed explication, she provides an alternative summary of this poem in which imagination and the reality of leaves and other natural objects become so confused in the poet's intentional turning and repeating, that reality and imagination fuse. From such alternative interpretations, she concludes that Stevens himself sensed an ambivalence about the proper relationship of imagination and reality.

In describing this ambivalence, Regueiro is more precise than she is in her discussion of Stevens's rejecting metaphor. On this latter topic she is unable to see a similar ambivalence in the poet's acceptance of a trope that enhances reality and his rejection of a trope that destroys reality. Like Yeats, Stevens turns, according to this critic, to the consciousness where no creative act can suffice. And, like Wordsworth, he quests for reality as a series of experiences. But, unlike Wordsworth, and Regueiro might have added Yeats, Stevens rejects transcendence as a way out of his dilemma, and turns to an affirmation of reality outside the realm of the imagination. Regueiro concludes from this not that Stevens's views changed on the proper relationship of reality and imagination, but that his poetry exemplifies a series of attempts to transcend its own "posing of reality within imaginative constructs" (p. 216). Stevens then, beyond Wordsworth and Yeats, has taken poetry into a realm where it denies "the validity of its recreation of the world in order to become a vehicle of experiences" (p. 218). This perspective is indeed an interesting one, but requires for full understanding a thorough knowledge of Stevens's images and theory. And, as Regueiro herself admits, it requires a rejection of criticism based on pure dialectic as practiced by Geoffrey Hartman, Paul de Man, and Harold Bloom.

Similar to McGrory and Regueiro, Newton P. Stallknecht notes in "Absence in Reality" (*Kenyon Review*, Autumn 1959) a relationship between Stevens and Wordsworth. Stallknecht classifies Stevens as neo-romantic (one who according to this critic, believes in Romanticism devoid of Platonism), but he also labels Stevens's "Sunday Morning" as a Wordsworthian "Intimations" ode tempered by doubt of the supernatural, and terms 'The Idea of Order at Key West" as Wordsworthian in its ' revelation of cosmic unity" (p. 546). Stevens's conception of the imagination is romantic, because for Stevens the faculty is capable not only of ordering, composing, inventing, and creating, but discovering as well. In general, the Romantic heritage is manifested in Stevens's celebration of life lived in a natural world.

In contrast, Kenneth Walker in the *Explicator* (April 1974), finds in Stevens's song and sea images from "The Ideas of Order at Key West" an indication of the poet's rejection of "older romantic" notions of the sea. According to Walker, the sea image lacks an anima, conscious spirit, or meaning one might find in Whitman's "Song of Myself" or Wordsworth's "Tintern Abbey." In Stevens, nature is merely the setting for the song and mind while both sea and song lack any transcendent reality. Only the song itself, by ordering chaotic sound, achieves more than mind or nature. A much earlier examination of Stevens's Romanticism by J. V. Cunningham in "The Poetry of Wallace Stevens" (*Poetry*, Dec. 1949) reached similar if broader, more developed conclusions. Cunningham characterizes Stevens as a conspicuously modern poet who writes in new and untraditional poetic forms about novel and daring subjects with attitudes consciously distinguished from any "old morality." Like all modern poetry and genuine art, according to Cunningham's definition, Stevens's poetry is obscure and impenetrable because it aspires to distinctiveness which is inherently uncommon and therefore inaccessible to the many. And, as one might expect in most moderns, Cunningham finds in Stevens a "disdain of the society and of the literary tradition in which he grew up" (p. 153). This dissatisfaction with the conventional in society and poetry drove a Stevens persona, Crispin, to wandering in a poem, "The Comedian as the Letter C," which resembles Wordsworth's "The Prelude" in its autobiographical nature. Like Wordsworth and Stevens, Crispin seeks a oneness of self and environment.

Cunningham views "Sunday Morning" as a modern poem speaking out against traditional Christianity, but also as a Wordsworthian expression in idea, detail, feeling, and rhetoric. Cunningham acknowledges the difference between Wordsworth and Stevens in the latter's denial of immortality, but finds equally important similarities in the two poets' use of natural landscape, syntax, and line-end emphasis. The central concern of Stevens's poetry is the poet's desire to be at peace with himself and his world. This desire is achieved in the Romantic tradition and in Wordsworth by a transitory experience of fulfillment that cannot be willed. According to Cunningham, Stevens attempted to will this experience in his poetry by constructing secular myths that affirm the unity of experience. Stevens attempts these constructions with metaphors resembling Wordsworth's doctrine of affinities, but in Stevens these affinities are frequently forced and unconvincing. Cunningham's comments are among the first on the Stevens-Romantic comparison and are among the best in their detailed explanation of Stevens's reworkings of selected Wordsworthian poetics.

J. Dennis Huston in " 'Credences of Summer': An Analysis" (*Modern Philology*, Feb. 1970) agrees with Cunningham's verdict that similarities between the poets do exist, but differs in his choice of Stevens poems examined as evidence for this comparison. According to Huston, Stevens is most clearly an heir of Wordsworth in "Credences of Summer," a poem in which Huston believes Stevens rewrote the Wordsworthian myth of "reciprocity between man and nature" (p. 263). In the work of both poets Huston finds that "the universe containing and contained in the consciousness of the observer is perceived directly" with no "mediating figure between the poet and the visible concrete natural world" (p. 263). Both poets turn to a merger of earth and imagination to provide the possibilities of creation that transcend the usual limits of time and place. The poem "Credences of Summer" moves toward the total transformation of nature in the human mind, and by viewing the world "without evasion by a single metaphor" Stevens achieves an apocalyptic vision not through art as Yeats and Blake did, but through nature. Huston compares this poetic vision to Wordsworth's delight when he viewed Tintern Abbey. And, like Wordsworth, Stevens examines the relationship of the perceiving mind to the external world of nature. In Wordsworth's "The Recluse" and in Stevens's "Credences" that mind and world are interdependent. Huston briefly roams beyond Wordsworthian Romanticism in his comparison of Stevens's seasonal images to Keats's usage of such images in "To Autumn" and in his comparison of Stevens's creative imagination and Coleridge's secondary imagination.

The study by Diane Wood Middlebrook, *Walt Whitman and Wallace Stevens*, reviewed earlier in this chapter, also compares Stevens with Coleridge. Based on her reading of John Shawecross's edition of the *Biographia Literaria*, Middlebrook discusses Coleridge's theory of the imagination based on the imagination as a power rather than one specific organ or faculty. As the power that allows the individual mind to attain a state of integration involving all of the individual's resources of feeling and thought, the imagination is divided by two phases: the abstracting phase in which stimuli are withdrawn from nature into the personal individual; and the symbol-making phase in which integration occurs between universal and particular elements. In this interchange the mind moves between the two poles of image and abstraction, while the imagination itself provides the power for this movement. Although Middlebrook only selectively attempts to relate her summation of Coleridge's theory to actual Stevens techniques, she does label the twentieth-century poet a Coleridgean and is one of a very few of his critics to isolate specifically what about Coleridge's imagination might be compared to Stevens's. In her one attempt to explicate details from Stevens in light of theory from Coleridge, she is perceptive. She examines the "It Must Give Pleasure" section of *Notes Toward a Supreme Fiction* as a development and interaction between the twofold movement of the creative mind identified by Coleridge as the primary and secondary imaginations but here personified as male and female personae. Her summary of the section's ten cantos is one of the more accurate explications of a Stevens poem. In canto I the intrusive, masculine, secondary imagination projects an idea of order to be received in canto II by the receptive, feminine, primary imagination that clears the sense of sight so the real can be seen. Canto III develops the poetic image of the masculine aspect; IV presents the allegory of marriage celebrating the union between the primary and secondary; V shapes the Coleridgean theme into a coherent narrative; V and VI oppose the masculine and feminine attempting to deal with the same problems; VII portrays the female as a possible muse and the male as implausible poet; VIII and IX develop the narrator as an individual discovering his identity as credible hero; and X unites the narrator with object, imagination, world, and female.

William Van O'Connor's previously cited early study of Stevens, *The Shaping Spirit*, also devotes significant attention to the Stevens-Coleridge relationship. O'Connor compares their theories of imagination as by no means identical but quite similar. Among the differences, O'Connor cites Coleridge's tendency to relate the imagination to the supernatural and Stevens's refusal to do so, as well as Coleridge's belief that the powers of the imagination were denied to the "sensual and the proud," an opinion not necessarily shared by Stevens. In comparing Stevens's and Cole-

ridge's theories of imagination, O'Connor notes that both oppose
as dichotomies the imagination and the rationalist mind; both view
the imagination as a way of establishing communion with nature;
and both employ light, particularly the moon and stars, as symbols
for the imagination.

Kenneth Burke in *A Grammar of Motives* (1955, pp. 224-26)
also focuses on Stevens's view of the imagination as it was inherited
from "idealists" such as Coleridge and Kant. Like O'Connor,
Burke thinks Stevens opposed the imagination with a rational
faculty, reason, but unlike O'Connor, Burke finds that this takes
Stevens beyond Coleridge who aligned the imagination and
reason against fancy and understanding. Burke's distinction is more
exact but no more revealing when applied to a Stevens poem. Not
only did Stevens outstep his Romantic counterpart in this align-
ment, but he also exceeded Coleridge in his "scientist" emphasis
on reality and the search for truth as a type of knowledge. According to Burke, Stevens epitomizes not simply the Romantic
but how an "idealist emphasis carries with it a scientist emphasis"
(p. 226).

Frank Kermode's *Romantic Image* (1957; pp. 47-48, 153-54)
also examines Stevens's mingling of poetic and philosophic theory
that produces a variation of Romanticism. According to Kermode,
Stevens resembles Blake, Coleridge, and Bergson in his assumptions about images. Kermode explicates "Anecdote of the Jar" as
a poem in which opposites are reconciled by Stevens's manipulation of the jar as a symbol of the fixed, orderly, and dead within
the natural, diffuse, and live landscape.

> I placed a jar in Tennessee,
> And round it was, upon a hill.
> It made the slovenly wilderness
> Surround that hill.
>
> The wilderness rose up to it,
> And sprawled around, no longer wild.
> The jar was round upon the ground
> And tall and of a port in air.
>
> It took dominion everywhere.
> The jar was gray and bare.
> It did not give of bird or bush,
> Like nothing else in Tennessee.

In the poem, the jar's meaning and being are the same because of
this inherent quality. Kermode finds in such poems Stevens's

unique resolution of the tension between image and discourse: the poet makes the problem itself the subject of his poetry.

The related problem of the poet's ability to re-create the world in his poetry and this general concern with all creation throughout Stevens's poetry leads Richard Gustafson in "The Practick of the Maker in Wallace Stevens" (*Twentieth Century Literature*, July 1963) to label Stevens particularly Coleridgean and generally Romantic. According to Gustafson, Stevens's concern with the process of creation is obviously a rephrased version of Coleridge's often discussed secondary imagination.

Harold Bloom maintains, in *"Notes Toward A Supreme Fiction*: A Commentary" (1963), that Stevens moves toward the creation of a fictive hero who, in "Notes," will climax this entire Romantic tradition. This most ambitious of Stevens's poems is, according to Bloom, his best as "an attempt at a final fiction in a fiction known to be a fiction, in the predicate that there is nothing else" (p. 77). In this Romantic tradition, Stevens mixes the modes of quest romance and poetry of vision in order to describe a poet withdrawing himself from the world into fabricated fictions. In the first section, "It Must Be Abstract," Bloom notes echoes of Keats's seasons, a Wordsworthian and Coleridgean belief in poetry's power, a wood dove/muse similar to Shelley's epipsyche or Blake's emanation, and times of excellence resembling similar moments in "Tintern Abbey." In the second section, "It Must Change," Bloom notes the romantic mutability of a Spenser or Wordsworth and the Keatsian recognition of the tragedy coupled with organic repetition in that mutability. Like other critics, Bloom notes the hints of Wordsworth in "Sunday Morning," the similarities with Coleridge in "Final Soliloquy of the Interior Paramour," and the echoes of Shelley in "Notes." Like Keats's Odes, Stevens's last section of "Notes," "It Must Give Pleasure," concerns itself with the poet's stance in relation to his own poetry. And, like Wordsworth and Coleridge, Stevens comes in this section to believe in the necessity of joy for the poet. In summary, Bloom interprets "Notes" as purely Romantic—and a flawless poem. In judging it as the "supreme achievement of post-Romanticism" his praise is too heavy-handed and his judgment too lightly weighed. Comments in this article were expanded and tempered by Bloom in his later book-length study (previously discussed in this chapter), *Wallace Stevens: The Poems of Our Climate*.

Critics have compared Stevens not only to Wordsworth and Coleridge, but to Keats as well. In the study by Doris Eder discussed earlier in this chapter, the critic, without noting her source, speculates that Stevens, while a student, read Keats for hours at a time. The only evidence Eder acknowledges to support this contention is a quote in a Stevens letter taken from a Keats verse letter to John Reynolds. She acknowledges Stevens's most consistent affinity with Wordsworth while also noting the two poets' differing views on the spirit that gives nature meaning. According to Eder this spirit is for Wordsworth supernatural but for Stevens human. The distinction is a perceptive one as is her comment comparing Stevens's sensuousness to that of Keats.

In a second previously cited study, *Wallace Stevens* by Lucy Beckett, the critic more thoroughly develops a Stevens-Keats comparison. Beckett contends that the young Stevens is like Keats in his seriousness, independence, and delight in the particular, real, and sensuous detail of the actual world. Beckett goes so far as to suggest a Keatsian complex of feeling behind all Stevens's poetry. This complex, a sense of loneliness and weakness in a world without absolutes, leads to an awareness that mere reality must be made, by the solitary mind, to suffice. She becomes more specific in her comparison of Stevens's "Sunday Morning" and Keats's May Odes. In these poems each poet attempts to accommodate death without aid from any structure of belief; and each considers the evils and sufferings of the real world as an essential element in poetic theory. What Beckett and Eder both fail to note is the difference in Keats's emphasis on the emotional aspect in life and creativity and in Stevens's emphasis on the intellectual and cognitive aspect of the imagination as it relates to life and creativity. Unlike most other critics concerned with Stevens's Romantic heritage, Beckett is not willing to label Stevens himself a Romantic or imply that Keats must therefore be "modern." Instead, she conservatively notes that both poets were confronted with similar challenges—an opinion that is safe in its ambiguity but less than revealing in its comparison of the poets' relationships to one another and their respective literary milieus.

The Modern Tradition

Although Stevens's poetry was created in the twentieth century, critics disagree about his "modernity." One of the earliest to attempt to analyze Stevens's modern heritage, J. V. Cunningham, published "The Poetry of Wallace Stevens" in the December 1949 issue of *Poetry*. The study was revised in 1960 and reprinted as "Tradition and Modernity: Wallace Stevens" in *The Achievement of Wallace Stevens* (1962) edited by Ashley Brown and

Robert S. Haller. Cunningham defines a modern poet as one who writes poetry that is different from older, more traditional, and expected verse. He acknowledges Stevens's debt to nineteenth-century Symbolists in the "brilliant" and "piquant" surface of the poet's work, but also finds in Stevens a disdain for society and literary tradition which is modern. According to Cunningham, "The Comedian as the Letter C" exemplifies Stevens's juxtaposition of the conventional and unconventional as a manifestation of man's relationship with his environment. Cunningham notes a similar combination of opposites in "Sunday Morning," a poem which he perceptively describes as an "undivine fiction that preserves the emotions of the old religion but attaches them to a poetry in which the sensory objects of a natural landscape enter into a union in celebration of the mortality of men" (p. 135). Such poems lead Cunningham to the conclusion that Stevens is modern *and* traditional because he relies on "inveterate violation of the old" (p. 139) in order to create the new.

Frank Kermode in his previously cited *Continuities* agrees with Cunningham's conclusion. For Kermode, Stevens is modern in his attempt to purge from poetry all remnants of "past imaginings," but traditional in his manipulation of blank verse and conventional American theme of isolation. Donald Davie in "Notes on the Later Poems of Stevens" (*Shenandoah*, Summer 1956) is less kind in his assessment of Stevens's mixture of traditions. In Stevens's unrhymed lines and "shameless ad-libbing" Davie finds an attempt to turn traditional poetic imperfection into modern virtue. He also criticizes Stevens's typically modern antirhetorical rhetoric and his persistent use of the indefinite article which precludes generalization in its singularity. Davie's criticisms are not unfounded, but his suggestion of only one alternative is a bit narrow minded. According to this critic, the only alternative to Stevens's modernism is "Renaissance poetics" in which rhetorical features do not communicate the poet's attitude but adorn the poem "not as expressive of the subject, but objective graces" (p. 41). In "An Audience for Wallace Stevens" (*Essays in Criticism*, April 1965), C. D. Cecil disagrees with Davie's condemnation by praising Stevens's use of words to communicate the impossibility of communicating with words; and Cecil disagrees with any critic linking Stevens to the past when he notes that "Like the American Dream it so often parodies, the poetry of Stevens refuses either laments for the rich past or despairs of the barren present" (p. 206). Although Cecil thinks that Stevens's intentional use of absurdity links him with Joyce and Shaw, the critic labels Stevens a "quintessential twentieth-century American" in his rotarian and comedian poses employed to rescue readers from complacency.

Similarly, Mildred E. Hartsock attempts in "Wallace Stevens and 'The Rock' " (*Personalist*, Winter 1961) to relate Stevens to the thought of his day. Hartsock explores Stevens's contemporaneity by examining his symbol of the rock, in which she finds the poet's acceptance of what *is*: nature with man as a part of it. Throughout his poetic expression, Stevens voices modern ideas about the revolutionary humanism, relativism, and pragmatism which have dominated twentieth-century American thinking, and in his last volume, *The Rock*, above all others, he acknowledges the need to see reality without metaphysical support. Unfortunately, Hartsock's analysis of the rock symbol is incomplete and her assumption that *The Rock* is Stevens's final statement on reality is incorrect. In "Wallace Stevens" (*Twentieth Century Literature*, Oct. 1955) Deatt Hudson glances briefly at Stevens's later poems as too abstract and philosophic but nonetheless modern American poetry. According to Hudson, Stevens found little in the modern American scene "worth salvaging for art." Such a negative assessment of a supposedly negative predisposition is correct in its terms "abstract" and "philosophic," but totally inaccurate in its assumption that Stevens rejected the world of reality around him as unworthy of art.

John Crowe Ransom (*The World's Body*, 1938, pp. 55-75) also views Stevens's poetry as separate from a social, political, or moral world. According to Ransom, Stevens belongs to a group of "poets without laurels," a few modernists read only by a small group and detested by the public. Unlike traditional poets who attempted to compound moral and aesthetic effect, such modern poets concern themselves, according to Ransom, with aesthetics devoid of moral implications. Poems like Stevens's "Sea Surface Full of Clouds" exemplify nontraditional poetry for its own sake, a poetry lacking in moral, political, religious, or social value. In Ransom's view, such modernists are reacting against Puritanism's mixture of aesthetics and morals, a mixture which weakened the aesthetic. Karl Shapiro seems to agree in "Modern Poetry as a Religion" (*American Scholar*, Summer 1959) which states simply that Stevens, in the modern tradition, "sets poetry apart from and above religion" (p. 298).

A few critics, however, have disagreed with Stevens's label as a modern. Among these, Leonard E. Nathan explains his thesis most thoroughly. In "Wallace Stevens and Modern Poetry" (*Indian Literature*, Jan.–Mar. 1967), Nathan contends that

Stevens develops in a direction counter to the trend of his time. Instead of moving away from rhetoric and toward the directness of the image, Stevens deliberately uses an inappropriate "epic meditation on an epicless era" (p. 83). In contrasting Eliot and Pound with Stevens, Nathan distinguishes between the formers' borrowing from traditional poetry in order to contrast the poverty of the present and the richness of the past and the latter's "more organic" use of the past. As an example, Nathan cites Stevens's "The Comedian as the Letter C" in which the poet uses Milton's epic meter and syntax to frame nonepic subject and diction. This technique is doubly effective because it communicates something about the convention it parodies as well as contrasts that convention with the present. In examining Stevens's borrowings from tradition, Nathan cites the poet's debt to Mallarmé's concept of the "pure poem" defying prose discourse, Valéry's model of the "speculative" poem, and Keats's definition of the relation between poetry and the literal world. Because of such borrowings, Nathan labels Stevens a traditional poet who, unlike moderns such as Eliot and Pound, viewed the past as an important part of a complex poetic relationship. Although such a comment is an appropriate analysis of Stevens's point of view, it is hardly accurate in its assessment of Eliot's and Pound's view of the past. Apparently not sure of his own opinion on the modernity issue, Nathan concludes that even Stevens is both traditional in his refusal to reject tradition and modern in that one cannot translate Stevens out of his twentieth-century American milieu.

John J. Enck also distinguishes Stevens from the moderns in "Stevens' Crispin as the Clown" (*Texas Studies in Literature and Language*, Autumn 1961). Unlike many modern artists, Stevens is able to confront modern man as a comedian but then move beyond this recognition to a sense of serenity. In contrast, Enck cites W. B. Yeats who, even in his poetry of old age, was troubled by the image of man as a fool. Enck bases his argument on a brief examination of twentieth-century literature's multiple use of the clown figure that in Stevens's work appears as Crispin, the persona who, because of his impractical enterprises, encounters difficulty in controlling his environment.

Randall Jarrell in "Fifty Years of American Poetry" (*Prairie Schooner*, Spring 1963) is less specific in his comparison of Stevens, Frost, and Eliot. Jarrell finds in Stevens a delight in existence and a late-life craftsmanship he finds in no other modern American poet. In an age when almost everyone "sold man and the world short," Jarrell also finds a Stevens "joy in life." Jarrell's idea is a pleasant one, but his characterization of Stevens as a poet of delight and joy is inexact. If Stevens did experience pleasure in the modern world around him and his own creativity, he also experienced unending doubt and uncertainty that manifest themselves in his late poems' acquiescence and acceptance of life's ambivalent nature.

Stevens as Imagist

Among those critics who more exactly attempt to place Stevens in some school or movement of this century, several have noted his contact with the Imagists. Stanley K. Coffman Jr., author of *Imagism: A Chapter for the History of Modern Poetry* (1951, p. 223), describes Stevens as Imagistic in some of his poems like "Study of Two Pears." Stevens's attention to metaphor, use of color, and fastidiousness in selecting material for poetry, recall for Coffman Imagist tendencies. Yet the critic is quick to add that Stevens's poetry is less Imagistic than that by William Carlos Williams and Marianne Moore, two other poets who began their career during the period of Ezra Pound's and Amy Lowell's Imagism. Coffman also adds that Stevens's interest in the world of actuality and the imagination's role in this world lead the poet beyond Imagist precepts to considerations of religion and aesthetics.

Other critics have looked to specific early Stevens poems for evidence of Imagism. Kenneth Lash's explication of "The Emperor of Ice-Cream" (*Explicator*, April 1948) describes this poem as the epitome of an excellent Imagist sample that combines clarity and compactness with significance of the individual images. Lash seems to misunderstand either the tenets of Imagism or the Stevens poem when he finds, in the poem's images, reference to a spiritual meaning—a reference forbidden by the famous "don'ts" of Imagism. In praising these images as "forceful" and "vivid," Lash is far more positive in his assessment of Stevens's Imagist tendencies than critics such as Laura Riding and Robert Graves. In their *A Survey of Modernist Poetry* (1927) which appeared before most critics even recognized a modernist trend, Graves and Riding pejoratively place Stevens in the "notoriously self-advertising institution" (p. 217) of Imagism and criticize his "enforced romanticism" as poetry avoiding a theme.

John J. Enck (*Wallace Stevens: Images and Judgments*, 1964) understands Imagism no better than Lash, but is more favorably impressed by Stevens than Graves or Riding seem to be. In his study of questionable merit discussed in chapter 1, Enck labels Stevens an Imagist and part of the early twentieth-century avant garde rejecting the clichés of the nineteenth century. He examines the poems of *Harmonium* as controlled by the precepts of Imagism, but cites as examples "Disillusionment of Ten O'Clock" and "Sea Surface Full of Clouds." Enck mistakes the impressionism of the latter poem for Imagism and seems to label "Disillusionment" imagistic because it develops as a single subject described through denial of positive terms. Neither Pound nor Lowell would have recognized the similarity. In a second study cited in chapter 1, *Wallace Stevens* (1960), Frank Kermode agrees with Enck that *Harmonium* owes something to Imagism, but unlike Enck, Kermode is able to specify what this something is, and more importantly, how it differs from pure Imagism. According to Kermode, *Harmonium* poems are Imagistic because they exemplify Stevens's interest in the fresh and concrete, while they are unlike Imagist poems because most of these poems involve abstract process.

Stevens and Eliot

Critics have also placed Stevens in or opposed to the tradition of T. S. Eliot's modernity. Thomas Vance performed a critical service in "Wallace Stevens and T. S. Eliot" (*Dartmouth College Library Bulletin*, Dec. 1961) by correcting a long-standing error. William Van O'Connor in *The Shaping Spirit* and Frank Kermode after him in *Wallace Stevens* attribute to Stevens a statement that the poet never made. O'Connor quotes from the Eliot issue of the *Harvard Advocate* (Dec. 1938), but denotes Stevens as the author of a comment actually written by Allen Tate. The quote cites Stevens as calling T. S. Eliot one of his two masters. When Stevens received a copy of O'Connor's book, he wrote O'Connor about the error and stipulated that he and Eliot were "dead opposites." Vance brings this point to critical light, and, counter to Stevens's own disclaimer, notes the milieu the two poets shared. Both absorbed, according to Vance, the atmosphere of "Harvard, French Symbolist poetry, Imagism, the American 'revolution' of 1910 and after" (p. 41-42). Both began as coterie poets and both, Vance agrees with Marianne Moore (*Poetry*, Feb. 1937), are kin in their self-directed irony which triumphs over pain by continually searching for what will endure. And, Vance perceptively notes the crucial differences between the two: Stevens faces the bareness of reality without "the piercing anxiety that has seemed to make Eliot the spokesman for the obsessions of an age" (p. 44). In this article by Marianne Moore, the poet reviews *Harmonium*, *Ideas of Order*, and *Owl's Clover*, praising Stevens highly for his verbal mannerisms, harmonics, persona disguises, and protest against modern disorder, while finding in Stevens what O'Connor and Kermode tried to find: a mutual influence between Eliot and Stevens. Only closer textual analysis than any critic has so far attempted might reveal such influence Stevens himself denied.

Wylie Sypher ("Connoisseur in Chaos: Wallace Stevens," *Partisan Review*, Winter 1946) couples a critical need to see Eliot and Stevens as similar, with a critical inability to appropriately develop that thesis. According to Sypher, the central problem in Stevens's poetry is the role of the imagination in *The Waste Land*. As poetic heir to Eliot's barren wilderness of disillusionment, Stevens proposes a violence within man to counter the violence around him, thus identifying poetry with counter pressures. Because Stevens demonstrates "the uses of imprecision" in his fictions that are feelings, Sypher places him in the Romantic tradition but insists that we measure the poet's success by comparing him to the Metaphysical tradition, a tradition in which Stevens has no part according to Sypher. Viewing most modern poetry as centripetal, with meaning moving inward to a precision of statement and only then issuing outward in a series of repercussions, Sypher contrasts Stevens's centrifugal poetic motion in which meaning abounds indefinitely outward. According to Sypher, Stevens sets one faculty, reason, against another, sensibility, and thus denies himself what a poet most needs, fictions. Sypher's argument is flawed on two counts: he uses Stevens's duality of faculties, a Metaphysical duality indeed, as evidence that Stevens is not a Metaphysical poet; and he concludes that Stevens's fictions are necessarily denied if faculties are placed in opposition, a conclusion contrary to evidence offered by the Metaphysicals themselves.

Sypher more and more entangles himself in his own contradictions when he terms Stevens, dispossessed of his fictions, a Prufrock, "a most inappropriate man in a most unpropitious place . . . a nomad exquisite of the Waste Land whose philosophy is an exercise in viewing the world" (p. 90). How Stevens's philosophy makes him inappropriate is never clearly stated by Sypher. Sypher does, however, accurately characterize Stevens as, unlike Eliot, endowed with a comic spirit to confront the absurdities of modern time. In this comic tone as opposed to Eliot's metaphysically ironic tone, Stevens is more appropriate to our time. Unfortunately Sypher never detects or mentions Stevens's ironic tone. And finally, Sypher criticizes Stevens because, in the poet's commitment to a poetry of the mind, he fails to achieve a meaningful myth. Sypher errs again seriously here because Stevens never wanted to establish a myth, but Sypher never sees that Stevens's poetry is a poetry aimed at recognizing the very fictional quality of our myths.

The ground on which to compare Stevens and Eliot varies greatly from critic to critic. Thomas R. Whitaker ("Voices in the Open: Wordsworth, Eliot, and Stevens," *Iowa Review*, Summer 1971) labels these three poets three versions of a "solitary voice" moving toward "complementary horizons." According to Whitaker, each poet "is most social when most solitary"; "is perplexed by an epistemological uncertainty"; believes "poetry must name"; "has been accused of the egotistical sublime"; and uses the long poem as a sustained voice attempting "to name its calling" (p. 96). Whitaker's undefined terms such as "horizon" and "poetic voice" fail to elucidate process or product in the work of the three poets. The reader becomes so entangled in Whitaker's "solitary voice" and "limited horizon" that any relationship among the three is indecipherable in Whitaker's terms. Even in his attempts to relate his muddled, poetically phrased thesis to poems, Whitaker is less than precise. He describes "The Prelude," "Four Quartets," and "Notes Toward a Supreme Fiction" as "problematic attempts of the solitary voice to name its calling" (p. 111), then leaves the reader with no clues for solving the problem or clarifying the attempts, much less for specifying any relationship among the three works.

Like Whitaker, Morris Greenhut attacks the difficulties of Eliot and Stevens. In his study "Sources of Obscurity in Modern Poetry: The Examples of Eliot, Stevens, and Tate" (*Centennial Review*, Spring 1963), Greenhut, unlike Whitaker, achieves some, though minimal, clarity of comment and interpretation. In analyzing obscurity and obscurantism in modern poetry, Greenhut contends that all serious writing presents various difficulties because of "the nature of language itself, the complexity of the matter to be communicated, the writer's imperfect mastery of his craft, the reader's inadequacy, the absence within a society of a commonly shared basic body of knowledge and experience" (p. 173). According to Greenhut, the difficulties that modern poetry presents to qualified readers may be traced to three sources: Eliot, Stevens, and Tate. In Eliot one finds an obscurity defined by Greenhut as an "absence of a common cultural and literary tradition" (p. 173), while in Stevens one finds a poetry whose very craft works itself into obscurity. As example of Stevens's obscurity, Greenhut cites poems in which connotation overpowers denotation, context fails to reveal necessary associations, and tone or nuance is inadequate to convey extended meaning. Greenhut thinks that Stevens's titles convey too much or too little and thereby confuse the reader. To support this contention, the critic cites "The Idea of Order at Key West" and maintains that a reader is unable to determine which phrase is most important, idea of order or Key West. Had Greenhut noted the volume in which this poem appears, *Ideas of Order*, and examined the poem's own ordering structure more closely, he might have avoided such a confession of needless confusion. His judgment, that "The Emperor of Ice-Cream" fails because its images are "undirected" and its juxtapositions of the gaudy and shabby are unable to reveal any meaning, is also a questionable and unsupported premise.

Greenhut is, however, more insightful than other previously cited critics in isolating comparisons between Stevens and Eliot. According to the critic, obscurity is not an end for Stevens as it seems to be for the school of poetry that followed *The Waste Land*. Stevens's poetry is obscure because it communicates too little directly by definition and statement while it communicates too much by possible connotation and allusion that take the character of indefinably subtle nuance rather than definitive focus. In this, Stevens resembles Eliot who in *The Waste Land* is difficult because he tries to amalgamate many disparates while he simultaneously becomes more allusive and indirect. And, this is similar to Tate in "Ode to the Confederate Dead," a poem which echoes *The Waste Land* in theme and treatment. Greenhut overlooks a crucial similarity that characterizes the obscurity of all three: their use of image and metaphor that defies paraphrase, merges disparates in language and concept, and ultimately eludes definition. A closer analysis of this technique's contribution to the difficulty in Stevens, Eliot, or Tate would have greatly expanded and strengthened Greenhut's study.

More precise than Greenhut and more accurate than Whitaker, William Van O'Connor isolates similarities and differences between the two poets. In "Wallace Stevens: Imagined Reality" (*The Grotesque: An American Genre and Other Essays*, 1962), O'Connor finds Eliot and Stevens comparable only in their skills but different in temperament, idiom, theme, and interest. Although Stevens is a hedonist and Eliot an ascetic, both are concerned with the role of the poet as well as the nature of poetry, belief, ideal, and morality. While Stevens approaches these concerns through the theme of the imagination, Eliot approaches them through traditional religion and cultural values. O'Connor labels Stevens the modern of the two because he, unlike Eliot, finds traditional beliefs obsolete. In contrast, Graham Hough (*Image and Experience,* 1960, pp. 3–84) places Stevens with Eliot and Pound as the founding fathers of modern poetry.

J. R. LeMaster in "Stevens and Eliot on the Mind of the Poet" (*Forum,* Winter 1972) starts where O'Connor stopped. LeMaster contrasts Stevens and Eliot by noting their differing definitions of the mind, the faculty in Stevens's poetry responsible for creation, but in Eliot's only a receptacle or medium. This difference is at least partially based on their different views of tradition. Eliot's view of tradition identifies him, according to LeMaster, with Ruskin and Burke who believed that the height of civilization was attained in the Middle Ages when art expressed common standards and values that provided a tradition. In contrast to Eliot's tradition, Stevens sees a world of flux in which man acknowledges the disappearance of god, finds no meaning beyond mere experience, and looks to the poet as a creator–god. For Stevens, poetry must lead to a revelation of nature impossible in Eliot's conception of the mind, and for Stevens, "Eliot's tradition is a receptacle from which the mind of the poet creates itself and its world" (p. 30). For Eliot, the poet's mind is merely a container in which tradition operates. LeMaster concludes this but never notes how Eliot's tradition is a receptacle for Stevens, and in fact contradicts his own conclusion by stressing the atraditional nature of Stevens's concern with flux. The study is not particularly enlightening because it draws little from the poets' exact theories and individual techniques. LeMaster fails to even acknowledge Stevens's *The Necessary Angel,* crucial to any discussion of the poet's theoretical approach to mind, creativity, or poetry.

In contrasting Stevens and Eliot, Roy Harvey Pearce includes two other poets, E. E. Cummings and William Carlos Williams. In "The Poet as Person" (*Yale Review,* Spring 1952), Pearce distinguishes this modern generation of poets by their choice between polar opposites: the denial of an irreducibly private and idiosyncratic man or the affirmation of him. According to Pearce, Eliot chooses denial while the other three affirm. In Stevens this affirmation proceeds through a celebration of the creative imagination, and in Stevens's early poetry this affirmation resembles Williams's awareness of reality and the thing-in-itself as factors enriching and limiting the experience of the self.

Stevens and Other Modern Poets

Other attempts to compare Stevens to specific modern artists include not only the critical followers and foes of Eliot, but those of E. E. Cummings and Hart Crane as well. In "The Imaginative Direction of our Time" (1962), Louise Bogan contrasts Stevens's *Collected Poems* and Cummings's *Poems 1923–1954*. She characterizes Cummings's poetry as a mixture of satire and sentiment epitomized by its attempt to break Victorian taboos on poetic subject. Stevens, according to Bogan, is not a satiric but a contemplative artist who is the first American poet to deal with America in imaginative rather than topical or regional terms. Her review praises both artists as complements of one another, honoring Stevens for his disciplined craft and Cummings for his boldness and verve.

G. S. Fraser's review of Stevens's *Collected Poems* and Cummings's *Poems*, "The Aesthete and the Sensationalist" (*Partisan Review*, Spring 1955), also juxtaposes the two as opposites, but in so doing, is less kind to both. As a British critic, Fraser condescendingly finds in Stevens and Cummings an extra-poetic fascination with American culture. In this culture, Fraser places Cummings in the tough, native tradition and Stevens in a more cosmopolitan and sophisticated American vein. Although he characterizes Stevens's language as opulent and Cummings's as sensationalist, he notes that neither poet fulfills Matthew Arnold's requirement that a poet strengthen and uplift the heart. Describing Stevens's subject as a "matter of mind," his tone as "polite irony" or "urbane mystification," his predicament as one of a "reflective aesthete," and his philosophy as that of a "pragmatic solipsist," Fraser judges him gifted but not great, because he finds Stevens's poetry lacks the life, urgency, and passion of work by an Eliot or Yeats. After damning Stevens to mediocrity, Fraser discloses that neither Stevens nor Cummings is adequate, but then, neither is society. The conclusion is a bit tangential, but cannot rival in irrelevance Fraser's final call for a more humane society enabling poets to be more humane.

Edmund Wilson in "Wallace Stevens and E. E. Cummings" (*New Republic*, March 19, 1924) reviews Stevens's *Harmonium* with Cummings's *Tulips and Chimneys*, and praises both poets for very different techniques. According to Wilson, Stevens is a master of style in his richness of verbal expression coupled with an absence of intense emotion. In contrast, Cummings exemplifies a boyish freshness and amateurishness coupled with immaturity. Yet, Wilson concludes that Cummings has the advantage as a poet because he is able to perceive and express deep "poetic feeling" not found in Stevens.

A third modern artist with whom Stevens is frequently compared is Hart Crane. Frank Kermode examined the two when their respective collected letters appeared. Kermode's study, "Strange Contemporaries: Wallace Stevens and Hart Crane" (*Encounter*, May 1967), asserts that both poets share "a proprietary attitude to language" (p. 66) which leaves to the reader the task of working out explicit meaning. In general, however, Kermode notes more differences than similarities in the two volumes. Crane's letters are more direct and personal but at times also more desperate, while Stevens's letters reveal a man who demanded privacy and the time to speculate before reaching a decision. Although Stevens's letters also reveal to Kermode a man "quietly absurd" in his "paraphilosophical games," they are praised by the critic because they indicate the direction of Stevens's frequent musings in poetry, and because they communicate ideas typical of modern poetry. According to Kermode, these Stevens letters exemplify how the poet shut out the passions of the world, while the Crane letters show how the poet dissipated those very passions. The distinction is important when comparing the two.

Harvey Gross ("Hart Crane and Wallace Stevens," *Sound and Form in Modern Poetry*, 1965) agrees with Kermode but is less precise in isolating the characteristics of the two poets' similarity or lack of it. Gross pairs the two only because they possess an "American sensibility" and lack of plain style. He distinguishes between Crane's alienated and scarred experience and Stevens's fastidious artistic distance between himself and "real life," while noting a concomitant variance in rhetoric: Crane voices a "stupendous reaction to experience" (p. 216), but Stevens attempts without "philosophical pompousness" to define the indefinable. Gross concludes that Stevens is Eliot's prosodic equal; that *Sunday Morning* is as significant as *The Waste Land* in confronting twentieth-century belief; and that "Le Monocle de Mon Oncle" rivals "The Lovesong of J. Alfred Prufrock" in seeking to establish a state of feeling through rhythm. The conclusions obviously do not relate to the Stevens-Crane theme. In general, Gross spends so little time on Crane and even less time discussing any similarities or differences between the two, one wonders why he titled his chapter to include the poet. In the course of the essay he briefly examines the Stevens-Eliot relationship, Stevens's musicality, Stevens's poetic method involving theme and variation, and scans Stevens's blank verse. Even such comments on technique are less than enlightening. When Gross notes Stevens's use of the caesura not only for a breath pause but also as an element of "rhythmic phrasing," one wonders why the critic wasted paper and ink on such an obvious statement.

An earlier study, "Thoughts on Modern Poetry" (*Sewanee Review*, Spring 1935), by Howard Blake focuses on Stevens and Crane but praises the latter at the expense of the former. According to Blake, Stevens's work is merely a miniature of Crane's "aesthetic on an epic scale," *The Bridge*. Contrasting Stevens's "tautness" and "restraint" to Crane's "flow" and "majesty," Blake clearly prefers what he terms Crane's "aesthetic absorbed into the subconscious" to Stevens's "selfconsciousness." Such a critical preference seems to reflect an appreciation for the undisciplined emotion of one poet without an awareness of appropriate aesthetic distancing in another poet.

In comparing Stevens with other modern poets several critics have moved beyond the English or American turf to poets in other languages. Michael Hamburger (*The Truth of Poetry: Tensions in Modern Poetry from Baudelaire to the 1960s*, 1969) and Ralph Freedman ("Wallace Stevens and Rainer Maria Rilke: Two Versions of a Poetic," 1967) have found a Stevens counterpart in the German poet, Rilke. In his chapter on "Absolute Poetry and Absolute Politics" Hamburger discusses Stevens's aesthetic of pure poetry, then labels Stevens a Romantic Symbolist in the tradition of Crane, Mallarmé, Rimbaud and Valéry, but also compares him with Yeats. In Yeats and Stevens, Hamburger finds poets who are "modern without being modernistic" (p. 113). The critic compares Stevens and Rilke on such modern ground and finds in both a mysticism that begins with the visible world as well as a mysticism that might be described as agnostic or secular.

Freedman's comparison of the two is far more developed, but similar in emphasis to Hamburger's study. According to Freedman, Stevens and Rilke are aesthetic poets in that both attempt to define a poetic idea, and both are philosophical poets because they view poetry as an "embodiment and immediate presentation of knowledge" (p. 61). Beyond theoretical concerns Freedman also examines external similarities between the two: both wrote a

great deal of obscure poetry, used painting and music for subjects, were influenced by philosophical and aesthetic ideas of the
late nineteenth century, admired Baudelaire and the *fin de siecle*,
absorbed Cézanne and post-Impressionism, and were engaged in
language experimentation.

Freedman also finds their poetry's common ground in their demonstrated need to see objects through the painter's eye. Accordingly,
both poets "partake not only of a general theory about the inter-
relation of the arts, but also of a virtual obsession with the way
artists see things" (p. 62). Both attempt to see objects simultaneously as they are and are not; and both create a relationship
between object and mind through the "reciprocal tensions" of
poetry. In his imitations of painting, Stevens is more abstract than
Rilke and more like Wordsworth. According to Freedman,
Stevens's "Peter Quince at the Clavier" and Wordsworth's "Tintern Abbey" resemble one another because both examine reflective
sight in which eyesight through meditation is converted to vision.
Stevens adopts this romantic function of the eye as a way of achiev-
ing imaginative power and adopts the stance of painter-poet in order
to distance himself from an object and thereby penetrate its
meaning. Freedman thinks that Stevens sought things as they are
and things of the mind in a reality that therefore is both mental
and physical and in an imagination that is dual because it is the
poet's eye grounded in the world and it is the intellectual supreme
fiction created by words. In contrast to Stevens's ambivalence
toward the imagination, Freedman finds in Rilke a single poetic
faculty in relation to a world that is dual in its organic and in-
organic nature. The poets then share a definition of the poet's
condition as part of the Symbolist experience; an awareness of a
fluctuating relationship between self and ever-changing world;
and a recognition that appearances to the eye are the mere starting
point for further reality. According to Freedman, this common
aesthetic of modern poetic theory emphasizing eye, sight, and
vision began with the Coleridgean imagination which analyzes,
dissects, and re-creates.

Freedman qualifies his assertions only by noting differences in
the two poetics, one exemplified by Stevens whose career extends
further into the twentieth century and into the American grain
that Rilke labeled a "mechanistic evil." Yet the primary difference
exists in the poets' varying tones: Stevens is more ironic, distanced,
witty, and detached while Rilke is more gentle, sentimental, varied
in theme, and comprehensive in method. Freedman's study is both
useful and interesting because of the thoroughness of his ap-

proach, attention to poetic emphasis, and ability to integrate the general literary milieu with the poets' individual concerns. No other studies comparing Stevens and other moderns are as helpful or as well developed.

Forging relationships where minimal comparisons exist, critics have occasionally compared Stevens to recent poets such as Conrad Aiken, John Crowe Ransom, Robert Lowell, E. A. Robinson, and Henry Green. R. P. Blackmur briefly compares Stevens and Conrad Aiken because both are concerned with the role of the imagination and actualizing that imagination in sophisticated, difficult, intellectual, and poetic language. In "The Composition in Nine Poets" (*Southern Review*, Winter 1937), Blackmur finds in the two poets an "ever-present particularizing intensity of process that gives their best poems an objective and inexhaustible vitality" (p. 572). Blackmur's vague terms do not elucidate any relationship between Stevens's and Aiken's poetic process, yet his general conclusion—that the two, like all modern poets, delete the superfluous elements of language for the inherent richness in the concreteness of words—is a valid, if oversimplified, statement. Reality in the words themselves is achieved by Stevens's use of the specific word to communicate a general meaning, while in Aiken the reverse is true. His poetic machinery is located not in his vocabulary but in the myths beneath that vocabulary.

Delmore Schwartz, in "Instructed of Much Mortality" *Sewanee Review*, Summer 1946), notes similarities between Stevens and John Crowe Ransom because "both poets make a like use of dandyism of surface, of irony, and of a mock-grand style" (pp. 440-41). According to Schwartz, both playfully and mockingly manipulate a grand style, then use colloquial and concrete vocabulary in order to undercut this very grandiloquence. Schwartz stipulates that the similarities of style may suggest influence, but more importantly suggest a style of the period in which writers of the age were caught in a shift from grand rhetoric to concreteness. The critic does concede that the ultimate direction of Stevens and Ransom differs. Stevens's irony is more defensive and used to discount his emotions as he moves toward "symbols and ideas abstracted from any time and place" (p. 444). Ransom's irony is more expressive and used to communicate the painfulness of his emotions as he moves toward a relationship among people as well as between people and the immediacy of existence.

Elizabeth Lunz's study of Stevens and Lowell, "Robert Lowell and Wallace Stevens on Sunday Morning" (*University Review*,

June 1971), focuses primarily on distinctions between the two poets' poetic ideas. Lowell himself twice criticized Stevens's poetry, once in a review of *Transport to Summer* (*Nation*, 1947) and in his own poem "Walking Early Sunday Morning" (*Near The Ocean*, 1967). Both are examinations of the metaphysical and political rather than poetic faults in Stevens's work. Lunz concludes from Lowell's assessments that the difference in the politics of the two is extreme. She interprets Stevens's "Sunday Morning" as a "hedonistic delight in luxury, in beauty, in the impermanent earthly paradise" (p. 269), while Lowell's later "Sunday Morning" poem confronts the disintegrating world that is a result of the death of god Stevens examined in his poem. If Stevens glimpses the demise of traditional religion, Lowell retrospectively reviews its value as an ordering principle. For their differing tasks, the two poets use different modes: Stevens, a dialogue, and Lowell, a confession. And, the two poets use differing techniques. Stevens's alliteration, sound effects, exotic vocabulary, and blank verse differ from Lowell's "rigid formalism," tight couplets, and lack of harmony in sound or development in imagery. Lunz eventually sides with Lowell and disagrees with Stevens's "untenable" position in "Sunday Morning" that the death of god brings a revival of the imagination. By criticizing Stevens's metaphysics, Lunz and Lowell, from their midcentury vantage point, seem to forget or overlook Stevens's early twentieth-century context. In "Sunday Morning," a poem that preceded World War I, international depression, and the exhaustion of modernist artistic tenets, Stevens, without benefit of prophecy, could view the role of the imagination optimistically in a world, from his point in time, that might have responded differently to the loss of its deity.

George Lensing's comparison of "Robinson and Stevens: Some Tangential Bearings" (*Southern Review*, Spring 1967) is both superficial and tangential. Lensing compares Robinson and Stevens as "two major American poets relying upon traditional metrical form, particularly blank verse" (p. 505). Both shared a New England environment according to Lensing, who seems to forget Stevens's Pennsylvania heritage. More accurately, Lensing notes that both began publishing in their student days when their poems appeared in the *Harvard Advocate*, and both looked to poetry for theology's replacement and a harmony between inner and outer world. After noting these surface similarities, Lensing devotes his article to summarizing other critics who have examined these poets individually, but he in no way integrates these critical ideas. He inadequately concludes by labeling Robinson the reflection of darkness in American poetry because of his tragic life, and by placing Stevens in this dark tradition because of the impossibility and elusiveness of his ideal poem.

Myron Turner's study of "The Imagery of Wallace Stevens and Henry Green" (*Wisconsin Studies in Contemporary Literature*, Winter 1967) is more successful than Lensing's in its examination of poetic techniques. Turner finds the Stevens-Green relationship evident in their "similarity of language and imagery" (p. 60), and focuses particularly on the poets' tropes. The poetry of both is characterized by "a vivid transfiguration of surface reality into something unreal yet tangible" (p. 61). The transfiguration is created when both artists use figures in the tradition of Yeats and the Symbolists. Both men then use tropes that, unlike traditional English similes, metaphors, and symbols based on correspondences, do not move toward correspondence, but contribute as images to a larger image pattern that communicates a state of consciousness or mood. Images become a means of defining a particular quality or attitude rather than conveying a "hidden meaning." For both, symbols are recurring and arbitrary with a logical basis but with no inherent reason for their selection. Such symbols must therefore be defined in every work in which they appear. According to Turner, both poets use such imagery and symbols to represent reality as it is, and, as heirs to *Ulysses*, both employ the individual consciousness as a faculty for interpreting that reality, while both extend the Joycean emphasis by exploring the shifting nature of reality. If Turner's comments are more enlightening when concerned with general modern manipulation of trope and reality, his interpretations are less accurate when concerned with specific Stevens characteristics. His contention— that neither Stevens nor Green attempts to see the surface of things more clearly but instead re-creates that surface—is imprecise. Stevens does re-create through poetry, but that re-creation occurs through a clarified vision focused on surface detail. And when he concludes that the two poets' harmony, permanence, and stability are found in a world of luxury, he totally disregards such Stevens poems as "The Rock" and "The Man on the Dump."

Unfortunately, perhaps some of the most fruitful ground for critics concerned with Stevens's modernity and contemporaneity is still relatively barren. Although Stevens's poetic career ended more than two decades ago and critics repeatedly emphasize his importance to twentieth-century verse, little attention has been devoted to his influence on those poets who lived during his time and even less attention devoted to his relationship with poets who have followed him. Here, more than anywhere else, critical attention seems deserved but obviously absent.

The Pre-Modern Tradition

Finally, critics have attempted to relate Stevens to various movements throughout traditional literature. Although extended studies devoted to this theme are not to be found, many critics in passing relate Stevens to various literary movements, and a few, those discussed here, attempt to specify a kinship with particular earlier artists.

From Plato to Dante in Western Thought

In J. Hillis Miller's "An Exercise in Discrimination" (*Yale Review*, Winter 1970), a previously cited review of Helen Hennessy Vendler's *On Extended Wings* (1969), Miller digresses from his reviewing task and examines Stevens as a participant in a tradition of language dating back to Plato. According to Miller, Stevens's use of metaphors typical of this Occidental tradition is fundamental to Western languages. Miller extends his analysis of Stevens as traditional by proposing that the individual affirmation giving Stevens's verse meaning is itself a traditional motif. The figures and concepts which, according to Miller, link Stevens with our cultural and language beginnings in Greece and Palestine are listed and briefly discussed by the critic. These include Stevens's affirmation of the present moment and speech as a product of that moment; dependence of his poetry on light and familial metaphors; use of space and spatial metaphors; emphasis on numerous terms for a rational or intellectual faculty in man similar to the Greek *logos* or Latin *ratio*; humanistic combination of man and this faculty; and the extensive treatment of the problems inherent in the creation and use of metaphor. Miller's points are interesting, but deserve supporting reference to Stevens's own poems as well as examples from that great, amorphous body of traditional literature to which Miller only generally refers.

Among other critics who seek to take Stevens out of his particular place and time, Glauco Cambon (*The Inclusive Flame*, 1963, pp. 79-119) and Karl P. Wentersdorf ("Wallace Stevens, Dante Alighieri, and the Emperor," *Twentieth Century Literature*, Jan. 1968) relate Stevens's poetry to Dante's *Divine Comedy*. Cambon specifically compares the three-fold structure of "Notes Toward a Supreme Fiction" to the three parts of the

Divine Comedy. In "Notes" Cambon interprets the first section "It Must Be Abstract" as a poem about the hell of the "estranged human condition" (p. 99); the second section "It Must Change" as a poem of alienation and exile in an intermediate, purgatorial stage of metamorphosis; and the third section "It Must Give Pleasure" as Stevens's terrestrial vision of paradise. To support this analogy Cambon cites Stevens's Dantesque, didactic language used to instruct the ephebe coupled with the ironic-dramatic role of the artist in a poem of architectural symmetries. Cambon's idea is a novel one, but seems to be more an indication of the critic's need for neat poetic structure than the Italian's influence on Stevens.

Wentersdorf is more general in his comparison of the two artists. To support his thesis, he cites Stevens's occasional borrowing from Christian mythology's treatment of evil and notes Stevens's several allusions to the *Divine Comedy*. According to Wentersdorf, the bitter cold as symbol for evil in Stevens's "No Possum, No Sop, No Taters" recalls the last of hell's nine circles in Dante's *Inferno* where the souls of the damned are frozen in ice. The mountain image in "Esthétique du Mal" reminds Wentersdorf of the *Purgatorio's* structuring image, and the purgatorial image in "Asides on the Oboe" recalls for Wentersdorf the Dantesque stairway which leads upward through suffering. The critic overemphasizes the influence of Dante on Stevens and overextends his Dantesque interpretations when he discusses Stevens's emperor of ice cream, in a poem by the same name, as a literary descendant of Dante's Satan, encased in ice in the pit of hell. And by characterizing Stevens's concept of evil as a traditional Christian horror of indifference, hypocrisy, greed, lust, and sadism, Wentersdorf overlooks Stevens's emphasis in "Esthétique du Mal" on evil and pain as important and valuable aspects of present reality.

Techniques from the Metaphysicals

Because of his techniques rather than his religious philosophy, Stevens has also been compared to the seventeenth-century Metaphysical poets such as Donne and Marvell. In a study by Hi Simons, "The Genre of Wallace Stevens" (*Sewanee Review*, Autumn 1945), the critic examines both Stevens's use of conceits (functionally yoking disparates rather than decoratively elaborating) and his manipulation of wit (to confront the reader with cryptic obscurities). According to Simons, these Metaphysical techniques define Stevens as a poet practicing in the genre of

Metaphysical poetry exemplified by Donne. Simons qualifies his judgment by noting differences in the two poets that appear to be differences in the poetic techniques demanded by radically different eras. Donne and Stevens employ different diction, prosody, and subject matter as a result of the differing psychology of creation in their respective periods. The most perceptive and indeed invaluable distinction that Simons makes between the two is exceptionally revealing when applied to Stevens's poetry: Stevens uses metaphor as a means of discourse with the metaphoric tenor left to implication and inference, while Donne manipulates traditional forms of the metaphoric tenor and vehicle. Simons terms Stevens's trope the "radical metaphor" and describes it as an inheritance, with Stevens's original variation, from French Symbolism.

Like Simons, Joseph E. Duncan (*The Revival of Metaphysical Poetry: The History of A Style, 1800 to the Present*, 1959, pp. 182-86) relates Stevens to Metaphysical poetry in his use of correspondences, conceits, paradox, and wit. More specifically, Duncan compares Stevens's caliper in "Last Looks at the Lilacs" to Donne's compass; Stevens's geometric parallel lines in "To an Old Philosopher in Rome" to Marvell's parallel lines; and Stevens's extended condensed metaphor in "The Curtains in the House" to similar metaphors in Herbert. Unfortunately, Duncan attempts to generalize from Stevens's use of Metaphysical poetic techniques, and labels Stevens a long-recognized Metaphysical in philosophical belief. This latter assertion is totally unfounded, and the comments on Stevens unnecessary after Simons's more penetrating analysis. Similarly, Walter Fuller Taylor's brief comparison of Stevens and the Metaphysicals (*The Story of American Letters*, 1956) adds nothing constructive to the Simons study, but does foolishly conclude that Stevens's poetry is written for a special few with special tastes because it "by-passes the overwhelming majority of the interests and values of civilized men" (p. 430).

As a brief footnote in the interest of critical disagreement, Harriet Monroe's "The Free-Verse Movement in America" (*English Journal*, Dec. 1924) and Howard Nemerov's "The Poetry of Wallace Stevens" (1963) must also be mentioned. These two critics become strange bedfellows in their agreement that Stevens is intensely individual and belongs to no school. Judging Stevens's poetry different "from almost everything else in English" (p. 75), Nemerov distinguishes Stevens as unique in the poet's preoccupation with the daily progression of trivial thought and his chosen mode of composition that is indicative of the mind in the act of deciding, rather than associational or logical in development. Nemerov also contends that Stevens differs in that he is most difficult at his moments of greatest simplicity, when he states direct equations. The simplicity, directness, and validity of Nemerov's and Monroe's comments make one question the critical witch-hunt for influence. Perhaps in Stevens's influence on students of poetry to follow, critics might find, as Monroe did, a unique and powerful school of poetics issuing not to but from Stevens.

References

Aiken, Conrad
  1919. "The Ivory Tower I." *New Republic* May 10, pp. 58–60.
Beckett, Lucy
  1974. *Wallace Stevens.* New York: Cambridge Univ. Pr.
Benamou, Michel
  1972. *Wallace Stevens and the Symbolist Imagination.* Princeton, N.J.: Princeton Univ. Pr.
Bewley, Marius
  1955. "The Poetry of Wallace Stevens." *Commonweal* Sept. 23, pp. 617-22.
Blackmur, R. P.
  1937. "The Composition in Nine Poets." *Southern Review* Winter, pp. 558–77.
Blake, Howard
  1935. "Thoughts On Modern Poetry." *Sewanee Review* Spring, pp. 187–96.
Block, Haskell M.
  1970. "The Impact of French Symbolism on Modern American Poetry." In *The Shaken Realist*, ed. Melvin J. Friedman and John B. Vickery, pp. 165–217. Baton Rouge: Louisiana State Univ. Pr.
Bloom, Harold
  1963. "*Notes Toward a Supreme Fiction*: A Commentary." In *Wallace Stevens: A Collection of Critical Essays*, ed. Marie Borroff. Englewood Cliffs, N.J.: Prentice Hall.
  1977. *Wallace Stevens: The Poems of Our Climate.* Ithaca, N. Y.: Cornell Univ. Pr.
Bogan, Louis
  1954. "*Harmonium* and the American Scene." *Trinity Review* May, pp. 18-20.
  1955. *Selected Criticism.* New York: Noonday.
  1962. "The Imaginative Direction of our Time." In *E. E. Cummings and the Critics,* ed. S. V. Baum, pp. 193–94. East Lansing: Michigan State Univ. Pr.

Brooks, Cleanth
1965. "Poetry Since *The Waste Land*." *Southern Review* July, pp. 487–500.

Burke, Kenneth
1955. *A Grammar of Motives*. New York: Braziller.

Buttel, Robert
1967. *Wallace Stevens: The Making of Harmonium*. Princeton, N. J.: Princeton Univ. Pr.

Cambon, Glauco
1963. *The Inclusive Flame*. Bloomington: Indiana Univ. Pr.

Cargill, Oscar
1941. *Intellectual America: Ideas on the March*. New York: Macmillan.

Carruth, Hayden
1955. "Without the Inventions of Sorrow." *Poetry* Feb., pp. 288–93.

Cecil, C. D.
1965. "An Audience for Wallace Stevens." *Essays in Criticism* April, pp. 193–206.

Coffman, Stanley K., Jr.
1951. *Imagism: A Chapter for the History of Modern Poetry*. Norman: Univ. of Oklahoma Pr.

Cohen, J. M.
1960. *Poetry of This Age 1908–1958*. London: Hutchinson.

Cunningham, J. V.
1949. "The Poetry of Wallace Stevens." *Poetry* Dec., pp. 149–65; reprinted in *The Achievement of Wallace Stevens*, eds. Ashley Brown and Robert S. Haller. New York: Lippincott, 1962.

Davie, Donald
1956. "Notes on the Later Poems of Stevens." *Shenandoah* Summer, pp. 40–41.

Deen, Rosemary F.
1957. "Wonder and Mystery of Art." *Commonweal* Sept. 20, pp. 620–21.

Duncan, Joseph E.
1959. *The Revival of Metaphysical Poetry: The History of a Style, 1800 to the Present*. Minneapolis: Univ. of Minnesota Pr.

Eberhart, Richard
1963. "Emerson and Wallace Stevens." *Literary Review* Autumn, pp. 51–71.

Eddins, Dwight
1971. "Wallace Stevens: America the Primordial." *Modern Language Quarterly* Mar., pp. 73–88.

Eder, Doris L.
1970. "Wallace Stevens: Heritage and Influences." *Mosaic* Fall, pp. 49–61.

Enck, John J.
  1961. "Stevens' Crispin as the Clown." *Texas Studies in Literature and Language* Autumn, pp. 389–98.
  1964. *Wallace Stevens: Images and Judgments.* Carbondale: Southern Illinois Univ. Pr.
Fraser, G. S.
  1955. "The Aesthete and the Sensationalist." *Partisan Review* Spring, pp. 265–72.
Freedman, Ralph
  1967. "Wallace Stevens and Rainer Maria Rilke: Two Versions of a Poetic." In *The Poet as Critic*, ed. Frederick P. W. McDowell, pp. 60–80. Evanston: Northwestern Univ. Pr.
Greenhut, Morris
  1963. "Sources of Obscurity in Modern Poetry: The Examples of Eliot, Stevens, and Tate." *Centennial Review* Spring, pp. 171–90.
Gross, Harvey
  1965. "Hart Crane and Wallace Stevens." In *Sound and Form in Modern Poetry: A Study of Prosody from Thomas Hardy to Robert Lowell.* Ann Arbor: Univ. of Michigan Pr.
Guereschi, Edward
  1964. " 'The Comedian as the Letter C': Wallace Stevens' Anti-Mythological Poem." *Centennial Review* Fall, pp. 465–77.
Gustafson, Richard
  1963. "The Practick of the Maker in Wallace Stevens." *Twentieth Century Literature* July, pp. 83–88.
Hamburger, Michael
  1969. *The Truth of Poetry: Tensions in Modern Poetry from Baudelaire to the 1960s.* New York: Harcourt, Brace.
Hartley, Anthony
  1960. "The Minimum Myth." *Twentieth Century* June, pp. 545–49.
Hartsock, Mildred E.
  1961. "Wallace Stevens and 'The Rock'." *Personalist* Winter, pp. 66–75.
Hays, H. R.
  1934. "Laforgue and Wallace Stevens." *Romantic Review* July-Sept., pp. 242–48.
Hoffman, Frederick J.
  1967. "*Symbolisme* and Modern Poetry in the United States." *Comparative Literature Studies*, pp. 193–99.
Hough, Graham
  1960a. *Image and Experience.* Lincoln: Univ. of Nebraska Pr.
  1960b. "The Poetry of Wallace Stevens." *Critical Quarterly* Autumn, pp. 201–18.
Hudson, Deatt
  1955. "Wallace Stevens." *Twentieth Century Literature* Oct., pp. 135–38.

Huston, J. Dennis

    1970. " 'Credences of Summer': An Analysis." *Modern Philology* Feb., pp. 263–72.

Jarrell, Randall

    1963. "Fifty Years of American Poetry." *Prairie Schooner* Spring, pp. 1–27.

Kalstone, David

    1971. "Conjuring with Nature." In *Twentieth-Century Literature in Retrospect*, ed. Reuben A. Brower, pp. 247–68. Cambridge, Mass.: Harvard Univ. Pr.

Kermode, Frank

    1957. *Romantic Image*. London: Routledge and Kegan Paul.

    1958. "The Gaiety of Language." *Spectator* Oct. 3, pp. 454–55.

    1960. *Wallace Stevens*. New York: Grove Pr.

    1967. "Strange Contemporaries, Wallace Stevens and Hart Crane." *Encounter* May, pp. 65–70.

    1968. *Continuities*, pp. 77–91. New York: Random House.

Kreymborg, Alfred

    1929. *Our Singing Strength: An Outline of American Poetry*. New York: Coward-McCann.

Langbaum, Robert

    1959. "The New Nature Poetry." *American Scholar* Summer, pp. 323–40.

    1970. *The Modern Spirit: Essays on the Continuity of Nineteenth and Twentieth Century Literature*. New York: Oxford Univ. Pr.

Lash, Kenneth

    1948. "Stevens' 'The Emperor of Ice Cream'." *Explicator* April.

LeMaster, J. R.

    1972. "Stevens and Eliot on the Mind of the Poet." *Forum* Winter, pp. 27–30.

Lensing, George

    1967. "Robinson and Stevens: Some Tangential Bearings." *Southern Review* Spring, pp. 505–13.

Lunz, Elizabeth

    1971. "Robert Lowell and Wallace Stevens On Sunday Morning." *University Review* June, pp. 268–71.

Matthiessen, F. O.

    1952. *The Responsibilities of the Critic: Essays and Reviews by F. O. Matthiessen*. Selected by John Rackliffe, pp. 71–74. New York: Oxford Univ. Pr.

McGill, Arthur C.

    1964. *The Celebration of Flesh: Poetry in Christian Life*. New York: Association Pr.

McGrory, Kathleen

    1970. "Wallace Stevens as Romantic Rebel." *Connecticut Review* Oct., pp. 54–64.

Middlebrook, Diane Wood
1974. *Walt Whitman and Wallace Stevens*. Ithaca, N. Y.: Cornell Univ. Pr.
Miller, J. Hillis
1970. "An Exercise in Discrimination." *Yale Review* Winter, pp. 281–89.
Monroe, Harriet
1924. "The Free-Verse Movement in America." *English Journal* Dec., pp. 691–705.
Moore, Geoffrey
1962. "Wallace Stevens: A Hero of Our Time." In *The Achievement of Wallace Stevens,* eds. Ashley Brown and Robert S. Haller. New York: Lippincott.
Moore, Marianne
1937. "Unanimity and Fortitude." *Poetry* Feb., pp. 268–72.
Morse, Samuel French
1957. "A Note on the Adagia." *Poetry* Mar., pp. 45–46.
Nathan, Leonard E.
1967. "Wallace Stevens and Modern Poetry." *Indian Literature* Jan.–Mar., pp. 82–101.
Nemerov, Howard
1963. "The Poetry of Wallace Stevens." In *Poetry and Fiction: Essays*. New Brunswick, N. J.: Rutgers Univ. Pr.
O'Connor, William Van
1948. *Sense and Sensibility in Modern Poetry*. Chicago: Univ. of Chicago Pr.
1950. *The Shaping Spirit: A Study of Wallace Stevens*. Chicago: Regnery.
1962. "Wallace Stevens: Imagined Reality." In *The Grotesque: An American Genre and Other Essays*, pp. 128–36. Carbondale: Southern Illinois Univ. Pr.
Pearce, Roy Harvey
1952. "The Poet as Person." *Yale Review* Spring, pp. 421–40.
1961. *The Continuity of American Poetry*. Princeton, N.J.: Princeton Univ. Pr.
Pinkerton, Jan
1970. "Wallace Stevens in the Tropics: A Conservative Protest." *Yale Review* Dec., pp. 215–27.
Poggenburg, Raymond P.
1968. "Baudelaire and Stevens: 'L'Esthetique du Mal.' " *South Atlantic Bulletin* Nov., pp. 14–18.
Ramsey, Warren
1954. "Wallace Stevens and Some French Poets." *Trinity Review* May, pp. 36–40.
1967. "Uses of the Visible: American Imagism, French Symbolism." *Comparative Literature Studies* pp. 177–91.

Ransom, John Crowe
1938. *The World's Body*. New York: Scribner.
Reguerio, Helen
1976. *The Limits of Imagination: Wordsworth, Yeats, and Stevens*. Ithaca: Cornell Univ. Pr.
Riddel, Joseph N.
1963. "Walt Whitman and Wallace Stevens: Functions of a 'Literatus'." In *Wallace Stevens: A Collection of Critical Essays*, ed. Marie Borroff. Englewood Cliffs, N.J.: Prentice-Hall.
1967. *The Clairvoyant Eye: The Poetry and Poetics of Wallace Stevens*. Baton Rouge: Louisiana State Univ. Pr.
Riding, Laura, and Graves, Robert
1927. *A Survey of Modernist Poetry*. London: William Heinemann Ltd.
Rosenfeld, Paul
1925. "Wallace Stevens." In *Men Seen—Twenty Four Modern Authors*, pp. 151–62. New York: Dial.
Schwartz, Delmore
1946. "Instructed of Much Mortality." *Sewanee Review* Summer, pp. 439–48.
1954. "In the Orchards of the Imagination." *New Republic* Nov. 1, pp. 16–18.
1955. "Wallace Stevens—An Appreciation." *New Republic* Aug. 22, pp. 20–22.
Shapiro, Karl
1959. "Modern Poetry as a Religion." *American Scholar* Summer, pp. 291–305.
Simons, Hi
1945. "The Genre of Wallace Stevens." *Sewanee Review* Autumn; reprinted in *Wallace Stevens: A Collection of Critical Essays*, ed. Marie Borroff. Englewood Cliffs, N.J.: Prentice-Hall, 1963.
1946. "Wallace Stevens and Mallarmé." *Modern Philology* May, pp. 235–59.
Southern Review
1971. [A Stevens Issue]. *Wallace Stevens and the Romantic Heritage*. July.
Stallknecht, Newton P.
1959. "Absence In Reality." *Kenyon Review* Autumn, pp. 545–62.
Sypher, Wylie
1946. "Connoisseur in Chaos: Wallace Stevens." *Partisan Review* Winter, pp. 83–94.
Taupin, René
1929. *L'Influence du Symbolisme Français sur la Poésie Américaine (1910-1920)*. Paris: H. Champion.
Tindall, William York
1955. *The Literary Symbol*. New York: Columbia Univ. Pr.

1961. *Wallace Stevens*. Minneapolis, Minn.: Univ. of Minnesota
Pr.
Tryford, John
1967. "Wallace Stevens." *Trace* Fall, pp. 339–44.
Turner, Myron
1967. "The Imagery of Wallace Stevens and Henry Green."
Wisconsin Studies in Contemporary Literature Winter, pp. 60–77.
Untermeyer, Louis
1919. "The Ivory Tower II." *New Republic* May 10, pp. 60–61.
Vance, Thomas
1961. "Wallace Stevens and T. S. Eliot." *Dartmouth College
Library Bulletin* Dec., pp. 37–44.
Vendler, Helen Hennessy
1969. *On Extended Wings: Wallace Stevens' Longer Poems*.
Cambridge: Harvard Univ. Pr.
Waggoner, Hyatt H.
1968. *American Poets from the Puritans to the Present*. Boston:
Houghton Mifflin.
Walker, Kenneth
1974. "Stevens' 'The Idea of Order at Key West'." *Explicator*
April.
Wentersdorf, Karl P.
1968. "Wallace Stevens, Dante Alighieri, and the Emperor."
Twentieth Century Literature Jan., pp. 197–203.
Whitaker, Thomas R.
1971. "Voices in the Open: Wordsworth, Eliot, and Stevens."
Iowa Review Summer, pp. 96–112.
Taylor, Walter Fuller
1956. *The Story of American Letters*. Chicago: Regnery.
Wilson, Edmund
1924. "Wallace Stevens and E. E. Cummings." *New Republic* Mar.
19, pp. 102–3.
Winters, Yvor
1959. "Poetic Styles, Old and New." In *Four Poets on Poetry*, ed.
Don Cameron Allen, pp. 44–75. Baltimore: Johns Hopkins Pr.

CHAPTER 3

Genre

> There is a universal poetry that is reflected in everything.
> This remark approaches the idea of Baudelaire that there ex-
> ists an unascertained and fundamental aesthetic, or order, of
> which poetry and painting are manifestations, but of which,
> for that matter, sculpture or music or any other aesthetic
> realization would equally be a manifestation.
>
> WALLACE STEVENS
> "THE RELATIONS BETWEEN POETRY AND PAINTING"

In Stevens's own theory of art proposed in his poems and essay collections, the poet frequently refers to philosophy, painting, and music as artistic endeavors not unlike his own choice, poetry, and even more frequently he draws from these genres when selecting images and metaphors for that poetry. Allusions to other forms and modes of communication are so numerous in Stevens's verse, and his involvement with and seeming imitation of other genres so pervasive, that the uninitiated reader and overread critic alike grapple for labels to describe Stevens's poetic genre. Does the poet fancy himself a philosopher, a painter, or a musician? That he defines himself as more than a traditional poet seems clear, if anything about Stevens is clear. But in which artistic or philosophic direction this "more than" leads, is still a matter of critical debate.

Philosophical Poet

By far the largest majority of critics who question what type of verse Stevens writes eventually confront the philosophical bent in Stevens's poetry and prose. Two camps distinguish themselves on this theoretical issue. Those who find that Stevens is indeed a philosophical poet emphasize the abstract quality of Stevens's discourse and his apparent need to intellectualize in verse, while they apply the term "philosophy" readily and generally with little attention to its precise domain. On the other hand, some critics acknowledge Stevens's abstract ideas but refuse to label him a philosopher or his poetry philosophic because they focus instead on the poetic nature of all that Stevens placed on paper. If the former critical position suffers from imprecision of definition, this latter position grows tedious with nuances and qualifications imposed on Stevens's verse that then becomes partially, quasi, or nonphilosophical depending on who performs the hair-splitting exercise. The debate has produced some of the worst—and best— criticism on this poet. A third group of critics begins with two assumptions: that Stevens is philosophical; and that the task of criticism is a search for the particular philosophers with whom Stevens has most in common. This chapter will examine these three approaches to the philosophic nature of Stevens's verse.

An Emphasis on the Philosophical in Poetry

The most comprehensive examination of Stevens as a philosophical poet may be found in *The Act of the Mind* (1965), a collection of essays edited by Roy Harvey Pearce and J. Hillis Miller. The specified purpose of the collection—to study the implications, range, and import of the philosophical label attached to Stevens—is achieved only unevenly by essays of varying scope and quality. Most of the studies collected originally appeared in various issues of *A Journal of English Literary History*, but those by Vendler, Hammond, Macksey, and Donoghue appeared first in this collected volume.

The initial essay in the collection, "Wallace Stevens: The Use of Poetry" by Bernard Heringman, asserts that Stevens's poetry is a poetry of interaction and synthesis between reality and the imagination; that the poet is himself a microcosm of the world; and that the supreme reality for Stevens is a combination of reality and imagination in poetry. To develop his contentions, Heringman examines Stevens's world as a dichotomy of images and symbols from the realm of reality and the realm of the imagination, but when the critic attempts to relate such images to the poet's philosophy in a poem such as "Notes Toward a Supreme Fiction," his explication of the poem is too terse and incomplete to congeal his critical approach with the poetry in question. Yet, at the core of Heringman's argument resides an assumption crucial to the understanding of Stevens's philosophical nature: the poet used poetry as a means of dealing with reality, escaping from it, ordering it, finding value in it, or simply describing it.

Frank Doggett's article, "This Invented World: Stevens' 'Notes Toward a Supreme Fiction'," which follows Heringman's, views "Notes" as an address to a young poet-ephebe and a personification of the poetic intelligence. Doggett examines Stevens's mode in the poem, personification, and his message on philosophy that defines poetry as a supreme fiction. According to Doggett, by employing personification, Stevens juxtaposes the poignancy of an individual with the distance of an idea, and by building a structure of these vignettes, Stevens constructs an allegory of supreme fictions. The term allegory seems a bit too rigid for Stevens's inconsistent use of cardboard figures whose equivalent abstractions, if any exist, metamorphose with each new image. In contrast, Doggett's comments are to the point when he explains Stevens's philosophy in the poem as a series of supreme fictions necessary for man to live his life. These fictions include the poet's assumptions that reality is a subjective act; that the idea of something solely in terms of existence apart from human perception is therefore impossible; that the idea of man takes the form of the giant-hero or the everyman-common-man; and that the invented world is a fiction that results from feeling. From these fictions Doggett attempts to deduce a moral in Stevens which praises experience as good in and of itself. Doggett's study is flawed in this conclusion because Stevens's philosophical stance on experience or on good is neither so simple nor so concrete.

The next three studies in the collection are discussed elsewhere because of their relevance to other Stevens themes. Robert Buttel's "Wallace Stevens at Harvard: Some Origins of His Theme and Style" may be found in chapter 1 where the focus is on Stevens's chronology; Michel Benamou's "Wallace Stevens and the Symbolist Imagination" is discussed in chapter 2 where emphasis is on Stevens's literary heritage; and Samuel French Morse's "Wallace Stevens, Bergson, Pater" is discussed later in this chapter.

The sixth study in the collection, Roy Harvey Pearce's "Wallace Stevens: The Last Lesson of the Master," suggests that Stevens begins with the philosophical problem, the relationship between imagination and reality, then attempts to find a poetic solution for the problem. Because of this, Pearce thinks that any discussion of Stevens must begin with his philosophy. Appropriately then, Pearce reviews Stevens's attitude as traceable to the subject-object relationship in Romantic poetry and to Stevens's own goal in his late poetry to celebrate the subject or power of the mind or to celebrate the object and unchanging reality. Pearce concludes that by arguing for a division between mind and reality, Stevens in his latest poems manifests the poet's central involvement with both. And, the critic accurately describes Stevens's combined poetic-philosophic process of creation as a continuing dialogue between mind and reality.

J. Hillis Miller in "Wallace Stevens' Poetry of Being" does not find in Stevens the dynamic philosophical process which revealed itself to Pearce. Like Pearce, Miller finds the subject-object, mind-matter, imagination-reality dichotomy in Stevens, but unlike Pearce, Miller traces it directly to the death of god and modern man's spiritual poverty in a barren land. For Miller, Stevens's imagination equals inner nothingness, his reality equals external barrenness, and his task, an impossible one of reconciling the two absences. The constant and endless search for such a reconciliation is the motive for all that Stevens creates. When Miller asserts further that "self-division, contradiction, perpetual oscillation of thought" (p. 146) are the constants of Stevens's philosophy, the critic distinguishes himself as the most pessimistic of those who analyze Stevens's ideas. The poet's world hardly seems so hopeless and his fluctuations between reality and imagination hardly so desperate as Miller would have us believe. But Miller is quite perceptive in stipulating how Stevens attempts to escape his mental oscillations: the poet attempts to create poetry that will simultaneously possess extremes.

Unfortunately the critic attempts to find further import by erroneously judging such simultaneous possession of extremes new to an art form that has always in its metaphors attempted the juxtaposition and merger of disparates and opposites. Stevens, according to Miller, achieves a resolution between the opposites, imagination and reality, in formulating a theory that identifies poetry and life. This poetic philosophy is developed in a poetry of "flickering mobility" which proceeds by momentary crystallizations and dissolutions of thought that sustain the identity of both poetry and life. Especially in the later poetry, Miller finds a movement toward nothingness that becomes, once nothingness is recognized, being. When Miller attempts to describe Stevens's ontology, the critic becomes ensnared in the vagueness of ontological terms such as "being" and "nothing," yet the strength of Miller's study must be acknowledged in his isolation of the cycles of creation and thought which become ordering principles in Stevens's poetry.

Unlike Pearce and Miller, Helen Hennessy Vendler ("The Qualified Assertions of Wallace Stevens") does not attempt to distill the doctrine of Stevens's philosophy from general theoretic concerns in his poetry. Instead, she focuses on the fine nuances and lack of certainty in poetic direct statements. According to Vendler, Stevens relies on "syntactic manipulations" to close statements on a tentative note and thereby provide his thought-endings with an ambiguity unique in English verse. To this end he uses model auxiliaries—may, might, must, could, should, would—to conclude his statements; uses questions as a qualified means of stating an argument; manipulates infinitives and shifting tenses as indications of movement toward the future and indefinite; inserts verbs at the end of poems, semantically implying a future; employs "seem" to introduce uncertainty or hesitation; and uses "if" to introduce hypothesis, supposition, or uncommitted assertions. In short, Vendler finds in Stevens the shadowy and ephemeral world only vaguely perceived in its ambiguity by a poet with many ambivalences.

To illustrate, she explicates the syntactic and image development in "Not Ideas about the Thing but the Thing Itself" and "The Idea of Order at Key West." Her summary of the latter poem is perhaps the most tersely enlightening one statement on the process in an overcriticized and too-anthologized sample of Stevens's verse:

> The structure of the poem is ostensibly one of logical discrimination, but actually the complicated progressions (even if . . . since . . . it may be . . . if . . . or . . .) simply serve to implicate the various alternatives even more deeply with each other so that the sea, the girl, the water, the song, the wind, the air, the sky and cloud, the voices of the spectators, all become indistinguishable from each other (p. 175).

By noting correspondences and indistinct mergings of imagination and reality through Stevens's syntax, Vendler, unlike most other critics, specifically identifies where Stevens's philosophy of duality meets his poetic practice of illogical juxtaposition. Other critics would do well to follow her close attention to text and chosen limited scope of analysis. By defining the nameable specifics of Stevens's individual poems, Vendler does not become trapped in the elusive contradictions of what others generally attempt to label Stevens's philosophy.

A similar approach with a less successful product is attempted by Mac Hammond in "On the Grammar of Wallace Stevens." According to Hammond, Stevens's late poetry is a poetry of grammar in which the repetition of words and phrases in proximity detaches the linguistic element from the concept it evokes. Although Hammond certainly devotes attention to such detail, unlike Vendler he is unable to reintegrate isolated particulars into a conclusion about the poem as a whole. Hammond finds in Stevens's metalanguage and metapoetry a poetry about poetry in which a grammatical drama unfolds in verse communicating concepts about its own poetic language. This final point is an important one but needs to become the starting point rather than the final line of an

essay. In such lack of appropriate emphasis and thorough development as well as in lack of integration, Hammond isolates a particular but never specifies its philosophical import to the Stevens
poetic whole.

Richard A. Macksey's "The Climates of Wallace Stevens" also
deals with what the critic terms particulars because, according to
Macksey, Stevens's world is a universe of particulars. In Stevens,
Macksey finds a poet whose landscapes mirror consciousness and
whose cyclical seasons mirror poetic moods. Asserting that for
Stevens philosophy provided a point of departure rather than jus-
tification for a poem, Macksey nonetheless warns against drawing
analogies between Stevens and philosophers. After issuing such a
warning, Macksey compares Stevens's cyclical mind to Leibniz's
monad; Stevens's confrontation of pure being so Hegel's, Stevens's
attention to the thing itself to Husserl's "third way" between realism and idealism; Stevens's creation and decreation to Heidegger's
and Sartre's; and Stevens's interacting imagination and reality to
Valéry's two universes. Macksey only in passing relates these comparisons to his central theme, Stevens's mind of winter, which the
critic attempts to reveal through analysis of three poems, "The
Snow Man," "The Course of a Particular," and "Not Ideas about
the Thing but the Thing Itself." According to Macksey all three
poems are characteristic winter pieces of Stevens's wintry imagination because each describes vacancy and negation in modern life.
In general, the focus of the entire essay is not philosophical affinities or themes in Stevens, but Stevens's use of the winter season as
a theme and ordering principle in the development of his poetic
form, and as the very source of his poetry. Macksey's approach
is only indirectly related to Stevens's philosophy and is much too
selective in its discussion of one "weather" in Stevens: Macksey
never even acknowledges the Florida sun and summer in so much
of Stevens's verse.

Denis Donoghue's study, "Nuances of a Theme By Stevens," is
more successful in relating Stevens's practice to philosophic theory.
Donoghue acknowledges Stevens's role as poet-philosopher and
the multiple contradictions in the poet's avowed philosophic com-
mitments, but he attempts to examine Stevens's philosophic ideas
in order to define their "poetic nature." Rejecting labels such as
ideal, metaphysical, mythological, or symbolist poet, Donoghue
types Stevens a "tropical poet" because his poetry depends on the
use of tropes as Santayana defined them in *The Realm of Matter*:
patterns indistinguishable in the movement of things. This tropical
environment is the world of *Harmonium*, while a Kantian universe

of aesthetic concern characterizes the universe of Stevens's second volume, *Ideas of Order*. The most promising but unfortunately the most vague assertion in Donoghue's article is his statement that the later poems such as those of *The Rock* describe a world in which the early concern for poet, rhetoric, and art has been replaced by an imagination that becomes humanist in its concern for the mortal element of life.

The final study in the collection, Joseph Riddel's "The Contours of Stevens Criticism," is one of the more useful in the volume. Riddel does not attempt to argue for one particular approach to the poet, but simply and effectively provides a general overview of Stevens criticism before 1964. Such a review of the criticism is appropriately placed in this philosophically oriented collection because Riddel finds, in the decade of criticism preceding Stevens's death, a predominant opinion that Stevens rather than Eliot speaks most authentically for modern man. As the "unofficial preceptor of the modern romantic self" (p. 245), Stevens provides ideas and poetics that faired poorly under critical review in the twenties and thirties but became more appreciated in the forties as practitioners of New Criticism looked closely at the poet's structures and textures. By the fifties, critics began delving into Stevens's total work by focusing on his chronology and pervasive themes. The general directions Riddel notes in Stevens criticism and the importance, acknowledged by Riddel, of criticism's role in revealing Stevens's thought, are the strongest points in his general summary. The critic, however, stops short of proposing any direction for the future criticism which he terms inevitable and desirable.

In his own book-length study of Stevens, *The Clairvoyant Eye* (1967), Riddel contends that Stevens is a philosophical poet while he questions critics who attempt to metamorphose a poet with unsystematic thought into a philosopher. The distinction is a fine but important one. As a philosophical poet Stevens suffers from limitations of abstractness and impersonality when he creates poetry without people and drama or a world in which passion and suffering are academic and intellectual. On the other hand, Riddel characterizes Stevens's philosophical tendency as evidence of a poet who read widely but understood philosophy only in general terms, and as evidence of a poet who stressed the ordering center of the mind, just as philosophers—Berkeley, Leibniz, Kant, Nietzsche, Schopenhauer, Whitehead, Croce, Bergson, Santayana, Jean Wahl, Ernst Cassirer, Henri Focillon, Ramon Fernandez—did. From Santayana and Bergson, Stevens also learned how to deny the transcendental in symbolism. From Bergson he learned a definition of the comic that involved man in a dramatic gesture which turned vice into human egocentrism; he learned that in seeing the world, man projects himself on it; and he learned that the self survives in time by continuing creation through the imagination in an intercourse between consciousness and flux. But, according to Riddel, Santayana's influence on Stevens is more direct and evident in Stevens's beliefs that imagination and art are central to life; that poetry is moral, religious, but secular in nature; and that all experience occurs in poetic terms.

Riddel places the beginning of Stevens's philosophic mode in the poems of the thirties such as "Owl's Clover" and "The Man with the Blue Guitar." In these, Stevens attempts to establish poetry as the center of experience and man as the center of reality. The mode moves in the forties to an examination of poetry's potential for knowing something beyond the world of reality while maintaining its existence amid reality's vulgarity. As Stevens's philosophic musings turn inward, his themes become academic and his style mannered, all merging together to create a genuinely philosophic poetry. Although this aspect is only one characteristic of Stevens's poetry examined by Riddel, the critic's comments achieve a welcomed balance between a discussion of Stevens's philosophic mode and a recognition of the poet's artistic merit.

In an earlier but meaningful study on Stevens's philosophic mode, "The Genre of Wallace Stevens" (*Sewanee Review*, Autumn 1945), Hi Simons acknowledges the debate about Stevens as philosopher or poet and suggests that one can trace through Stevens's volumes a developing attitude toward some very specifically philosophic subjects. Simons lists these subjects as the socioaesthetic problem in the relation of the artist to his environment; the aesthetic, epistemological problem in the relation of imagination to reality; the problem of belief in its theological and metaphysical aspects; and a concern with humanism. Simons notes that Stevens is, above all else, a poet, but he also notes that Stevens's poetry is, above all else, an intellectual poetry. The adjective "intellectual" seems for Simons synonomous with philosophic, but it also yokes Stevens with traditional Metaphysics in poetry which Simons traces back to Donne and Marvell. (Simons's notation of Stevens's Metaphysical inheritance postulated in this study was discussed in chapter 2.)

Other critics such as Marianne Bankert in "The Meta-Metaphysical Vision of Wallace Stevens" (*Renascence*, Autumn 1971) and M. L. Rosenthal in "Stevens in a Minor Key" (*New Republic*, May 7, 1951), also tie Stevens's philosophy with traditional meta-

physics. Bankert's study depends on two assumptions: to define the
relationship between imagination and reality in terms of a dualism
that places them in opposition is inaccurate; and Stevens eschewed
such a Platonist dualism but held the conviction that reality and
the imagination are interdependent. At the core of Stevens's poetics, Bankert finds a movement from duality through unity and
conflict to harmony between reality and imagination, and she finds
a poet whose role is defined as mediator between the two aspects
of experience. In this Stevens awareness of the interdependence of
all dualities, the poet affirms a traditional metaphysic inherited
from the Thomistic "real distinction." Bankert also lumps Stevens
with all Western philosophers concerned with ontology, then
reads his "Sea Surface Full of Clouds" as an example of unpredictable Being associated with such ontology. By using undefined
philosophical labels such as "Thomistic" and interspersing these
with a Christian interpretation that Stevens, unlike Donne. failed
to find man an image of "the Word," Bankert weakens a discussion that otherwise reveals an ambivalence toward dualism evident
in the poet.

Rosenthal also acknowledges the complexity of Stevens's treatment of reality, pure idea, and imagination, but does not specify
the components of this complexity and does not attempt to relate
his comments to any individual poems. His study, a review of only
one volume, *The Auroras of Autumn*, is naturally quite brief and
more generally descriptive. He does, however, provide an opinion
divergent from Bankert's. According to Rosenthal, Stevens longs
for rather than rejects a Platonic world, but Rosenthal bases his
conclusion not on the issue of dualism, but on the ultimate happiness and knowledge Stevens supposedly found guaranteed by
Platonism. Stevens was hardly so nostalgic as Rosenthal would have
us believe.

In a similar attempt to relate Stevens's philosophy to some established branch of that genre, Judith McDaniel in "Wallace Stevens and the Scientific Imagination" (*Contemporary Literature*,
Spring 1974) focuses on how Stevens deals with abstractions by
manipulating ideas from modern philosophy of science. McDaniel
places Stevens in the line of Romantic poets descended from
Wordsworth, a line of reaction against the scientific discoveries of
the eighteenth century. Like Wordsworth, Stevens must confront
a mechanistic universe, but unlike his nineteenth-century predecessor, Stevens reacts to, not against, scientific ideas. To support
McDaniel's thesis, that Stevens is influenced by philosophy of science, she notes that the poet quotes from Whitehead's *Science and*

the Modern World and seems familiar with physicist Max Planck. McDaniel limits most of her examination of Stevens's verse to one volume, *The Rock,* and correctly acknowledges that these poems deal with advancing age and approaching death as personal concerns while they explore cosmic implications of order and disorder in the universe. In poems such as "The Philosophical Significance of the Theory of Relativity" and "The Reader," McDaniel finds Stevens confronting concepts of energy, matter, space, time, and relativity. Other poems like "Prologues to What Is Possible" and "An Old Man Asleep" create the theoretical world of physics in which nothing is certain, only probable. And, in conclusion, McDaniel finds in *The Rock* a sense of the task which the poet shares with philosopher and scientist: all attempt to describe or illuminate the universe.

In "On Speaking Humanly" (1970), Thomas R. Whitaker disagrees with critics such as McDaniel, Rosenthal, Bankert, and Simons who approach Stevens by examining philosophical tendencies in the verse. Instead, Whitaker proposes that Stevens's real philosophy may be ascertained not by comparing the poet's thought to other men's, but by examining the poet's act of speech which for Stevens provided "actual and potential value" (p. 68). The study is very ambiguous because Whitaker never clarifies his definition of "speech." At various times the word seems to refer to linguistic theory, style, word choice, poetic technique, poetic voice, and persona voice, but as the meanings accumulate and become interchangeable, one is lost in imprecise communication and unclear emphasis. Only in his conclusion does Whitaker relate this magic speech vaguely to a loosely defined linguistic theory when he specifies Stevens's governing philosophy: "*We speak,* therefore we are" (p. 86). He extends his description of Stevens's philosophic position when he notes that for Stevens belief precedes final belief in a fiction because a faith in true speech is itself "affirmation, commitment, and acceptance" (p. 86). Whitaker's entanglement in overgeneral and undefined terms merits mention only because of his unrealized attempt to relate language to philosophy in the poet.

A bit more lucid if not more exact, Katharine Gilbert's "Recent Poets on Man and His Place" (1952) also attempts to relate language and philosophy in Stevens. Gilbert's comments are especially noteworthy because they originally appeared in the form of an address delivered at a 1946 Yale meeting of the American Philosophical Association's Eastern Division. Here, Gilbert introduced to philosophers a poet who believed that man's situation in the world could be salvaged by the gaiety of man's language. According to Gilbert, recent poets such as Stevens reveal new experience through linguistic invention while they intensify the problem of "doing and undergoing" (p. 81). Although brief, Gilbert's comments are important only as a perspective from the vantage point of one concerned primarily with philosophy rather than poetry.

In examining Stevens's philosophical nature, critics have disagreed about not only his relationship to areas of philosophical inquiry but also his merit as a philosophical poet. In "Reality and the Imagination: The Poetic of Wallace Stevens' 'Necessary Angel' " (*University of Kansas City Review*, Autumn 1954), Steve Feldman's criticism degenerates into mere paraphrase and blind praise. Feldman characterizes Stevens as a skeptic who distrusts philosophers but hopes that poetry as unitive truth will equal or surpass the intellectual genre. According to Feldman, Stevens's prose theorizing about poetry is thorough, complete, useful, up-to-date, and difficult to summarize, while the poet is himself an inspiration to other poets because he is able to combine the theories of Coleridge, Wordsworth, Shelley, French poets and philosophers in the Symbolist movement, as well as modern philosophy and psychology in order to distill his own personal philosophy. Such uncontrolled lauding ignores Stevens's superficial understanding and occasional hodgepodge conglomerations of philosophy—a subject, most critics agree, in which Stevens dabbled as a novice, not a master.

A. Alvarez (*Stewards of Excellence*, 1958, pp. 124–39) and M. Whitcomb Hess ("Wallace Stevens and the 'Shaping Spirit'," *The Personalist*, Spring 1961) are less kind on this count to Stevens. Although Alvarez initially praises Stevens as the most "perfectly finished poet" (except Eliot) produced by America, he ambivalently criticizes Stevens for borrowing from some indistinct, unnamed poetic predecessor and for contriving a style of endless repetition and triviality. He thinks that Stevens writes philosophical poetry because such poetry depends on a "clarity of abstractions rather than of experience" (p. 126), and because Stevens moves through a logical process from pure description to the idea of the thing described, thereby moving into a Platonic world of ideas. In short, Alvarez praises Stevens for the poet's coherence typical of a philosopher, but criticizes him for a contrived artistry typical of a poet. Alvarez himself deserves criticism for his lack of attention to his supposed chosen subject in this chapter subtitled "Platonic Poetry." What Alvarez really seems to discuss is not poetry in the Platonic vein, but his own muddled paraphrase of a few Stevens ideas and his own ambivalence toward the poet. The study, a more appropriate first-draft, working-out of thesis, reveals more about the inadequate development of a critic's argument than a philosophical tendency in a poet.

Hess's study briefly compares Alvarez's 1958 book, titled *The Shaping Spirit* in its British printing, and William Van O'Connor's study by the same name (1950). Hess departs from the comments of both earlier critics to launch into a scathing attack on Stevens's philosophy. Hess labels Stevens's doubt of the external reality of sense knowledge as a "pernicious" theory traceable to Descartes, and finds the poet's concern with man's creative imagination based on the "unsound" metaphysics of Aristotle's matter-form hypothesis. In Stevens's world, Hess discovers a philosophical breakdown exemplified in poems like "Bantams in Pine-Woods" where one finds "spacious-reasoning-set-to-poetry" (p. 211). Concluding that Stevens's philosophy is as bleak, pessimistic, and inescapable as Kafka's view of man, Hess misinterprets the poet and poetic persons who are clearly not paralyzed pawns or puzzled beings in a world of unintelligible and inexorable forces. The Kafka analogy is not defensible.

Like Hess, Lewis Turco ("The Agonism and the Existentity: Stevens," *Concerning Poetry*, Spring 1973) damns Stevens as an "agonist" who works his theoretics out in poems rather than essays. According to Turco, poets may be divided into three types: the professionals who dedicate their lives to writing poetry; the amateurs who use poetry as a means to an end; and the agonists such as Stevens who construct and embellish a particular theory of poetry. Turco thinks poetic techniques are manipulated by Stevens in order to communicate abstractions, but, because of the poet's single concern with abstraction, the poetic result is the same poem written over and over. In "An Ordinary Evening in New Haven" Turco attempts to find evidence of Stevens's predominant abstract theme, the subjectivity of reality, but Turco's explication of this complex poem is no more enlightening than his oversimplification of Stevens's career in general.

Like Turco, J. V. Cunningham in "The Styles and Procedures of Wallace Stevens" (*University of Denver Quarterly*, Spring 1966) criticizes what he describes as Stevens's preoccupation with philosophizing. In the name of beneficence, Cunningham claims to save Stevens from himself and his friends by discriminating among and describing the poet's "simple-minded ideas and procedures" (p. 11). These ideas include Stevens's loss of implicit belief in the Christian God as well as his desire for "rest" and "peace." Labeling Stevens a "Hartford Hegel" whose mode develops by a dialectic that includes a statement of position, presentation of opposites, and intervention of resolution, Cunningham devotes most of his study to a discussion of Stevens's imagination and reality. But, Cunningham never bothers to explore fully the philosophical inadequacies he notes in a poet he criticizes so sharply in one sentence and objectively relates to Royce, William James, and Santayana in another. In one of his more negative and unfounded statements about Stevens, Cunningham describes the poet as an amateur writing poetry for his own sake and the sake of experience rather than for the "thing's sake." If this judgment were not so vague, it might be accurately applied to Cunningham.

Elizabeth Jennings's *Every Changing Shape* (1952) devotes a chapter to the same lack of Christian faith in Stevens that Cunningham notes, but Jennings defines her central focus more clearly and develops it more thoroughly than Cunningham does. In her chapter about Stevens, "Vision Without Belief," Jennings characterizes Stevens as a poet who lacks faith in the religious sense and affirmation in the human sense. In such an absence, Stevens searches for reality using the imagination. This is the subject of every poem and this is the enactment of his philosophy that cannot be separated from his poetry without stripping his poems of meaning. More than a philosophical poet, Stevens is to Jennings a visionary poet whose vision includes a philosophical search for reality. Drawing on Stevens's "The Comedian as the Letter C," "Peter Quince at the Clavier," "Sunday Morning," "Credences of Summer," and "Notes Toward a Supreme Fiction," she attempts to elucidate Stevens's vision as a faith in creation based in the mind of man. To the creative aspect of poetry Stevens assigns attributes that other men assign to religion and philosophy. Acknowledging this, Jennings seems to contradict herself by also asserting that Stevens does not elevate art into philosophy. Her study is also marred by the assertion that Stevens lacks faith and belief. On the contrary, the poet's belief in a creative power and faith in an interactional and experiential universe are adamant. Jennings appears to assume that a lack of orthodox faith in traditional religion is synonomous with an inability to believe in any greater meaning. Stevens's faith in his own supreme fiction belies such a critical conclusion.

An Emphasis on the Poetic in the Philosophy

In contrast to these critics who emphasize the philosophical nature of Stevens's poetry, one finds the critics who reemphasize the poetic aspect of Stevens's philosophical musings. James Baird's *The Dome and the Rock: Structure in the Poetry of Wallace Stevens* (1968) is the best example of this latter tendency. Baird suggests that philosophical approaches to Stevens are limited because they impose the critic's approach rather than elucidate the poet's work, but Baird also acknowledges the philosophical nature of Stevens's musings and characterizes such musings as "self-contained." The subject of Stevens's poetry is, according to Baird, poetry as poetic process. To understand Stevens's work, Baird suggests then that one must examine the entire "poem-as-process." Because this poem-as-process is created as a poet's grand design, Baird uses the metaphor of architecture to unify his study.

To Baird, Stevens's work is organized with architectural precision, the mind taking shape as a building and the grand poem evolving into a dome crafted upon the rock of being. Baird selects architecture as an appropriate metaphor for Stevens's method because in architecture and in a Stevens poem the artist shapes a creation in which the living idea of that object resides beneath the surface of its craft. As examples of this method, Baird cites Stevens's poems "To an Old Philosopher in Rome," "St. Armorer's Church," and "Architecture." In these poems and others, Stevens's symbols of achieved structure are dominated by images of the dome, while in other poems such as "The Good Man Has No Shape" and "A Lot of People Bathing in a Stream," the concepts of shape and structure of the self are poetic subjects. Baird uses this interdependence and interaction of form and content as evidence that Stevens is not a philosopher. Philosophers, in Baird's characterization, begin with the imposition of an idea on the world while poets begin with the phenomena of the world and use them ultimately to reach an idea. For the philosopher, an idea proceeds to an object, while for a poet as for an architect, the object proceeds to an idea. Yet, Baird concedes, Stevens is philosophically related to Santayana's *The Sense of Beauty*, Berkeley's "Essay on Vision" and "Concerning Motion," and Bradley's *Appearance and Reality*, but the poet is not in any way related to phenomenologists. Baird bases this last conclusion on Stevens's attempt to portray the poet as a shaper defining the poetic personality that determines structure. In other words, Stevens seeks an architecture of the self rather than allows the mind to merely present the phenomenal world.

Baird attempts to trace Stevens's philosophical structure to various strains of literature including nineteenth-century English Romanticism and French Symbolism, as well as to an oriental influence discernible in the haiku-like "Thirteen Ways of Looking at a Blackbird" and "Six Significant Landscapes." Stevens's American antecedents Baird finds not in Poe but in the aphorisms and riddles of the poet's Pennsylvania Dutch heritage. And, according to Baird, the architectural shaping of the self may be traced back to the poetic theorizing of Emerson, Thoreau, Whitman, and Dickinson, but Stevens's version must ultimately be considered his own.

According to Baird, Stevens, like Cezanne, viewed objects as depending on a total visual field including the attitudes, experience, and organization of the observer. Baird thinks the arc is Stevens's choice of metaphor to communicate this vision; and as examples the critic cites the spherical curvature in "A Primitive Like an Orb," the rounding of ideas into cocoons in "Ghosts as Cocoons," and arching cloths related to parasols in "Certain Phenomena of Sound." When the arcs of self and life, real and unreal conjoin, Baird finds what he terms Stevens's creation of a dome. The critic's own use of geometric and architectural metaphor is more prominent here than the art it describes, but seems obviously appropriate to describe such an art in which the poet creates precise relationships through his act of poetic composition. By analyzing this poetic composition, Baird attempts to isolate specific visual aspects of Stevens's poetry that relate to the poet's philosophical position. Accordingly, Baird interprets Stevens's use of the sun image as not a poet's attempt to create a sun myth but to recognize a major fact of physical and external being (the sun) in its relationship to a perceiving consciousness (artist's imagination). He examines the poet's definition of light as a power that illuminates and provides the perceiver with a means of possessing an object visually. The light and imagination meet in poems such as "Tattoo" and "Glass of Water" in which the light reveals but the imagination adds color. Baird notes that recent scientific inquiry into the perceptual nature of color authenticates Stevens's theory of color that emphasizes the role of the perceiver.

From the sun, light, and color, Baird moves to a consideration of Stevens's theoretical position on the eye. The importance of the mind to the power of sight is emphasized by Baird because in Stevens the same emphasis occurs and leads to an abstract art in which the poet assumes no obligation to a representational art that focuses on external truth rather than the perception and organization of the mind. With strict attention to physical experience communicated through images of sun, light, color, and perceiving eye, Stevens introduces his setting, the reality of the rock around which symbols of leaves, wind, weather, clouds, frost, and moon

multiply as indications of the builder attempting to link the parts
of his work in conjoining arcs. Baird again utilizes the term "arc"
metaphorically as a unifying theme in Stevens's poetry and stipulates ten such arcs for consideration: symbols of the imagination;
encounters of the eye; masques and festivals; ritual presences;
land-made men; transitions in the American community; the difficulty of being; aspects of the supreme fiction; the descent of the
rock; and the poet as priest. To each of these Baird devotes a chapter of analysis and to each he prescribes a poetic image associated
with the theme by Stevens in his poetry. In their respective order
these images include wing and claw, the painter, the comedian,
the mythological canon, American place, society, existence, the
hero, the northern quarter, and the chapel of wind and weather.

As symbols of the imagination and as examples of Baird's first
arc, wings, birds, clawed and fanged animals communicate the
poet's savage scrutiny of the imagination's power. As a raw,
fanged, snarling but visually oriented faculty, Stevens's imagination
differs from Wordsworth's and Coleridge's philosophical faculty
which patiently synthesizes. The painter who personifies for Stevens encounters of the eye is a poet-painter who uses words and
colors to elaborate on a design. Stevens's creative method is, according to Baird, like Cezanne's subjective objectivism in which
the artist meets reality. Yet Baird is quick to agree with the most
noted critic on Stevens's painterly nature, Michel Benamou (to be
discussed later in this chapter), who stipulates that the affinity
between poetry and painting must be found in a comparison of the
artists' use of words and colors. In Stevens, unaccustomed verbal
usage and diction are used to create the newness, speed, and momentariness of impressionism. But as Stevens progresses, Baird finds
a growing need in the poet for expressing something beyond mere
color on canvas. Because of this need, painting becomes for Stevens a metaphor, not an end, of mimetic poetry.

Baird's second arc for consideration, Stevens's personification of
masques and festivals in the comedian, is most obvious in "The
Comedian as the Letter C." In this poem Baird finds a "masque
projected from the disarray and the poverty of the national imaginative experience" (p. 206). And, in the tradition of commedia
dell'arte, Baird finds, in many Stevens poems, actors who mime
parts but are totally mute while the poet alone speaks. This point
is an important explanation of the one-dimensional characters for
which so many critics fault Stevens. Other figures in Stevens's
verse such as the central man and paramour woman are labeled by
Baird as mythical presences who enact the ritual of creation in

Stevens's shaping of his dome. Even the land-made men, who personify for the poet the American place, become almost mythical as Stevens approaches Emerson's conception of poet-as-namer. For Stevens, contemporary place compelled language, and speech of the now became all that man could possess or know. This philosophical position coupled with the poet's view of the American community in transition, manifested in his symbol of society as granite monotony, characterize Stevens's more social middle poetry in which he explores mass consciousness.

According to Baird, in Steven's later work the poet turns to symbols of existence in order to focus more on the individual self and the difficulties inherent in that self's being. In this focus, Baird compares the poet's ideas with those of existential philosophy. Both poet and existential philosopher study the immediacy of being, but Stevens views being in a mode entirely his own, emphasizing singular perception which revitalizes the process of the mind and requires, according to Baird, description in poetry. Although Baird compares Stevens's and the philosopher's concern with existential immediacy, the critic categorically denies that the poet borrowed from such philosophers. Stevens moves beyond existential philosophy when he proposes the hero figure as alive and functioning in modern time. According to Baird, Stevens's hero is a major man associated with all men and therefore a human who is capable of postulating and believing in supreme fictions. If the chance of transcendence exists for such a man or any man in Stevens's poetry, Baird finds it in the poet's paradox: by denying the self faith in the superhuman, Stevens affirms faith in the human. This transcendence and the celebration of age as the poet's design fulfilled, Baird lodges in the Stevens theme of descent to the rock and reality prevalent in the late poems that explore the northern quarter.

The final theme Baird examines, the poet as priest practicing in a chapel of wind and weather, is the supposed culmination of Stevens's design. In the late poems that typify this theme Stevens's language becomes priestly as he attempts to transform the real into the unreal by consecrating the imagination. Poetry then for Stevens is redemptive because it provides evidence of health and a shaping power within man. This conclusion is well stated, but Baird's means of arriving here are far less direct. The critic's style is difficult and abstruse, often depending on formal somewhat archaic diction; lengthy complex aperiodic sentences; and extended, oblique, and mixed metaphors. That is not to say that the study is not worth the effort in concentration required of the reader. On the contrary, Baird's command of the Stevens criticism as well as his ability to paraphrase and summarize theoretical import in individual Stevens poems is admirable. If one reads the study as a metaphorical memorial to one poet's process and as a critical architectural superstructure utilized to order a philosophical poetry of process, Baird's book is exceptionally helpful. If, however, simple elucidation is one's need, Baird's own metaphors intrude and force the critic's poetic language into the sensibility of the reader for interpretation rather than functioning as explanatory comments on the poet. In exploring the poet's and his own grand design, Baird slights individual poems and a multiplicity of themes in Stevens not subsumable under the dome and rock metaphor.

Joseph Riddel's review of Baird's study ("The Dome and the Rock" *American Literature*, Jan. 1970) criticizes Baird more generally for a lack of unifying central theme as well as for inattention to particular poems. Riddel senses in Baird a difficulty reconciling the architectural metaphor and poetry as process, a difficulty which does occasionally near the surface in Baird's study. Baird, in setting himself against most philosophical criticism of Stevens, refuses to acknowledge what Riddel terms a "criticism of consciousness" which enables a critic to examine the making of the poetic self in structures of language. (The very phenomenological analysis of self-reflexive poetics rejected by Baird may be found in Riddel's book-length study to be discussed in chapter 4.) Hyatt Howe Waggoner's review of the Baird study (*Modern Philology*, May 1970) also criticizes Baird for rejecting criticism that philosophically examines Stevens because, according to Waggoner, after the rejection, Baird acknowledges evidence in the poems to support their philosophic meaning. Waggoner, like Riddel, mentions his own book-length study (discussed in chapter 2), but Waggoner expends so much energy describing his own approach that Baird's study gradually fades from his focus as a result. One might add to Riddel's and Waggoner's comments, if the world were just, book reviewers would require of themselves the same attention to the text they so often require of their subject.

Baird himself seems to clarify his position on the philosophical element in Stevens when, in an earlier shorter study, "Transvaluation in the Poetics of Wallace Stevens" (1961), he discusses Stevens's contribution to poetic theory. Listing those poets who throughout literary history have changed the nature of poetic theory, Baird judges Stevens's supreme fiction as important as Wordsworth's analysis of the imagination's process, Coleridge's theory of poetic synthesis, Poe's concept of poetic unity and impressionistic totality, Baudelaire's doctrine of poetic symbol as structure of polyvalence, and Mallarmé's ideas on poetic surrealism. In acknowledging Stevens's place in the theory of poetics, Baird acknowledges his primary role as poet but also notes the "philosophical color" that gives the poet's remarks an air of combined theory and description. Although deemphasizing Stevens's relationship to philosophy, Baird nonetheless examines the poet's theory of supreme fiction in its affinity with existentialism and the relativity of modern absolutes as well as with French poetics and modern painting. According to Baird, Stevens, like Tillich, rejects philosophy because it attempts a false synthesis, but like Tillich he adheres to a concept of art that calls for a limitation of reality. Like other studies by Baird this one is intense, meaty, definitive, but abstruse in analyzing its subject, here the artistic philosophies important to the understanding of Stevens. And, like other Baird studies, this abstract synthesis demands a reader quite familiar with the poet and his critics.

A second, book-length study of Stevens is also devoted primarily to an analysis of the poet's philosophical mind. Frank Doggett in *Stevens' Poetry of Thought* (1966) stresses the importance of philosophic concepts while also acknowledging the miscellaneous character of these concepts which are not refined into a consistent philosophy but are bound together in a type of "naturalism" evident in Stevens's allegiance to earth and reality. The major emphasis of the study then is the "nature and function of idea in the poetry of Stevens" (p. x), and the major strategy is an examination of the poet in light of philosophical writings. Doggett does not assign Stevens to a particular school of thought, nor does he contend that specific philosophers influenced Stevens. He simply holds that philosophy helps elucidate concepts in Stevens's poetry. According to Doggett, Stevens's idea of individual being which occupies most of his poetry depends on mortality and subjectivity, the interdependence of mind and reality. Because of the emphasis on mind and reality, the specific moment of experience is crucial in Stevens, and the mind's humanizing of reality through created forms becomes crucial in the poetry. With a "rudimentary naturalism" that rejects transcendence and accepts the flux and change in time and experience, Stevens defines the mind as a faculty capable of forming relationships within itself and interpreting the world anthropomorphically. Doggett traces this definition to Schopenhauer and Santayana, while he traces Stevens's idea of flux to Bergson, William James, and Whitehead as well as San-

tayana. For understanding Stevens's view of the self interpreting
experience, Doggett recalls Whitehead's definition of past as part
of the self living into the present and definition of self as locus
within the general unity of the world.

Doggett is most helpful when he traces philosophical ideas of
the self, mind, or reality as they appear in the poetry. Stevens's
belief that the self may take other forms is manifested, according
to Doggett, in poems such as "Notes Toward a Supreme Fiction"
in which the poet splits into an alter-self, the ephebe. The duality
of existence in Stevens's thought takes the form in many poems of
simple opposition such as that found in "The Snow Man," a poem
juxtaposing that which exists and that which is nonexistent. For
Stevens, duality also prevails in man's ways of knowing the world
either through physical life or a supplemental way, through cognition. Both mind and reality then as forces in nature become confronting opposites that are yet a part of each other. He as poet
wishes to be part of this dual self of nature. Here again, Doggett
notes Stevens's "inherent naturalism."

Stevens's poetry is to Doggett basically a poetry of thought because, in the verse, abstraction is a major element. Yet, ideas in
Stevens have a poetic rather than philosophic function and the ultimate goal is not, as in philosophy, the assertion of statement, but
typical for poetry, the implication of a fictive statement. Doggett's
distinction between the two genres is clear and appropriately applied to this poet, as is his conclusion that Stevens often reverses the
traditional poetic paradigm by reversing the experience to cognition movement, starting with an idea, and only then moving into
matters of experience. Doggett is also useful when he notes affinities
with the ideas of Schopenhauer, James, Santayana, Bergson, Jung,
Cassirer, Whitehead, Hume, Kant, Nietzsche, Croce, and Bradley;
when he examines not-so-well-known and seldomly examined
samples of Stevens's work; and when he ties his assertions and Stevens's poetics to the poet's important essay on the relationship of
philosophic and poetic ideas, "A Collect of Philosophy." But, his
approach is problematic when his search for philosophy causes
him to miss the poetry of the poems entirely; when he fails to value
any one major poem above any of Stevens's minor mediocre
poems, equalizing all as bearers of philosophy; and when he imposes the rigors of systematic theorizing on Stevens's constantly
fluctuating asystematic perception of changing reality. Even Doggett himself tentatively acknowledges this last problem when he
notes that Stevens's ideas have purposes other than philosophic ones

and at times are really only "half ideas." Doggett further asserts that Stevens's effect is achieved because these ideas are not elaborated. This latter assertion partially lightens the load of philosophical import cast by Doggett and other critics too frequently as burdens on Stevens—and reader. Interestingly enough, Doggett himself must have felt this burden when he asserted in "Wallace Stevens' Later Poetry" (*English Literary History*, June 1953), a study discussed more fully in chapter 1, that Stevens is never a philosophical poet except when he delves into a theory of reality. Otherwise, his ideas are "systemic," not "thematic."

In his "Abstraction and Wallace Stevens" (*Criticism*, Winter 1960), Doggett correctly assesses Stevens criticism as too preoccupied with the poet's ideas. That Stevens reintroduced the idea into poetry after Imagism Doggett also acknowledges, but distinguishes between such ideas which are abstract assertions presented as general summary rather than fully supported philosophical premises. Noting Stevens's declaration in *Opus Posthumous* that he did not employ poetry as a medium for philosophy, Doggett proposes that Stevens manipulates "philosophic themes." Much in this study and in most Doggett articles before 1966 may also be found in slightly altered form in Doggett's *Poetry of Thought*. The critic compares excerpts from works by philosophers like Santayana, James, and Bradley with poems by Stevens in order to reveal the differences in poetry and philosophy as the differences between direct statement and a created statement in a fictive world with further implications. Doggett asserts that Stevens uses philosophical ideas as most poets use dramatic content, to provide a surface, guise, and role for the poem. In this way the poet inverts the relationship of idea and experience in such a way that action is not a representation of abstraction but the specified thing becomes a general conception instead. The similarities between this and Doggett's longer study are obvious. Yet in its brevity, "Abstraction and Wallace Stevens" is superior to the *Poetry of Thought* because the former possesses the clarity of concise argument and defined focus without the latter's burden of extended proof and imposed systematization. In "Abstraction and Wallace Stevens" Doggett clearly distinguishes where Stevens borrows from philosophy, where the poems differ from philosophy, and how they differ.

Isabel G. MacCaffrey in "The Other Side of Silence 'Credences of Summer' as an Example" (*Modern Language Quarterly*, Sept. 1969) takes up where Doggett's article stops. Like Doggett, MacCaffrey bases her study on the assumption that Stevens is a poet of ideas, but that his mode of development—the poem moving gradually toward a discovery of its subject—differs from typical methods of philosophy. According to this critic, Stevens's relationship to philosophy has been overexamined because his concerns overlap with those of philosophy; because many of these concerns are repeated often in many poems, inspiring conjecture about a philosophical system; and because he often imitates the logic of philosophical discourse. Yet she agrees with Doggett that Stevens's mode includes but exceeds aspects of a philosophical mode. MacCaffrey summarizes that Stevens "moves through philosophy, the attempt to make logical sense of being, to poetry, the attempt to make imaginative sense of being" (p. 420). To support her contentions, MacCaffrey examines Stevens's "Credences of Summer" as a statement embodying "the strange relations of life's nonsense" (p. 420) that must be read not as a philosophical discourse but a poetic discourse on the interdependence of being and saying. She distinguishes poetic discourse from philosophic discourse by suggesting the importance of syntactic arrangement and form in poetry. From this basis she develops an extended and penetrating explication of "Credences" as a poem about the nature of belief and man's fictions, but her other comments add little to Doggett's often stated and often published ideas on Stevens and philosophy.

Like MacCaffrey, Frank Lentricchia, Jr. ("Wallace Stevens: The Ironic Eye," *Yale Review*, Spring 1967) finds that most Stevens criticism inadequately labels him a philosophical poet. Such a label emphasizes the poet's theory but thereby neglects the ironic tone of his poetry. Lentricchia thinks that Stevens starts with philosophic ideas but uses them as vehicles of expression for his lyricism. The philosophical perspective then is the poem's perspective, but irony is the dominant tonality used by the poet in the poem. In Stevens's poetry one finds a Kantian epistemology not as a theoretical postulate but as a poetic possibility in an "unresolved dialectic," Lentricchia's term for the form of Stevens's poems. By this the critic seems to mean a tension between the poet's antithetical motivations. The dialectical process is operative in the development of Stevens's primary concern, the relation of the perceiver and the perceived, and unfolds as a thesis in which the poet recognizes the world as objectively real and the source of his *materia poetica*, opposite an antithesis in which Stevens thinks the world has no existence except in the mind. Regardless of how the poem resolves the issue, a tension is produced by the poet's acknowledgment of dualistic nature. Using poems like "Sunday

Morning" and "The Snow Man" as examples, Lentricchia concludes that this unresolved dialectic defines the form and tension
in Stevens's poems.

Elder Olson's earlier study, "The Poetry of Wallace Stevens"
(*College English*, April 1955), is less exact in isolating the parameters of Stevens's philosophical poetry. Olson, like Lentricchia,
criticizes Stevens criticism, but Olson faults it for metamorphosing
a good poet into a bad philosopher. That Stevens is a poet of ideas,
Olson acknowledges, but that he uses such ideas with an emotional
as well as an intellectual dimension, Olson also asserts. Agreeing
that philosophic concerns are a part, but only a part, of Stevens's
poems, Olson thinks Stevens does not describe ideas using rational
discourse, but evokes them using images that are poetic and emotional in character. The study becomes diffuse and is weakened
when Olson attempts to explicate several poems at length by isolating in each the poetic and the philosophic elements. Contrary to
most Stevens criticism, Olson stipulates that the later poems are
inappropriately described as more difficult and philosophic. In a
moment of basic insight certainly worthy of exploration (which
does not occur), the critic states that if anything is difficult in
Stevens's poetry it must be the images that lack total description,
development, or specification of relationship.

Far more enlightening is Marjorie Perloff's "Irony in Wallace
Stevens' *The Rock*" (*American Literature*, Nov. 1964). Slamming
previous discussions of Stevens's *The Rock* as "unnecessarily sol-
emn and doctrinaire" (p. 327) in their focus on the philosophical
nature of Stevens's poetry, Perloff characterizes the speaker in these
late poems as an ambivalent, aloof, sophisticated spectator rather
than a philosopher. Acknowledging a more doctrinal and philosophical concern in Stevens's middle period typified by "The Idea
of Order at Key West," Perloff traces a deepening irony and
double vision that began in the early *Harmonium*. She examines
this deepening irony in poems such as "The World as Meditation"
in which the daydream of the poem serves as an ironic comment
on the poem's epigraph, an interesting and cogent reading to say
the least. She also examines what she terms the life cycle poems in
The Rock, such as "The Green Plant," in order to discuss the
chronic tension between meaninglessness becoming awareness and
awareness becoming meaninglessness. Her intent in this study,
clearly stated, is to divert attention from the poems as philosophical
argument to the poems as poems. In this task her explications are accurate and revealing, her review of Stevens criticism relevant and

thorough, and her argument well defined and supported. She perceptively notes that these late poems are disappointing if one searches for philosophical theory because one then finds that these poems lack, as critics have charged, humanity and particularization. If instead they are read as poems, a task she attempts, a reconciliation of opposites reveals itself in the imagination and reality which in *The Rock* become equals. In short, her study is one of the most convincing on Stevens's poetry as part of the genre of poetry not philosophy.

R. P. Blackmur ("The Substance That Prevails," *Kenyon Review*, Winter 1955) and Horace Gregory ("An Examination of Wallace Stevens in a Time of War," *Accent*, Autumn 1942) are even more adamant in lodging Stevens firmly in a poetry genre, defined by them as totally nonphilosophic. Blackmur states Stevens is not a man of intellect, and when he as poet attempts to delve into concepts, his work becomes "merely discursive" and a "disorder of sensation" (p. 95). Blackmur admits that Stevens is a poet of ideas, but even qualifies this by noting that the poet's abstractions simply provide a means for a show of "the sheer preciousness of his beliefs" (p. 97). Originally delivered as an address in the Braden Lecture series at Yale in 1954, Blackmur's comments lack the specificity, and one might add the insight, of Perloff's study. Gregory's study, on the other hand, though early in the criticism and therefore more tentative, is quite specific in focus. Gregory maintains that Stevens is not a philosopher or an intellectual, and the value of his poetry cannot be measured in intellectual terms. Distinguishing between intellectual poetry and a poetic intelligence with wit, Gregory places Stevens in the latter category. Acknowledging that poems like those in *Parts of a World* originate in philosophic discourse, Gregory finds that Stevens ultimately uses philosophic language to express a poetic sensibility. However, Gregory's greatest contribution rests in his perceptive, almost prophetic assessment, considering his study's date, of a notable strength and weakness in the poet. This strength Gregory lodges in Stevens's poems that may be read as analogies for observations of the world. The weakness in Stevens's longer poems Gregory describes as a confusion in aesthetic values. In poems after *The Man with the Blue Guitar*, Stevens whimsically treats the relationship of poetic mind and external world and thereby blurs the distinction between Coleridgean methods of fancy and the imagination. The shock value of such surprising incongruity in form and content may eventually distinguish Stevens, Gregory speculates, but its cost must be assessed in these mildly argumentative and repetitious poems.

An Emphasis on Specific Philosophers

Rather than define or trace the philosophical elements in Stevens's poetry, some critics have attempted to show that Stevens was influenced by particular philosophers. Using various poems as keys to the poet's affinity with individual philosophers, critics have examined Stevens's relationship to Santayana, Bergson, and William James among others. The Stevens-Santayana relationship concerns the most critics because of the poet's obvious admiration for Santayana communicated clearly and masterfully in the late poem "To an Old Philosopher in Rome." Santayana taught at Harvard during the years Stevens studied there, and the two are known to have written poems for one another's perusal. David P. Young in "A Skeptical Music: Stevens and Santayana" (*Criticism,* Summer 1965) reports that Samuel French Morse told him Stevens owned everything Santayana published. Based on this information, Young concludes that the relationship between the two was not one of friendship or even extended acquaintance but of study. Young labels Stevens a poet because he communicates not the truth of a philosopher but the experience of truth, but Young also thinks that Stevens mixes poetry and philosophy because his mentor, Santayana, found an affinity between the two.

Young's study is quite useful because, unlike many other statements about the Stevens and Santayana relationship, Young's explores in some detail the beliefs shared by the two men: Santayana viewed the universe as an irrational chaos of flux, a principle found in Stevens's images of natural disorder; Santayana viewed such chaos as the basis for a knowledge devoid of metaphysical falsifications of order, a view expressed by Stevens in images of progressing seasons that move from portents of skepticism to the reconstitution of belief; Santayana suggested a rejection of past beliefs as well as a scrutiny of all knowledge's validity, a concern confronted in Stevens's redefinitions of reality and imagination; and Santayana emphasized the aesthetic character of all knowledge and experience and thereby emphasized the imagination, a focus found in Stevens's imagination as central faculty. In short, Young suggests that Stevens found the basis for his ideas about poetry in Santayana's theory of knowledge and imagination which stressed aesthetic value and experience. Santayana himself discussed the ideal possibilities of philosophical poetry in his *Interpretations of Poetry and Religion* (1900). In this study Santayana proposed an affinity in the universal and moral functions of poetry and religion, both utilizing imagery, fiction, and idealism in their interpretations of reality. This same comparison of poetry and religion Young

correctly finds in Stevens's poems such as "Sunday Morning" and
"A High-Toned Old Christian Woman." Stevens responds to
Santayana's noted affinities by substituting poetry for religion, and
by experimenting with the four types of poetry which Santayana
describes as phases of progress leading to the best poetry: phase
one is concerned with sound and euphony; phase two with a
meter and sound enhanced by vocabulary and style; phase three
with a depiction of sensuous experience; and phase four with the
poet's reordering and reconstructing of experience. Santayana's
theories were attractive to Stevens because in them all experience
as well as all knowledge are poetic in character while the human
imagination is the supreme fiction. So similar in belief are Stevens
and Santayana, Young suggests, that Stevens's poem on Santayana
might be applied to the poet himself. The point is perceptive and
the study well executed in its elucidation of philosophic affinity
only skirted by other critics.

Joseph N. Riddel's "Visibility of Thought" (*Publications of
the Modern Language Association*, Sept. 1962b) precedes Young's
study with similar conclusions. In "To an Old Philosopher in
Rome" Riddel finds a blending of Santayana's philosophy and
Stevens's aesthetic, and in Stevens's world view, like Santayana's,
Riddel finds an awareness of man's mortal condition as well as a
concomitant skepticism coupled with humanism. The world
Santayana posited in the imagination is like the meditative world
revealed in Stevens's late poetry. For both men, these inner worlds
are based in a physical, outer world. Riddel's study is strongest
not in any detailed delineations of similarities in the two men, but
in the critic's accurate summary of Stevens's theme in "To an Old
Philosopher in Rome."

> On the threshold of heaven, the figures in the street
> Become the figures of heaven, the majestic movement
> Of men growing small in the distances of space,
> Singing, with smaller and still smaller sound,
> Unintelligible absolution and an end—
>
> The threshold, Rome, and that more merciful Rome
> Beyond, the two alike in the make of the mind.
> It is as if in a human dignity
> Two parallels become one, a perspective, of which
> Men are part both in the inch and in the mile.
>
> How easily the blown banners change to wings . . .
> Things dark on the horizons of perception,

Become accompaniments of fortune, but
Of the fortune of the spirit, beyond the eye,
Not of its sphere, and yet not far beyond,

The human end in the spirit's greatest reach,
The extreme of the known in the presence of the extreme
Of the unknown. The newsboys' muttering
Becomes another murmuring; the smell
Of medicine, a fragrantness not to be spoiled . . .

In this poem, according to Riddel, Stevens translates ideas into a
sense of dramatic experience based on a tension between life and
death, and thereby communicates Santayana's dual commitment
to spirit and matter as well as his sense of the origin and end of
all things.

Riddel's focus is more limited but more thoroughly developed
in his "Stevens on Imagination—The Point of Departure" (1971).
In this study, Riddel proposes that the most appropriate philosophical analogue to Stevens's ideas on imagination is Santayana's
concept of epiphenomenalism. Riddel develops his study by
attempting to define Stevens's conception of the imagination.
According to Riddel, the poet rejects the polarities of imagination
and reality as individual entities within themselves and comes to
see them as opposites between which life fluctuates. Summarizing
Stevens's theory of imagination as "his search for a theory of
imagination" (p. 82), Riddel suggests that Stevens rejected any
final definition of the faculty as too fixed, requiring that he as
poet must always view the imagination as part of a flux. Yet, for
Stevens, imagination is a process of a beginning that starts at the
moment of the modern annihilation of god. According to Riddel,
this annihilation demanded of man an inevitable first creative or
initiating act, a new beginning brought about by man's own
faculties. Such "new beginnings" Riddel traces throughout
Stevens's poetry from Crispin's story in "The Comedian as the
Letter C," a parable about the beginnings of modern imagination,
to "The Man with the Blue Guitar" in which the structure
exhibits an "imagination imagining itself in a series of self-
inventions" (p. 71), and ultimately to the late poems such as
"Notes Toward a Supreme Fiction" and "An Ordinary Evening
in New Haven" in which the imagination attempts to forge a
new order out of chaos. The study is not as helpful as the earlier
"Visibility of Thought" by Riddel because in "Stevens on Imagination" the critic relies heavily on direct quotes from the poet and
philosophical paraphrases of Stevens's theory. The complexity and

confusion in Stevens's thought is not reduced by such direct
quotation or restatement, and the analogy with Santayana is not
developed enough to be enlightening.

Daniel Fuchs's "Wallace Stevens and Santayana" (1967) focuses
attention on Santayana's poetry and maintains that his naturalistic
sonnets in *Poems* (1922) influenced Stevens. In Santayana's first
sonnet sequence with its poetic argument, naturalism, and memories
of Christianity, Fuchs finds the antecedents to Stevens's "Sunday
Morning." The similarities are those of tone, world view, rhythm,
and diction, but the differences, also noted by Fuchs, include
Stevens's discovery of the fresh idiom Santayana lacked when
he used the sonnet form. By implying that Santayana provided
the innovative approach to religion and naturalism but Stevens
only supplied the innovative form, Fuchs sells Stevens short. Also
analyzing the philosophical affinities between the two, Fuchs
suggests that from Santayana Stevens learned a disapproval of
sentimentalism in the romantic; satiric dismissal of archaic concepts;
appreciation for a mind of winter and cold; a sense of divinity
within individual man; and a role for the poet. In Stevens's early
"Peter Quince at the Clavier" Fuchs notes a Santayana-like belief
in the interdependence of aesthetics and emotions as well as a
Santayana-type meditation on ideal immortality. More generally,
Fuchs also notes Stevens's programmatic concern with Santayana's
imagination theme, and the two men's shared conviction that
poetry at its best is a replacement for religion. Yet Fuchs forces
a comparison when he juxtaposes Santayana's shift from philosophy of history to systematic ontology with Stevens's shift from
sensuous world to a mental conception of that world, from
hedonist to meditator, and from comedy to satire. That Stevens
made such "shifts" is certainly debatable, and that such shifts inherently relate the poet to a philosopher who coincidentally also
changed his mind is a dubious conclusion at best. Fuchs does accurately note that knowledge of Santayana's ontology is helpful
in penetrating the cantos of "Notes" because Santayana's belief
that the world must be invented permeates "Notes," but Fuchs
unfortunately misunderstands the Santayana-Stevens imagination
as process (described by Riddel). This misunderstanding is most
obvious in Fuchs's statement that Stevens's poetry is inconsistent
with Santayana's philosophy when the poetry develops as direct
cognition examining the thingness of things.

Unlike Fuchs, Guy Davenport in "Spinoza's Tulips: A Commentary on 'The Comedian as the Letter C'" (*Perspective*,
Autumn 1954) only superficially compares Stevens and Santayana

then throws in Spinoza for good measure. Davenport's article is not long enough to suffer from the number of critical errors noted in Fuchs's study, and his study, Spinoza excepted, contributes nothing above and beyond what can be learned from Riddel. According to Davenport, Stevens's major theme is his philosophical analysis of the mind struggling between the two worlds of the real and the fictive. Davenport describes Stevens as a philosophical landscapist who, through his imagery, objectifies philosophical ideas. To develop this idea, Davenport expends minimal energy explicating "The Comedian as the Letter C," but he spends even less energy defining the kinship he suggests among Stevens, Santayana, and Spinoza.

Critics have also noted the affinities between Stevens and Henri Bergson. Frank Kermode focuses on this theme in his study "The Words of the World" (*Encounter*, April 1960). According to Kermode, Stevens adhered to Bergson's concept of nature's defense against domination of the intellect stemming from the belief that myths can and do become obsolete. Bergson's *Fonction Fabulatrice* manifests itself in Stevens's ephemeral myths and heroes who become casualties in the conflict between reality and the imagination. Bergson thought that the counter pressures between the imagination and reality could be maintained only through metaphysics, and Stevens borrowed this concept for his poetry. Acknowledging Santayana's importance in the study of Stevens's verse, Kermode asserts that Santayana and Bergson provide a strong philosophical link with the Romantic–Symbolist tradition in which Stevens found himself.

William Noon (*Poetry and Prayer*, 1967, pp. 157-92) places Stevens in a tradition of empiricists who followed Henri Bergson, but Noon also mentions Stevens's debt to such strange bedfellows as William James, Charles Pierce, Santayana, Ralph Waldo Emerson, and Plato. Noon suggests that Stevens's thought falls within multiple philosophical schools but that Stevens himself, by virtue of his role as poet, is not a philosopher. The critic mentions that in "Notes" Stevens examines the question of how a mind can find and express the absolute in ways that do not include metaphor and fiction, yet Noon never notes this question's obvious affinity with Bergson's ideas. Unfortunately, the study degenerates further when Noon labels Stevens's imagination "god" and proposes that Stevens was therefore closer to god than he himself realized. Thinking that Stevens did not believe his own dictate that the final belief must be in a fiction, and that Stevens probably knew, despite his comments to the contrary, that god is not an illusion,

Noon carries his own critical comments beyond unsupported
assertions when he preposterously attempts to Christianize a pro-
fessed nonbeliever.

Samuel French Morse's study, "Wallace Stevens, Bergson,
Pater" (*Journal of English Literary History*, Mar. 1964), also
suggests a Stevens–Bergson tie but is more specific in its reference
to Stevens's poetry than Kermode's comments, and more accurate
in its description of Stevens's attitude toward the world than
Noon's study. According to Morse, Stevens adapts Bergson's
theory of comedy to his own needs. Although Bergson elevates
the social implications of comedy to a level of greater significance
than Stevens, the poet nonetheless echoes Bergson's idea that
comedy exists only in the human domain. Morse specifies that
Stevens's Crispin resembles Bergson's comic madman, but unfortunately does not develop this potentially enlightening point by
looking at other poems, or at Crispin in more detail. The poem
in which Crispin appears, "The Comedian as the Letter C," provides Stevens with an opportunity to test the appropriateness for
poetry of Bergson's theory of comedy. Hence, in the "Comedian"
one finds a Bergsonian use of language in which a comic effect is
obtained when language is used figuratively but with the pretense
that it should be taken literally. Morse seems far more concerned
with analyzing the "Comedian" than the title of his study denotes,
and he devotes far more verbage to a discussion of Stevens's notes
on the poem and his correspondence with Harriet Monroe which
preceded its creation, than to the philosophies of Bergson or Pater.

Margaret Peterson in "*Harmonium* and William James" (*Southern Review*, July 1971) answers those who find Santayana's influence in the late poetry and those who note Bergson's ideas present
in the early poetry by proposing that William James is the philosophical father of Stevens's first volume, *Harmonium*. According
to Peterson, James supplies the subjects, terms of conflict, and
philosophical point of view in these early poems. Citing James,
Bergson, and Santayana as the three significant opponents of the
German idealist doctrine fashionable in Stevens's Harvard days,
Peterson describes the *Harmonium* emphasis on beauty in the
temporal world as a reflection of the philosophical spirit of the
times. Three philosophical themes predominate in this volume: a
loss of Christian faith and collapse of traditional values; inadequacies in the period's opposing philosophies, empiricism, and
idealism; and the aesthetic consequences of these first two. Such
themes, according to Peterson, are voiced in the rejection in "Sunday Morning" of religious complacency and philosophical idealism

coupled with its shift from an intellectualized post-Kantian God to the immediate preoccupations of the world. Peterson also traces to James these ideas along with Stevens's anti-idealist stance in in "Disillusionment of Ten O'Clock" and "The Emperor of Ice-Cream" and "Disillusionment of Ten O'Clock" as companion pieces deriving from James's "The Present Dilemma in Philosophy" in which the state of religion is discussed. The modern crisis in religion, according to James, has resulted in philosophical and social extremes exemplified, according to Peterson, by "sleep-walking idealists" who are the elite and "atheistic empiricists" who are the poor. These extremes are rendered without social comment in "Disillusionment of Ten O'Clock" and "The Emperor of Ice-Cream," respectively. These overreadings seem to reveal a critic who cannot see the poetic forest for the philosophical trees. Yet, in her general comments on "Sunday Morning" and on poems in *Harmonium* reflecting a Jamesian "pragmatic critique of rationalism," Peterson is quite helpful; and her approach to *Harmonium*, not as gaudy poetic wordplay but as philosophically influenced verse, is unique and refreshing.

Disagreeing with Peterson's view of Stevens as a post-Kantian poet, John Crowe Ransom in "The Concrete Universal: Observations on the Understanding of Poetry" (*Kenyon Review*, Summer 1955) and in "The Planetary Poet" (*Kenyon Review*, Winter 1964) compares the poet's ideas to those of Kant and Hegel. In the earlier study Ransom borrows from Kant's and Hegel's terminology in order to examine how one understands poetry in general. His allusions to Stevens are brief and vague, but he does suggest that Stevens's "The Motive for Metaphor" resembles Kant's idea of a relationship between the Universal and metaphor. In the later article Ransom spends some time recalling his exposure to Stevens when Ransom was editor of the *Kenyon Review*. The reminiscences lead to a discussion of Stevens as a "good Kantian" though, as Ransom acknowledges, no evidence exists to suggest Stevens read this philosopher. Ransom uses Kant's three modes with which the mind is capable of ordering behavior as keys to Stevens's poetic career. Stevens was engaged in the first and third modes, the scientific-business economy from which man derives a livelihood and the "grace" economy in which man is concerned with beauty, but not in the second mode, the moral economy in which man participates in institutionalized religion. The first economy Ransom traces to Stevens's profession as business executive and the third to his avocation, writing poetry. Examining poems in *Harmonium*, Ransom concludes that Stevens wages a

small, personal war against the moral economy and traditional
religious belief.

Labeling Stevens a "philosopher who never stops being a poet"
and a "philosophical naturalist, perhaps a logical positivist" (p.
254), Ransom judges Stevens's "Notes Toward a Supreme
Fiction" the poet's masterpiece philosophical poem. If this judgment is critically debatable, Ransom's description of Stevens's
creative strategy is more elucidating and more easily defended.
According to Ransom, Stevens employs two methods of development: he creates extraordinary images and situations in extended
passages of pure poetry lacking argumentative structure; and he
uses these same images and situations to embody and objectify the
argument. Scanning Stevens's career and some of Kant's ideas,
Ransom finds the two selves of Stevens traceable to Kant's two
economies, serenely coexistent in the last years of Stevens's life
when he refused to abandon either his business endeavors or his
poetic attempts. In general Ransom's comments such as this last
one occasionally border on oblique comparisons of Stevens's life
and poetry and Kant's philosophy. But, this study is far more
specific than his earlier one and is of interest in its critical combination of recollection, speculation, and interpretation.

Richard P. Adams's "Wallace Stevens and Schopenhauer's *The
World As Will and Idea*" (*Tulane Studies in English*, 1972)
focuses on Stevens's relationship to the one volume of the study's
title, and assumes only that Stevens read part of the book and
borrowed ideas from it. Adams bases this assumption on a Stevens
quote found in "A Collect of Philosophy," a quote taken by
Stevens from a summary of the Schopenhauer volume. Examining
Stevens's poem "Not Ideas about the Thing but the Thing
Itself," Adams asserts that this title corresponds to one of the
central themes in *The World*, and, consistent with Schopenhauer's
ideas, the poem is about rebirth in terms of a contrast between the
thing itself and ideas about the thing. Also consistent with Schopenhauer, who contends that music represents the will, the thing
itself, and not an abstract idea, Stevens manipulates musical imagery
in the poem. Adams finds hints of Schopenhauer's influence in
"The Snow Man," a poem in which Stevens attempts to escape
from the will, the world, and one's individuality in order to
create a state of mind in which pure subject and its correlative,
the pure idea, exist; and in "The Man with the Blue Guitar," a
poem in which Stevens attempts to speak or play "things as they
are," an attempt closely allied with Schopenhauer's definition of

genius as the will's highest level of objectification attempted in order to obtain self-knowledge.

Adams cites Stevens's letter to Henry Church (Dec. 1942) as evidence that the late poem, "Notes Toward a Supreme Fiction," is not a philosophic poem. Disagreeing with Ransom who labels it Stevens's philosophic masterpiece, but agreeing with Peterson, Adams finds in Stevens an adoption of William James's pragmatism which, according to Adams, is a "philosopher's attempt to deal with the gap Schopenhauer demonstrated, but could not bridge, between reality and the mind" (p. 157). Stevens also attempts to do what Schopenhauer claimed impossible: "make his individual mind and art completely express, and thereby dominate and subdue, the reality of things as they are" (p. 149). Adams concludes that Stevens is not a disciple of Schopenhauer because he stops short of Schopenhauer's pessimism and at times approaches the pragmatism and optimism of William James. He is a poet, not a philosopher, concerned with metaphysical ideas which he communicates not through abstract logic but by way of feeling, intuition, aesthetic value, and moral attitudes. Adams achieves precisely what he intends: by scrutinizing the similarities and differences between the poet and philosopher he develops an admirably unified study which provides one philosophical perspective on a poetry with multiple philosophical concerns.

Marjorie Buhr is more general and her focus less defined in her study "The Impossible Possible Philosopher's Man: Wallace Stevens" (*Carrell*, June 1965). Rather than confine herself to affinities between the poet and one philosopher, Buhr acknowledges the effect of Santayana's and Bergson's ideas on Stevens, but turns her attention to phenomenologists such as Heidegger and Husserl. The poet's affinity with such men whose ideas were popular in his youth may be seen in his concern with exact and extensive description of the obvious and of the importance of the imagination in the poetic process. Buhr draws analogies between Stevens and phenomenologists, all of whom attempt an explanation of man devoid of transcendent power. Rather than find god in the universe, such men attempt to provide the world with value, and attempt to portray death as an intensification of experience. Heidegger, like Stevens in "The Snow Man," makes a distinction between the nothing that is merely nonexistence and that-which-is-not which functions as being. Without fully examining the Stevens-phenomenologist similarities, Buhr moves to a comparison of Stevens and the English philosopher she thinks influenced him

most, Alfred North Whitehead. According to Whitehead, an
individual's experience of the world is the most significant fact of
existence, but man is beset by conflicting desires for a future of
variety as well as for an immutable absolute. That such tenets may
be found in Stevens's work, Buhr assumes but fails to demonstrate.
Such lack of in-depth development characterizes this article that
simplistically skims several philosophic schools and usually fails
to apply them to specific poems.

Following Marjorie Buhr's lead Thomas J. Hines explores the
Stevens-phenomenologists comparison in a book-length study,
*The Later Poetry of Wallace Stevens: Phenomenological Parallels
with Husserl and Heidegger* (1976). In this study Hines suggests
that Stevens, at the "height of his power," the later poems, questions Being itself as well as the very process and product of observation. Such questioning led the poet to derive a new form based
in both prolonged meditation and instantaneous vision. Hines
contends that Husserl's meditations on the creative imagination
and Heidegger's original visions of the poetic process reveal much
about Stevens's own development. Admitting that such comparisons are fortuitous, Hines nonetheless thinks that these German
philosophers provide the vocabulary for discussing Stevens's
"modes of questioning" as well as his "meditations on the function
and possibility of poetry as a quest for the full sense of Being
itself" (p. 13). Hines seeks "to make Stevens' later work more
accessible by showing, through Husserl and Heidegger, some of
the meditational processes and . . . some of the visionary forms
that Stevens incorporates in his poems" (p. 13).

Hines's study suffers primarily not from any flaw in this argument or inadequacy in these objectives, but in the dissertationlike
language which characterizes this study. His introduction not only
draws from and builds on earlier critical work, but provides research paper type footnotes to list evidence for summaries that
in his narrative would have sufficed. He clearly states where his
study resembles and differs from its predecessors, then follows
his preparatory comments with a direct statement of "My thesis
is," and finally with a summary description of ideas to appear in
later chapters. He is quick to specify what he does not claim lest
a too rigorous oral examination find implied contentions where
supporting evidence is absent. And, he once again, as the student
of so many critics before him, argues both sides of the question,
"Is Stevens a poet or philosopher?" For Hines, like so many
critics who preceded him, Stevens must be examined within the
context of his most obvious domain, poetry.

The only direct relationship Hines notes between Stevens and Husserl must rest on a vague statement by Stevens in "A Collect of Philosophy," alluding to an idea suggested by Jean Wahl and recalling for Hines the meditations of Husserl. Of the Heidegger-Stevens relationship, Hines freely acknowledges the poet's statement that he was unable to obtain works by this philosopher, but Hines maintains that the poet's "interest" in the philosopher is an indication of affinity rather than influence.

Quickly discarding *Harmonium* as a flashy experiment, an anomaly in the development of this philosophical poet, Hines moves into his subject, the later poetry, which he apparently defines as all of the verse except *Harmonium*. His explications of poems in later volumes seldom, if ever, add original insight into well-worn poems such as "The Idea of Order at Key West," "The Man with the Blue Guitar," and "The Man on the Dump." When Hines examines poems such as "The Glass of Water," "Crude Foyer," and "The Latest Freed Man," poems less worn by critics' decreation, he does so with an eye not for poetic explication, but for philosophic example. In short, he discusses such Stevens poems as nothing more than verse manifestations of simplified philosophic thought. His interpretation of "Yellow Afternoon" provides an example.

> It was in the earth only
> That he was at the bottom of things
> And of himself. There he could say
> Of this I am, this is the patriarch,
> This it is that answers when I ask,
> This is the mute, the final sculpture
> Around which silence lies on silence.
> This reposes alike in springtime
> And, arbored and bronzed, in autumn.
>
> He said I had this that I could love,
> As one loves visible and responsive peace,
> As one loves one's own being,
> As one loves that which is the end
> And must be loved, as one loves that
> Of which one is a part as in a unity,
> A unity that is the life one loves,
> So that one lives all the lives that comprise it
> As the life of the fatal unity of war.
>
> Everything comes to him
> From the middle of his field. The odor

Of earth penetrates more deeply than any word.
There he touches his being. There as he is
He is. The thought that he had found all this
Among men, in a woman-she caught his breath-
But he came back as one comes back from the sun
To lie on one's bed in the dark, close to a face
Without eyes or mouth, that looks at one and
    speaks.

To Hines, this poem is simply an exercise in the poets discovering "Being-in-the-world" through the female persona that is nothing more than an "abstract notion of Being" (p. 128). Such a reading superimposes Heidegger's Being as the basis of all things on a poetry that through sensual and antithetical images may communicate some of the complexity in existence, but may also communicate so much more about sense perception, the poetic process, the nature of language in "any word," and the interaction of abstract and concrete facets of reality. Such is the "so much more" Hines never mentions.

Such singularly simplistic explications lead Hines to a singularly inadequate conclusion. According to this critic "Stevens is the poet of the poetry of Being" (p. 273). Accurate on the surface, such a conclusion typifies Hines's approach and reduces the poet's view of his own world to a critic's myopic vision of that poet's mind and world. If Hines really accepts his own definition of Being as the source of both the mind and the world, he is required by this poet's struggle with such dichotomous terms as imagination and reality, mind and world, to deal with the complexities of these term's interaction. These are the complexities at the heart of Stevens's poetry, and these are the aspects of the poet's undisciplined phenomenology and ontology that the critic neglects.

For the reader specifically interested in the similarities between a poet's thought and the more disciplined expression of that thought in philosophy, Hines provides an extended if uneven analysis of affinities between the poet's verse and these philosophers' ideas. Like Husserl's methods of reduction and decreation, Stevens's poems often describe for Hines the reductive and decreative processes of an artistic mind in the process of describing itself. This reductive process, which according to Hines characterizes *Ideas of Order* and *The Man with the Blue Guitar*, is replaced in *Parts of a World* and *Notes Toward a Supreme Fiction* with a more ontologically oriented search, beyond mere perception, for a relation between self and world. In analyzing this phase of Stevens's development, the critic utilizes Heidegger's concept of the difference between Being (mind and world) and beings (things that exist in the world). This concept demands an acknowledgment of existence in the temporal world and thereby provides Hines with an approach to Stevens's concern in the late poems with time, the relationship between time and experience, and the relationship between Being (mind and world) and poetry.

Painterly Poet

Doris Eder ("Wallace Stevens' Landscapes and Still Lifes," *Mosaic*, Summer 1971) labels Stevens a "painterly poet" because his poems are comparable to painted landscapes and studio pieces "whose titles read like an art exhibition catalogue" (p. 4). Various critics such as Eder have found in Stevens's concern with nature and man as perceiving mind or eye not an indication of philosophical affinity, but rather a strong hint of a visually oriented genre. A few such as Eder view this hint rather harshly. Others, to be discussed later, find the painterly tendency both interesting in itself and appropriate to the interaction of modern art forms in general, as they trace the interaction of artistic movements in the visual and verbal genres.

A Focus on Visual Perception

In examining Stevens's visual perceptions, Doris Eder criticizes the poet for his flat characters which she thinks mirror a distaste for people. This inaccurate assumption becomes even more absurd and incorrect when Eder explains it by comparing Stevens's landscapes to the "unpeopled" landscapes of Wordsworth. The critic seems to have read little from either poet. Noting that Stevens is more adept at visualizing objects than man, Eder approaches an accurate point which she inadequately extends by merely noting the interaction of landscape and perceiving eye in Stevens's verse. She contends that Stevens composes still lifes when he places objects in relation to one another and when he works with forms that undergo external rather than internal changes. The vagueness of this comment makes it useless. In general, this study adds little if anything to Stevens criticism because Eder fails to sustain her examination of Stevens's visual aspects. She brushes lightly many attributes of the Stevens visual, but in her brief jumping about from one undeveloped and unsupported point to another, she lacks any cohesive analysis of particular visual characteristics.

George McFadden takes an entirely different approach but with a minimally successful result. In "Probings for an Integration: Color Symbolism in Wallace Stevens" (*Modern Philology*, Feb. 1961), McFadden bases his analysis on two premises: in Stevens's poetry one finds the process of plastic perception in which one makes one's own world according to the way one perceives it; and in Stevens's verse one finds an imagination that is capable of developing the forms of ordinary perception. McFadden suggests that Stevens's poems are not about objects which are perceived but are about the act of perception. In this view the poems themselves become the process of composition, as the poet develops his own symbolism of color to unify the process of composition. Utilizing a broad spectrum, Stevens manipulates color as an abstraction which connotes a wide range of attitudes toward experience. In this way, according to McFadden, the poet gives form to experience. This approach simplistically characterizes Stevens's use of color as an imposition of symbology that, though never rigorously structured or consistently applied by the poet, is formulated in such strict terms by the critic. Such a contention reduces Stevens to a second-rate poet in search of symbolic reference, or worse, in search of stock images to convey those references. Ignoring this inadequacy in McFadden's conclusion, one may find interesting points along the way. McFadden describes the poet's use of black as a frame for all life and imagination, and he associates Stevens's use of white with a stasis in form such as one might find in an image of ice. Such descriptions do not reveal great insight and they do not elucidate ultimate meaning in the poetry, but they do contribute some value to the study.

In analyzing the painterly aspects in Stevens, a study previously discussed as philosophical in emphasis is by far one of the best examinations of visual manipulations and concerns in Stevens's poetry. James Baird's *The Dome and the Rock* (1968) suggests that sight, color, and light are important interactional forces in Stevens's work. Asserting that Apollinaire's insistence upon the invention of color by each perceiver is an important antecedent to Stevens, Baird emphasizes that Stevens equates seeing in painting with seeing in poetry. The endless present difficulty in seeing for poet and painter is described by Baird as an attempt to render a unified vision of external sight and internal idea. Baird more specifically yokes poetry and painting when he notes that the same compositional principle may be applied to both: the poet imposes words while the painter imposes colors upon a basic design. Stevens epitomizes this similarity when he uses words "in their existential meaning" (p. 174) to create a sense of color. Comparing Stevens's use of gray to Klee's use of the same color as indicative of a point between dimensions of color, Baird concludes that in such definitions of color one finds the essence of Stevens's relationship with painting. Baird narrows his focus by even more specifically relating Stevens to Impressionist painters whose objective is to capture the "momentariness in sight" (p. 183). Stevens's "true experiments with painting in poetry" (p. 183) Baird finds in the early "poised on water" poems in which unaccustomed verbal usage and diction are manipulated to create Impressionism's sense of the fleeting moment. According to Baird "Sea Surface Full of Clouds," described as Stevens's five Impressionist paintings in which color is the only subject, is the poet's masterpiece in the painterly mode. After this, and the later *Ideas of Order*, Stevens's painterly poems are directed more and more to ideas outside the canvas. Painting then becomes for Stevens a metaphor, and color, a means not an end.

A Focus on Artistic Movements

Most critics who attempt to study visual aspects of Stevens's genre turn to a discussion, as Baird does, of what specific artistic movements seem most relevant to Stevens's techniques. Michel Benamou's *Wallace Stevens and the Symbolist Imagination* (1972) is the most thorough examination of this topic. Throughout Stevens's work Benamou finds an affinity with painting. Benamou notes that Stevens read exhibition catalogues; referred in lectures and poems to Cezanne and Picasso; collected French paintings with Impressionistic and Cubist strains; and was exposed early to Cubism through Henry Arensburg, a friend of Stevens and Duchamp. The most lasting influence on Stevens's poetic vision seems to have come from Impressionism. In Impressionistic painting and Stevens's poetry Benamou finds a fluent universe as the stage for wind, rain, sun, and moon; an art based on weather but filled with the vastness of sky and water; and an acute sense of visible change as it is detected in conditions of lighting. Among Stevens's Impressionist poems, Benamou names "Evening without Angels," "Blue Building in the Summer Air," "Variations on a Summer Day," "Of Hartford in a Purple Light," and "Sea Surface Full of Clouds" as examples of Stevens's desire for a fresh, translucent vision comparable to the Impressionists' search for the restored innocence of the eye.

The Impressionist strains in Stevens, Benamou finds coupled

with signs of Cubism. In *Parts of a World* and later collections Benamou notes the "paraphernalia of Cubism, the guitars and mandolins, the still lifes arranged on tables, the plaster heads, the bits and odds that painters hoard for their collages" (p. 8). In Cubist paintings as in some Stevens poems the subject of creation is the artistic imagination. This is an art of the imaginative eye exploring many facets of reality; an art defined as a hoard of destructions; and an art whose merit is derived from "the degree of concentration with which the imagination refracts the object" (p. 8). Benamou suggests that Stevens's poetry incorporates conflicting elements from Impressionism and Cubism—such as naturalness and artificiality as well as delight in appearances and metamorphosis of appearances—by incorporating change in poetry. In short, the passive change in the Impressionists' world perceived by the artist and the active change wrought by the Cubist on his environment may both be found in Stevens.

More generally, Benamou characterizes Stevens as a visual poet concerned with pictorial composition, vivid visual images, and the pure forces of light and color. Benamou avoids an erroneous equation of painting and poetry when he distinguishes the forms of the two media by differentiating color in painting as the "real thing" from color in poetry as a "reflection of words." With such precise terms, Benamou's study is a classic in Stevens criticism. He establishes beyond a doubt the presence of a poetry-painting affinity in Stevens, defines the limits of that affinity, and examines the importance of that affinity to art in general. His astute assessment of *Harmonium* as Steven's theory of poetics in practice and *Ideas of Order* as the theory itself deserves further analysis with the perceptive acuity he brings to the poetry-painting subject. Such promising, undeveloped hypotheses reflect the meatiness of his work and mar the surface of his analyses only by demanding further study.

Benamou's chapter on Stevens and Apollinaire, though not as important to Stevens criticism as the painting-poetry study, is certainly worth reading. Admitting that no massive evidence links Stevens and Apollinaire, Benamou establishes a parallel in their poetic development: the stylistic transformations in Apollinaire's poetry of 1910–12 are comparable to similar transformations in Stevens's verse of 1930–37. Both attempts to change are caused, according to Benamou, by a crisis in Symbolist values coupled with extensive thought about Cubist painting. The critic bases his comparison on painters mutually admired by Stevens and Apollinaire, painters who provided the two poets with examples of modern

style. Among the similarities in the two, Benamou cites their belief in the limited social function of art; in the nobility of the
imagination; in a split between the imagination and reality; and in
the role of the poet as decreator in an art form, poetry, that is itself de-creative.

In *Wallace Stevens: The Making of Harmonium* (1967), Robert Buttel also provides a helpful discussion of Stevens's debt to
painting. Buttel's comments are more general, but are similar in
emphasis, as he acknowledges, to Benamou's study. Asserting that
Stevens exhibits an Impressionist sensibility in his use of mutated
objects under varying light conditions, Buttel traces the mode of
"Sunday Morning" to Matisse's "Odalisque" paintings and the
mode of "Hibiscus on the Sleeping Shores" to Dufy. Buttel does
not limit his discussions to one or two movements but mentions
elements in Stevens that remind him of the Pointillists, Fauvists,
Expressionists, and Cubists. He finds in Stevens's lines hints of
paintings by Chagall, Kandinsky, Klee, Van Gogh, Gaugin, and
Cezanne, but generalizes that Stevens used many techniques of
modern painting to present pictorial formulations of dream scenes
that are part of an individual's unconscious experience. Stevens
learned most, however, from the Impressionists' attempt to render
reality's immediacy, but he also learned from the Cubists' tendency
to fragment and restructure which revealed the multiplicity of experience as well as the simultaneity of different perspectives. According to Buttel, such painting dramatized for Stevens the artist's
function, reconciling a need for order with the unordered force
of life. And, despite Stevens's experimentation with various modes
of painting, Buttel asserts that he never resorts to art for art's sake,
a failure of Imagism and Cubism alike. This last point is certainly
debatable and viewed quite differently by critics who condemn
Stevens's art as having no purpose but its own creation.

Written as a historical narrative, Buttel's discussion of Stevens
includes mention of artistic events contemporaneous with Stevens's
writing. The music of Debussy and Stravinsky, the lectures of
Henri de Regnier at Harvard, and the Armory Show of 1913
Buttel relates to the poet. In extensive footnotes with everextend-
ing references and bits of interesting literary paraphernalia, Buttel
enlivens his study but occasionally borders on tangential association. He ties and crossties relationships among aesthetes and lit-
erati of the time through such colorful associations, and usually
supports his remarks and relates his wanderings to Stevens by citing pertinent comments in the poet's letters. At times the reader
wishes for less of Buttel and more of Stevens, but, as noted in dis-

cussion of this same study in chapter 2, more often that same reader welcomes the more lively analysis Buttel's narrative style communicates.

Other critics, in a more specialized vein, have attempted to relate Stevens solely to the Impressionists. In "Wallace Stevens: The Delicatest Eye of the Mind" (*American Quarterly*, Summer 1962) Emilie Buchwald argues that by fragmenting the world into colors and parts, then questioning the eye's power to see, Stevens makes the artist an American Adam who names and shapes his own world. Stevens attempts "to come to terms" with the dilemmas of Impressionism and Symbolism by replacing traditional ways of seeing and relating. Because of this, Stevens's most important "struggle," according to Buchwald, may be viewed as an artistic attempt to achieve composition, to establish a relationship between what is included and omitted in a verbal picture. She compares Stevens with Cezanne because both seek to control chaotic matter through accents, refractions, and color usage, and both attempt to unify composition as well as express emotion. As an example of Stevens's Cezanne-like use of color, Buchwald examines "Sea Surface Full of Clouds," while in poems such as "Disillusionment of Ten O'Clock," "Domination of Black," and "The Man with the Blue Guitar" she finds color expressionistically employed as a vehicle to communicate or stimulate emotion. That Stevens adopts this expressionist color-emotion equation, Buchwald concludes, but adds that he is more successful in his poems about the absence of color or a unified color spectrum symbolized in images of crystal, diamond, or glass. Her comments about Stevens's Impressionist tendencies are more limited and less precise than Benamou's, while her speculations about Stevens's use of color add little to the texture of the poems themselves.

A later discussion of Stevens and Impressionism, "Pure Poetry: Wallace Stevens' 'Sea Surface Full of Clouds'" (*Tulane Studies in English*, 1974) by Richard P. Adams, confines itself entirely to an analysis emphasizing the artistic milieu of the poem in the title.

I

In that November off Tehuantepec,
The slopping of the sea grew still one night
And in the morning summer hued the deck

And made one think of rosy chocolate
And gilt umbrellas. Paradisal green
Gave suavity to the perplexed machine

Of ocean, which like limpid water lay.
Who, then, in that ambrosial latitude
Out of the light evolved the moving blooms,

Who, then, evolved the sea-blooms from the clouds
Diffusing balm in that Pacific calm?
C'était mon enfant, mon bijou, mon âme.

The sea-clouds whitened far below the calm
And moved, as blooms move, in the swimming green
And in its watery radiance, while the hue

Of heaven in an antique reflection rolled
Round those flotillas. And sometimes the sea
Poured brilliant iris on the glistening blue.

II

In that November off Tehuantepec
The slopping of the sea grew still one night.
At breakfast jelly yellow streaked the deck

And made one think of chop-house chocolate
And sham umbrellas. And a sham-like green
Capped summer-seeming on the tense machine

Of ocean, which in sinister flatness lay.
Who, then, beheld the rising of the clouds
That strode submerged in that malevolent sheen,

Who saw the mortal massives of the blooms
Of water moving on the water-floor?
C'était mon frère du ciel, ma vie, mon or.

The gongs rang loudly as the windy booms
Hoo-hooed it in the darkened ocean-blooms.
The gongs grew still. And then blue heaven spread

Its crystalline pendentives on the sea
And the macabre of the water-glooms
In an enormous undulation fled.

Stevens's technique in this partially quoted poem, representing a
scene several times by using different amounts of light which suggest varying moods, recalls for Adams Impressionism and post-
Impressionist painters. Like Benamou, Adams cites the similarity
between Stevens's "Sea Surface" and Monet's *Water Lilies*, and
supports his comparison by citing a Stevens letter to Henry

Church. In this 1943 letter Stevens reports that he read the *Ga-zette des Beaux-Arts*, a publication which in 1909 carried a lengthy discussion of a *Water Lilies* exhibition. Adams also speculates that Stevens probably saw *Revue des Deux Mondes* (December 1918) in which Henri de Regnier published twenty poems on various painters, especially French Impressionists. Adams attempts to establish that when Stevens viewed the Gulf of Tehuantepec, he viewed it with a vision educated by Monet's *Water Lilies*. This point is crucial to Adams's argument because the critic concludes that Stevens, like Monet, communicates a sense of changing experience in a changing world by combining repetition and variation. The point is well taken, but some other antecedents to "Sea Surface" suggested by Adams are not so carefully considered. According to the critic, "Sea Surface" may have been influenced by Melville's use of the sea in *Moby Dick* and Poe's progression from naive to sophisticated disillusionment in "The Bells." One would not be unjust in judging such comparisons farfetched. Yet, Adams's discussion must be recognized as a rather thorough analysis of the visual elements in the poems and the affinities existing among Stevens, Baudelaire, Mallarmé, Laforgue, and Valéry.

Beyond Impressionism, some critics have focused on Stevens's relationship to other artistic movements. Louis Untermeyer in *American Poetry Since 1900* (1923, pp. 323–28), contends that Stevens is a Pointillist rather than an Impressionist. Untermeyer bases his use of this label on Stevens's habit of disregarding perspective and emphasizing blocks of pure color juxtaposed in chromatic clashes. This assertion as well as Untermeyer's conviction that Stevens lacks an appreciation of language but exhibits "obscure verbalism" are neither evidenced in the poetry nor supported by further critical explanation. Much later, Marcus Cunliffe (*The Literature of the United States*, 1967, pp. 269–72) provides a more positive assessment of Stevens's capabilities but also differs with critics who label the poet an Impressionist. According to Cunliffe, Stevens's poems approach Dadaism and Surrealism in their use of inconsequential detail and bizarre effect, while Stevens himself is labeled one of the most accomplished twentieth-century poets. Horace Gregory and Marya Zaturenska in "The *Harmonium* of Wallace Stevens" (1946) more specifically relate Stevens to another artist rather than a movement. These two critics term Stevens the James McNeill Whistler of twentieth-century American verse. According to Gregory and Zaturenska, Whistler, a painter's painter, becomes a rhetorician in his painting while Stevens, a poet's poet, becomes a painter in his verse. What both artists share is a tendency to add intelligence and wit to their creations. The comparison is really too general to be helpful. Wylie Sypher (*Rococo to Cubism in Art and Literature*, 1960, pp. 318–21), in a similarly general fashion, stresses Stevens's indebtedness to painting and describes the poet's art as a decorative approach to post-Cubist form. Sypher also notes Stevens's tendency to play with words as pure sound, a technique that links the poet's work with musical form.

Musical Poet

Most critics who choose Stevens's musical elements as the topic for their study confine themselves to individual poems. The most often cited example of the poet's musicality, "Peter Quince at the Clavier," is the focus of studies by Newell F. Ford ("Peter Quince's Orchestra," *Modern Language Notes*, May 1960); Wendell S. Johnson ("Some Functions of Poetic Form," *Journal of Aesthetics and Art Criticism*, June 1955); and Joseph N. Riddel ("Stevens' 'Peter Quince At the Clavier': Immortality as Form" *College English*, Jan. 1962a). Various other critics have pursued this topic, including William York Tindall in his aforementioned pamphlet *Wallace Stevens* (1961). While Tindall provides a good, short explication of the poem as an imitation of a symphonic form in four movements, Riddel suggests that the poem develops a musical analogy by varying a three-part sonatina framework including exposition, development, and recapitulation with coda. According to Riddel, the poem operates on two levels, as a parable that dramatizes the need for vital form in the experience of beauty and as a statement of abstract theory which epitomizes all art forms in music. Riddel's comments provide the best explication and the most exact specification of musical elements and their role in the poem.

Johnson's study is not as successful. According to this critic, "Peter Quince" exemplifies the structure of a clavier (not violin, we are told) sonata with four parts evolving as a fairly fast first and fourth movement establishing then summarizing a theme, respectively, changing to a second movement of slow deliberate progression to a climax in contrast to a third scherzo movement. Although the poem evokes musical effects, those effects also embody what the poem means in structure and statement. In this way Stevens unifies the theme of creative imagination with the idea and realization of music also found in the form. Johnson's comments are explicit if brief, but seem to deluge the poetics in too-elaborate

and too-limiting orchestrations. Newell Ford criticizes such fixity
of interpretation, but fairs little better himself by suggesting one
read the poem as Peter Quince's baroque string ensemble. According to Ford, Peter Quince conducts, calling for, with his
baton, the entrance of bass viols, treble viols, legato or pizzicati
passages, and the crash of symbols or horns. Ford appears to be
carried away with his own metaphor when he characterizes Susanna as the supreme conductor of a male orchestra and herself an
instrument of immortal music. Yet his article, not without redeeming comment, accurately notes that the poem-in-music hovers
between sacramental eroticism and urbane comedy.

Some of the earliest notes on Stevens's musical Peter Quince
appeared in the *Explicator* (Nov. 1955) and were written by
Mary Joan Storm. Storm's comments are basic but accurate in
their simple statement of relationship. She finds that music in the
poem plays a double role by furnishing the imagery to carry the
conceptual meaning and by functioning, through meter and
rhyme, as a signal of subtle changes in tone which parallel gradual
changes in character or plot. In other words, the poem's structure
of meaning and structure of sound are closely allied with music.
The form of the poem thereby parallels a musical composition in
which meaning, sound, and structure cohere inherently in the art
form. Without overreading, Storm offers a simple explication that
leaves the poem intact.

Other poems examined for their musical elements include
"Asides on the Oboe" and "Variations on a Summer Day." In
Merle E. Brown's "A Critical Performance of 'Asides on the
Oboe' " (*Journal of Aesthetics and Art Criticism*, Fall 1970), the
critic provides an exegesis on the role and function of criticism,
then decides to "perform" the poem. After noting that explanations of allusions and references in a poem are as useless as attempts to memorize the notes of a sonata, both endeavors lacking
artistic meaning, Brown proceeds to examine references in the
poem to Stevens's concept of fiction and tragedy. How this examination becomes a performance is certainly unclear, as is why it was
ever attempted. Brown blows his own horn without elucidating
any poetic instrumentation.

Edward Butscher's "Wallace Stevens' Neglected Fugue: 'Variations on a Summer Day' " (*Twentieth Century Literature*, July
1973) devotes more attention to the poem in question. According
to Butscher, "Variations" is Stevens's ultimate attempt to paraphrase musical composition. Much of the poem's strength rests
in its organization as a fugue which develops one or two major

themes contrapuntally from a polyphonic base but with the introduction of different voices as it progresses. Butscher thinks this musical organization allows Stevens to create an artistic experience in which the reader participates in a musical metaphor which defies linguistic barriers that separate form and content. The point is an interesting one.

Perhaps the ultimate comment on Stevens's musical nature must be found in John Gruen's "Thirteen Ways of Looking at a Blackbird: A Song-Cycle" (*Trinity Review*, May 1954). Rather than write an article, Gruen composed a song-cycle which he explains in his *Trinity Review* comments. Viewing the very structure of the poem as similar to a theme and variation motif in music, Gruen focuses on the blackbird itself as an indicator of mood. Attracted to the poem because of its rich sounds, physical detail, and strange gestures, Gruen attempts to capture in musical notes the ambiguity of the blackbird figure Stevens achieved. As one version of another man's thoughts only hinted in a different medium, Gruen's interpretation, though musical rather than verbal, is highly speculative but no less valid than traditional criticism in its representation of Stevens's intent. The cycle, recorded by soprano Patricia Neway who is accompanied by Gruen himself, appears on *Contemporary Records*. John Logan ("John Gruen's Settings for Wallace Stevens," *Hudson Review*, Summer 1956) reviews the Neway-Gruen performance and notes the importance of a piano in the cycle which creates the mood of individual ways of looking at the bird. The piano, like the poet's infinite ways of viewing reality, refuses to finish its line and hangs suspended at the end of thirteen ways. No more appropriate comment on Stevens could have been penned.

Psychological Poet

In the Stevens criticism, many critics touch upon the ulterior or psychological motives of a man who divided his life between a profitable profession and an artistic obsession. Among these only a few critics to date have delved into Stevens's own version of psychology. The topic seems far less fruitful than more textually oriented approaches, but it early attracted critical attention. In "Wallace Stevens and Other Poets" (*Southern Review*, Autumn 1935) Howard Baker examines Stevens's first two volumes and finds interests that parallel those of psychologists in the poet's time. Baker suggests that the air of the times, laden with psychoanalysis and free association, probably influenced the poet, then compares Jung and Stevens as contemporaries interested in abiding images of sun, moon, and sea, and interested in exploring man's consciousness in an attempt to understand the archetypes of experience and the detachment in the human consciousness. In order to compare Jung and Stevens, Baker contends that critics must postulate an unchanging spiritual world independent of the times, a dictate entirely unrelated to Stevens's work. Labeling Stevens's verse a mental poetry concerned with consciousness, Baker formulates his single cogent point. Needless to say, the study may provide an interesting diversion if one can ignore its lack of unity and coherence in analyzing Stevens.

In a more successful study, "The Gestalt Configurations of Wallace Stevens" (Modern Language Quarterly, Mar. 1967), Steven Foster focuses on Stevens's responses to the world as these responses may be conceptualized through a theory of Gestalt psychology. Stevens's interest in "things-as-they are" and in perceptual observation Foster uses to ally the poet with Gestalt dogma. The critic clearly states that his intention is to ignore traditional approaches to the poet and to combine the Stevens verse with inferred psychological meaning "whether Wallace Stevens would roll over in his grave or not" (p. 62). According to Foster, Stevens aligns himself with Gestalt principles through his vivid perceptions of the world, his insistence on forms in the mind, and his preoccupation with epistemological questions. In his critical endeavor, Foster summarizes Gestalt psychology, drawing from Gestalt Psychology: A Survey of Facts and Principles (1935) by George W. Hartman, with specific reference to principles formulated by Raymond H. Wheeler. The Wheeler principles—Law of Field Properties, Law of Derived Properties, and Law of Determined Action—Foster applies to Stevens's prose statements and poems. The Law of Field Properties stipulates that any item in reality equals more than the sum of its parts; the Law of Derived Properties states that parts derive their properties from the whole; and the Law of Determined Action specifies that the whole determines the activities of the parts. Applying these laws to poems such as "Three Academic Pieces" (proem section), "A Primitive Like an Orb," and "Sea Surface Full of Clouds," Foster also discusses the figure-ground issue in Gestalt psychology as it relates to "Anecdote of the Jar." The figure-ground principle dictates that an object and its background interact according to perception. In Stevens's concern with composition as a means of establishing perceptual relationships, Foster finds evidence of a Gestaltist approach. Little more than a diversion, this study provides a general psychological perspective without specifying how that perspective enriches or even elucidates the poetry.

Regardless of Stevens's psychological, artistic, or philosophical genre, critics repeatedly seem fascinated by the poet's combination of business career and verse creation. Reviewing the sum of this verse shortly after Stevens's death, Elizabeth Green ("The Urbanity of Stevens," *Saturday Review*, Aug. 1956) asserts that "it seems incredible that these particular poems, so continuously concerned with the imagination, so full of references to painting and sculpture and music, to faraway places and fantasy, should have been written by a man who spent his days dealing with the intricacies of insurance law. But a closer reading of his work suggests that there is no essential paradox after all. Stevens is a man completely at home in his environment" (p. 11). How he viewed this environment and how "at home" he felt are matters for the continuing critical discussion explored in chapter 4.

References

Adams, Richard P.
   1972. "Wallace Stevens and Schopenhauer's *The World As Will and Idea*." *Tulane Studies in English*, pp. 135–68.
   1974. "Pure Poetry: Wallace Stevens' 'Sea Surface Full of Clouds'." *Tulane Studies in English*, pp. 91–122.
Alvarez, A.
   1958. *Stewards of Excellence: Studies in Modern English and American Poets*. New York: Scribner.
Baird, James
   1961. "Transvaluation in the Poetics of Wallace Stevens." In *Studies in Honor of John C. Hodges and Alwin Thaler*, ed. Richard Beale Davis and John Leon Lievsay, pp. 163–73. Knoxville: Univ. of Tennessee Pr.
   1968. *The Dome and the Rock: Structure in the Poetry of Wallace Stevens*. Baltimore: Johns Hopkins Pr.
Baker, Howard
   1935. "Wallace Stevens and Other Poets." *Southern Review* Autumn, pp. 373–96.
Bankert, Marianne
   1971. "The Meta-Metaphysical Vision of Wallace Stevens." *Renascence* Autumn, pp. 47–53.
Benamou, Michel
   1972. *Wallace Stevens and the Symbolist Imagination*. Princeton, N.J.: Princeton Univ. Pr.

Blackmur, R. P.
   1955. "The Substance That Prevails." *Kenyon Review* Winter,
   pp. 91–110.
Brown, Merle E.
   1970. "A Critical Performance of 'Asides on the Oboe'." *Journal
   of Aesthetics and Art Criticism* Fall, pp. 120–28.
Buchwald, Emilie
   1962. "Wallace Stevens: The Delicatest Eye of the Mind." *American
   Quarterly* Summer, pp. 185–96.
Buhr, Marjorie
   1965. "The Impossible Possible Philosopher's Man: Wallace
   Stevens." *Carrell* June, pp. 7–13.
Butscher, Edward
   1973. "Wallace Stevens' Neglected Fugue: 'Variations on a Summer Day'." *Twentieth Century Literature* July, pp. 153–64.
Buttel, Robert
   1967. *Wallace Stevens: The Making of Harmonium*. Princeton,
   N.J.: Princeton Univ. Pr.
Cunliffe, Marcus
   1967. *The Literature of the United States*. Baltimore: Penguin.
Cunningham, J. V.
   1966. "The Styles and Procedures of Wallace Stevens." *University
   of Denver Quarterly* Spring, pp. 8–28.
Davenport, Guy
   1954. "Spinoza's Tulips: A Commentary on 'The Comedian as the
   Letter C'." *Perspective* Autumn, pp. 147–54.
Doggett, Frank
   1958. "Wallace Stevens' Later Poetry." *English Literary History*,
   June, pp. 137–54.
   1960. "Abstraction and Wallace Stevens." *Criticism* Winter, pp.
   23–37.
   1966. *Stevens' Poetry of Thought*. Baltimore: Johns Hopkins Pr.
Eder, Doris L.
   1971. "Wallace Stevens' Landscapes and Still Lifes." *Mosaic* Summer, pp. 1–5.
Feldman, Steve
   1954. "Reality and the Imagination: The Poetic of Wallace
   Stevens' 'Necessary Angel'." *University of Kansas City Review*
   Autumn, pp. 35–43.
Ford, Newell F.
   1960. "Peter Quince's Orchestra." *Modern Language Notes* May,
   pp. 405–11.
Foster, Steven
   1967. "The *Gestalt* Configurations of Wallace Stevens." *Modern
   Language Quarterly* Mar., pp. 60–76.
Fuchs, Daniel
   1967. "Wallace Stevens and Santayana." In *Patterns of Commit-*

ment in American Literature, ed. Marston LaFrance, pp. 135–64. Toronto: Univ. of Toronto Pr.

Gilbert, Katharine
1952. "Recent Poets on Man and His Place." In *Aesthetic Studies: Architecture and Poetry*, 49–81. Durham, N.C.: Duke Univ. Pr.

Green, Elizabeth
1956. "The Urbanity of Stevens." *Saturday Review* Aug., pp. 11–13.

Gregory, Horace
1942. "An Examination of Wallace Stevens in a Time of War." *Accent* Autumn, pp. 57–61.

Gregory, Horace and Marya Zaturenska
1946. "The Harmonium of Wallace Stevens." In *A History of American Poetry 1900–1940*, pp. 326–35. New York: Harcourt, Brace.

Gruen, John
1954. "Thirteen Ways of Looking at a Blackbird: A Song-Cycle." *Trinity Review*, May.

Hess, M. Whitcomb
1961. "Wallace Stevens and the 'Shaping Spirit'." *The Personalist* Spring, pp. 207–12.

Hines, Thomas J.
1976. *The Later Poetry of Wallace Stevens: Phenomenological Parallels with Husserl and Heidegger*. Cranbury, N.J.: Associated University Presses.

Jennings, Elizabeth
1962. "Vision Without Belief." In *Every Changing Shape*, pp. 201–12. Philadelphia, Pa.: Dufour.

Johnson, Wendell S.
1955. "Some Functions of Poetic Form." *Journal of Aesthetics and Art Criticism* June, pp. 496–506.

Kermode, Frank
1960. "The Words of the World." *Encounter* April, pp. 45–50.

Lentricchia, Frank, Jr.
1967. "Wallace Stevens: The Ironic Eye." *Yale Review* Spring, pp. 336–53.

Logan, John
1956. "John Gruen's Settings for Wallace Stevens." *Hudson Review* Summer, pp. 273–76.

MacCaffrey, Isabel G.
1969. "The Other Side of Silence: 'Credences of Summer' as an Example." *Modern Language Quarterly* Sept., pp. 417–38.

McDaniel, Judith
1974. "Wallace Stevens and the Scientific Imagination." *Contemporary Literature* Spring, pp. 221–37.

McFadden, George
1961. "Probings for an Integration: Color Symbolism in Wallace
Stevens." *Modern Philology* Feb., pp. 186–93.
Morse, Samuel French
1964. "Wallace Stevens, Bergson, Pater." *Journal of English Literary History*, March; reprinted in *The Act of the Mind*, ed. Roy
Harvey Pearce and J. Hillis Miller. Baltimore: Johns Hopkins Pr.,
1965.
Noon, William T
1967. *Poetry and Prayer*. New Brunswick, N.J.: Rutgers Univ. Pr.
Olson, Elder
1955. "The Poetry of Wallace Stevens." *College English* April, pp.
395–402.
Pearce, Roy Harvey, and J. Hillis Miller
1965. (editors) *The Act of the Mind*. Baltimore: Johns Hopkins
Pr.
Perloff, Marjorie
1964. "Irony in Wallace Stevens' *The Rock*." *American Literature*
Nov., pp. 327–42.
Peterson, Margaret
1971. "*Harmonium* and William James." *Southern Review* July,
pp. 658–82.
Ransom, John Crowe
1955. "The Concrete Universal: Observations on the Understanding of Poetry." *Kenyon Review* Summer, pp. 383–407.
1964. "The Planetary Poet." *Kenyon Review* Winter, pp. 233–64.
Riddel, Joseph N.
1962a. "Stevens' 'Peter Quince at the Clavier': Immortality as
Form." *College English* Jan., pp. 307–9.
1962b. "Visibility of Thought'." *PMLA* Sept., pp. 482–98.
1967. *The Clairvoyant Eye: The Poetry and Poetics of Wallace
Stevens*. Baton Rouge: Louisiana State Univ. Pr.
1970. "The Dome and the Rock: Structure in the Poetry of
Wallace Stevens," *American Literature* Jan., pp. 609–11.
1971. "Stevens On Imagination—The Point of Departure." In *The
Quest for Imagination*, ed. O. B. Hardison Jr., pp. 55–85. Cleve-
land: Case Western Reserve Univ. Pr.
Rosenthal, M. L.
1951. "Stevens in a Minor Key." *New Republic* May 7, pp. 26–28.
Simons, Hi
1945. "The Genre of Wallace Stevens." *Sewanee Review* Autumn,
pp. 566–79.
Storm, Mary Joan
1955. "Stevens' 'Peter Quince at the Clavier'." *Explicator* Nov.
Sypher, Wylie
1960. *Rococo to Cubism in Art and Literature*. New York:

Tindall, William York
1961. *Wallace Stevens*. Minneapolis: Univ. of Minnesota Pr.
Turco, Lewis
1973. "The Agonism and the Existentity: Stevens." *Concerning Poetry* Spring, pp. 32–44.
Untermeyer, Louis
1923. *American Poetry Since 1900*. New York: Henry Holt.
Waggoner, Hyatt Howe
1970. [Untitled Review]. *Modern Philology* May, pp. 392–96.
Whitaker, Thomas R.
1970. "On Speaking Humanly." In *The Philosopher-Critic*, ed. Robert Scholes, pp. 67–88. Tulsa, Okla.: Univ of Tulsa Pr.
Young, David P.
1965. "A Skeptical Music: Stevens and Santayana." *Criticism* Summer, pp. 263–83.

CHAPTER 4

World View

> Poetry is the statement of a
> relation between a man
> and the world.
>
> WALLACE STEVENS "ADAGIA"

According to Frank Doggett ("The Poet of Earth: Wallace Stevens," *College English*, Mar. 1961), the two subjects with which Wallace Stevens's poetry is most frequently concerned are mortality and the interdependence of the mind and world, imagination and reality. Doggett's comment, if broadened a bit, summarizes the focus of this chapter: Wallace Stevens's world view which seems to have two primary themes, mortal man and the interaction of mind and world in poetry.

Several attributes characterize the criticism that focuses on Stevens's world view. First, most studies approach the poet's theoretical stance as a series of merging concepts—reality, imagination, supreme fiction, evil, death, flux, nothingness—rather than as clearly defined and distinguishable terms. This critical ambiguity is partially a function of the interaction of these concepts in the poetry, but also a function of critical imprecision. Second, faced with such ambiguity, complexity, and occasional contradiction, many critics resort to lengthy quotations or direct paraphrase, neither of which inherently explains itself. As a result of such imprecision and paraphrase, this criticism is the most generally unsatisfactory of works dealing with Stevens. Again, the complexity of the subject, the contradictions of the poet, and the shoddiness of the studies produce articles and books that, failing to find exact definitions in Stevens, utilize undefined terms to explain themselves, or worse, ignore the need for precise definition and focus in criticism. Finally, a basic difficulty in examining a "world view" must be acknowledged. The problem of indirect inference—reading the mind of the poet—is inherent in any such discussion. Unlike textual analysis or biographical conjecture, interpreting or explaining a poet's idea of the world requires several critical jumps: one must review the text itself, move inside that text to literal and figurative meanings of content and form, and then make the often

fatal leap into the poet's cognitions, where at some conscious, subconscious, or unconscious level a "world view," composed of concepts, ideas, and opinions, is purported to exist. The problem is
complicated in Stevens by the poet's productivity in essays, poems,
and letters that abound in apparent contraditions; by his poetic
style that defies logical progression and traditional syntax; by the
obliqueness of his prose statements; and by his tendency, when
asked to clarify a passage, to verbalize more abstract poetic prose.
The task of deciphering Stevens's statements in prose and poetry
has become a search for his elusive world view.

Toward this end, critics have examined Stevens's comments on
poetry, a theory of world and mind in interaction; Stevens's practice of poetic techniques, themselves inherently bound with the
interaction of reality and imaginations; and Stevens's ideas on man,
as a greater than life hero and as the epitome of life's transience
and mortality. If we make that cognitive leap from text to poet's
mind to critics' interpretation, these seem to be the primary concerns of Stevens's world view.

Stevens on Poetry: The Theory

That Stevens was himself concerned with a theory of poetics is
abundantly clear, not only in the common subject in his poetry,
aesthetic theory, but in the topics for discussion in his essays and
letters. Stevens's own statements on poetics will be discussed in
chapter 5, while for now discussion will be limited to the critics'
perceptions of that theory.

General Introductions

Those critical studies that are most hampered by the complexity in Stevens's theory are those that attempt to explain it in its
entirety or attempt to isolate many or all of its multiple components. Among these Ronald Sukenick's *Wallace Stevens: Musing
the Obscure* (1967), Henry W. Wells' *Introduction to Wallace
Stevens* (1964), Herbert J. Stern's *Wallace Stevens: Art of Uncertainty* (1966), and James G. Southworth's "Wallace Stevens"
(1950) are most notable. Sukenick's book, the most recent of these
problematic critical exercises, attempts to provide all things for all
Stevens readers. This study is divided into three sections: an introductory chapter on the poet's theory and practice; "readings" of
the poems; and "a guide" to the collected poems.

The introductory chapter describes Stevens's subject as a search for an attitude that would adequately confront the difficulties in contemporary, American, secular life. Toward this end, Stevens hypothesizes fictions and creates heroes in an attempt to capture an "intense state of mind." These fictions, according to Sukenick, are not ideological formulations of belief, but are statements of "favorable rapport with reality sufficiently convincing that disbelief may be suspended" (p. 3). This definition of Stevens's fictions is Sukenick's most original contribution in a study littered with old and often repeated assumptions including: Stevens's poetry deals in antithetic terms such as chaos and order, imagination and reality, or stasis and change; Stevens's history is a changing process in which no idea of reality is final, poetry is a constant metamorphosis of reality, and reality itself is characterized by flux; and Stevens's poetry is the act of transforming reality by turning chaos into a reality perceived with some order. Sukenick stresses the importance of the ego in perceiving this ordered reality, and further asserts that the imagination must establish a bond between the ego and the real. Here Sukenick differs from more precise critics who find the poetic process in Stevens characterized by imagination interacting with reality while both imagination and reality are influenced by and part of the experiencing self. By stressing the "ego," Sukenick introduces an unnecessary and undefined third construct where the poet manipulated only two.

Sukenick more accurately notes that Stevens's sense of reality depends on resemblance, a resemblance created by the imagination through metaphor, a technique that enhances reality. And, Sukenick also accurately notes that this is the theoretical source of Stevens's poetic preoccupation with the variation form. This leads the critic to describe Stevens's genre as not discursive or didactic but as unsequential reflections in which the theme is the sum of the poet's reflection, and in which no progressive argument or logical conclusion exists. The end of such "a psychological mode of meditation" (p. 24) is resolution rather than the "demonstrated truth" Sukenick describes as the usual end of discursive and didactic verse.

In general, this introductory chapter varies in quality, but is basically sound for the beginner in Stevens's verse. Sukenick notes many of the major concerns in the poetry as well as the more important poetic techniques such as emphasis on sound and the uses of language that distinguish Stevens. At best the critic strays noticeably when he interjects the ego into Stevens's work, and at worst he adds little original thought to the body of criticism, burgeoning by the 1967 date of this study's publication.

Unfortunately, the remaining two parts of Sukenick's endeavor
are not as harmless in their faults. The readings of the second section also vary in quality, format, and length, but focus on individual poems as they are arranged in the *Collected Poems* and
Opus Posthumous. Some of these readings are explications, others
are merely summaries of theme, and still others, brief examinations
of selected elements in the individual poems. A lengthy explication of "Notes Toward a Supreme Fiction" is concluded with a
summary of that explication, while the comments on all of the
other long poems are not blessed with such a recapitulation of
theme. Such inconsistencies abound. The reading of "Sunday
Morning" is valid, but that of "Peter Quince at the Clavier" too
simplistic, and that of "The Idea of Order at Key West" far too
literal. Even worse, important poems such as "Anecdote of the
Jar," "The Snow Man," and "The Auroras of Autumn" are not
deemed worthy of a reading and are left to brief notes in the
third section.

The latter section purports to provide a guide to Stevens's collected poetry but offers instead a conglomeration of loose ends.
Here Sukenick cites comments made by Stevens, makes various
interpretive asides, explains several allusions, and provides an al-
phabetical list of poems. The latter functions as a type of index to
Sukenick's book, but like the other elements of this section, is
neither complete nor thorough.

In short, the study produces more problems than insights. The
accurate assumptions in the first section are usually less than original, the choice of poems for "readings" or for "guide" notes seems
arbitrary, and the critical comments for beginners, too general for
any but the most uninitiated novice reader. At best the study has
a limited audience and for that audience provides often misleading
emphasis.

Henry Wells's study is similar to Sukenick's both in purpose and
in problems. Wells claims to write an introduction to the poet
which will serve as a companion to the poems. As introduction or
companion, the book is misleading. Wells asserts that none of
Stevens's works is imitative, a false statement to any critic who has
perused the poems of Stevens's Harvard years. After this initial slip
Wells seems to move rapidly into unsupportable interpretations
and unfounded statements. He notes that the poet's style is "un-
rhetorical and unadorned" (p. 5), and that Stevens himself, divided
between the pull of poetry and philosophy, was not a happy man.
While pitching his book to the nonexistent student of Stevens who
has read the poetry "several times" but is not concerned with the

"esoteric problems" raised by the poet, Wells promises to review
the best and most typical of Stevens's poems but only briefly
glances at "An Ordinary Evening in New Haven" and "Notes
Toward a Supreme Fiction." He adds professional insult to critical
injury when he asserts that "The Comedian as the Letter C" is
"graced with a straightforward narrative, so that it is less in need
of explanatory comment" (p. 16), and when he judges "Owl's
Clover" one of Stevens's better works.

Wells's study is also weak when he speculates about some personal emotion in the poet without providing evidence from biographical fact. In the poem "Esthétique du Mal" Wells finds clear
evidence of some "violent experience, a bereavement and a grief"
behind the poet's lines. Yet, his study is even weaker when, without
reliance on the poet's emotions or personal life, the critic attempts
paraphrases without reference to text or use of supporting quotations, and develops such paraphrases as simplistic "the meaning is"
equations. Such readings are indefensible when he ignores the lines
of a poem such as "Anecdote of the Jar" and describes the object
of the title as ceramic clay, hardly the reflective surface the poet
created. When he attends more closely to the poem itself, as he
does in his interpretation of "Sunday Morning," he exemplifies a
lack of critical perceptiveness in his description of the poem as
marred by the very lush rhetoric and tension between its form
and content that are the basis for its masterful execution.

In moving away from individual interpretation, Wells fares little better with general statements about pervasive themes and techniques. He asserts that the techniques of art seldom, if ever, concern Stevens; that Stevens perceived life through a telescope or
microscope but seldom through the power of his eyes; that Stevens's conception of god is "Emersonian" and his place in American literature, firmly rooted in the New England, Anglo-Saxon
Protestant tradition; and that Stevens's views of man's social predicament are "broad, imaginative, and penetrating" (p. 186).
These contentions rival one another in absurdity. Wells's book is,
however, not without redeeming critical merit. He does accurately
note the musical element in many of the poet's shorter poems, and
perceptively notes that Stevens is capable of creating a sense of
emotion through gestures of his own and the created personae in
his poems. Such emotions are, according to Wells, expressed
neither as a bang nor a whimper, but as a pianissimo. How Stevens
evokes such emotion certainly deserves exploration, but here again
Wells fails us.

In short, Wells's companion to Stevens is critically uncompanionable. Unsound, misleading, even totally false statements accumulate in a study lacking a coherent structure. Wells begins with a discussion of a late, difficult, philosophical Stevens, then jumps about in chapters about Stevens's form, style, and themes only to move into discussions about humor, art, psychology, insight, emotion, the Hero, social predicaments, and Yeats. Discerning the order of the critic's mind requires more perseverance than the complexity of the poet's mind demands. Even individual chapters lack unity, but suffer also from brevity and elusive, undefined subjects. The haphazard approach to subject and arrangement of chapters, to selection of subjects and poems for discussion, as well as to the critical analysis and execution, is unrivaled in Stevens criticism.

A third book-length study, Herbert Stern's *Wallace Stevens: Art of Uncertainty*, is also flawed by an unsystematic approach to the critic's subject. Stern notes three aims for his exercise: he attempts to demonstrate that for Stevens poetry functioned as a test of aesthetic and philosophical principles; that Stevens abandoned poetry after *Harmonium* because of his insurance career and forces within his art which denied the possibility of art; and that the poet as hedonist and humanist, skeptic and romantic, was one integrated artist. The first aim is not explored thoroughly because Stern does not examine the poet's aesthetics or philosophy in detail. The second aim is emphasized at the expense of Stern's own credibility. The critic never explains completely those destructive forces in Stevens's art, and he never accounts for Stevens's revitalized profundity of creation after his post-*Harmonium* period of silence. The final aim is based on Stern's assumption that Stevens's mind was split by an internal struggle which, nonetheless, produced a vital poetry based on self-questioning. This idea certainly merits exploration, but Stern becomes too distracted by flaws that he cites in *Harmonium* and by critics' errors in the *Harmonium* period to review the poems in detail. He never examines the logical extension of the internal struggle, Stevens's quiet poetic resolution in the interaction of reality and imagination.

Stern's study is further limited by his decision to confine his comments primarily to *Harmonium;* by his tendency to refer briefly to other Stevens periods; and by his selectivity in analyzing relatively few poems from the *Harmonium* era. In the examination of poems Stern does review, misreadings predominate. Stern suggests that in Stevens's poetry one finds a disdain for tradition, the confusion of modern times, and a definition of poetry as mere decorative "embroidery." These three judgments expose a critic unfamiliar with his subject. As critic he misreads an entire volume when he says of *Harmonium:* "The figure of the somewhat ridiculous poet engaged in a somewhat ridiculous pursuit appears most commonly in the work of the *Harmonium* period, when Stevens' relations with his own art were particularly strained" (p. 68). While most critics who examine these early poems judge them Stevens's best, Stern extends his pejorative analysis by damning "Sunday Morning" as a "counterfeit" which adopts the style of a former tradition in order to deny the validity of that tradition. Stern, like Sukenick, fails to see the mastery in Stevens's manipulation of traditional form in this poem.

Misreadings are accompanied by unresolved critical contradictions. Stern describes the ideal approach to Stevens's verse as a tracing of correspondences among all that the poet wrote, then Stern immediately abandons such an approach as "impossible." He asserts that the early charges against the "cloistered" character of Stevens's art were accurate, then indicts himself by questioning the "limited perceptions" on which such judgments were based. He warns against interpreting budding genius in early verse when reviewing it from the vantage of late masterpieces, and then adopts this very approach to Stevens's Harvard sonnets. And he notes the profusion of critical attention devoted to the first edition of *Harmonium,* then on the same page praises critics for examining this work when few were willing to peruse it.

The list of offenses grows. As one wades through Stern's comments summarizing his first chapter as an outline of Stevens critics, one wonders why such an outline neglects to mention Doggett, Riddel, and Morse among other notables in the Stevens domain. One winces at the unfounded biographical allusions when Stern compares Stevens to the poet's father because they both wrote poetry as a mere amusement, and when Stern invokes Freudian criticism as the key to Stevens's honorific descriptions of Florida. According to the critic, such praise reflects the poet's search for a pleasure principle and concomitant retreat from a reality principle. The contention is not only tangential to the poetry, but scholarly unsupportable as well.

As a study that attempts to combine a review of previous criticism with a historical and biographical perspective, Stern's book fails because of his invalid historical comparisons, unfounded biographical conjecture, and oversimplified critical generalizations. An annoyingly overdramatic rhetoric both attacks and praises a poet who demands more objective, systematic analysis than this study provides. Stern, as the most negative critic who has written a book-length study on Stevens, would have done well to focus his attention on a poet he found more palatable.

James G. Southworth's "Wallace Stevens" epitomizes all that is bad in critical summaries of ideas. Like the three books just discussed, Southworth's earlier study attempts to isolate and discuss all of Stevens's major poetic tenets and, not stopping here, tries to list all of the demands such ideas place on the reader. According to Southworth, Stevens's world view includes a definition of man as a poor, worthless, specimen; a definition of poetry as a force leading man to a higher spiritual life; and a definition of Stevens himself as an idealist. Among these ideas, Southworth interjects Stevens's distrust of nature as cruel oppressor, of the mind as inadequate when confronted with absolutes, and of the masses as an obstacle to the pursuit of life. If these summaries of primary ideas seem less than perceptive, they do not compare in misjudgment with Southworth's omissions; he never mentions two of Stevens's most important themes, the interplay of reality and imagination, and the mortality and humanity of man.

Southworth does accurately describe the demands of Stevens's poetry as inspired by unfamiliar vocabulary, manipulation of sound, sustained images, and variations in rhythm, but in summarizing ideas the critic apparently devotes little attention to the text. Of Stevens, Southworth tells us the poet had "a sense of the islands of goodness," a feeling he sensed "as he walked to church." The statement is as critically inappropriate and unsupportable as it is unduly pious. However, like the three books previously discussed, this earlier, shorter study is far from harmless when one reviews its misplaced emphasis. Southworth asserts that above all else Stevens searched for truth and appealed to his reader to find a greater truth beyond fact. In stressing truth, Southworth misses entirely Stevens's emphasis on the real as the focus of imaginative perception and his emphasis on the role of fiction—not truth—in fact.

Imagination and Reality: Divine Force or Human Faculty?

The most perceptive critic to examine this all-important imagination and reality in Stevens is J. Hillis Miller (*Poets of Reality*, 1969, pp. 217–84). Miller's book-length study focuses on six twentieth-century writers who, faced with the death of god, turn to reality for meaning. His comments on Stevens also appear in *The Act of the Mind* (1965), a volume he edited with Roy Harvey Pearce. The basis of all of Stevens's thought and poetry is, accord-

ing to Miller, the vanishing of god which left nothing but man and
nature, subject and object. Stevens, then, defines poetry as the
substitute for religion. The creation after the death, of new fictions
which pretend to be no more than fictions, is the act of poetry, and
the central theme of that poetry is the dialogue between subject
and object, the interaction between imagination and reality. According to Miller, all of Stevens's work is an exploration of "varia-
ble perspectives from which reality can be viewed by the imagination" (p. 225). Although Miller asserts that Stevens eventually
adopts a dualistic acceptance of both reality and imagination, Miller
is a bit off base when he finds in early Stevens a temporary but
total acceptance of reality and a concomitant rejection of imagination. And, by contending that reality becomes a temporary
"unchallenged king" in Stevens, Miller neglects much that is important about the imagination in the poetic process of Stevens's
poems about pure reality.

Yet, these points are minor and far outweighed by Miller's explicit definitions of constructs used by the poet. Miller notes that
to Stevens "abstraction" means man's power to separate himself
from the impinging real, and by "idea" Stevens means a direct
sense image, a definition drawn from the word's etymology. And,
Miller accurately defines the life of Stevens's poetry as a struggle
with the impossible task of reconciling the imagination and reality.
According to this critic, the poet is able to find momentary balance, but is caught in fluctuations between the two forces. Miller
further contends that Stevens's chief contribution to literature is
the elaboration of a poetic mode that allows the poet simultaneously to possess seemingly mutually exclusive terms. Stevens
achieves this as his later poems progress toward an acceptance of
one realm in which imagination and reality are conjoined. Miller
concludes that ultimately for Stevens reality and imagination are
not poles but two names for the same thing, an identity of poetry
and life. In this way, Stevens is able to deny ultimate being in
some transcendent realm but still postulate being and meaning
within things.

By trying to specify exactly what Stevens means in several
phases of his poetry, Miller confines and limits a poet whose inconsistencies often defy resolution. In this attempt Miller contradicts himself because the poet contradicts himself; and in this
admirably systematic attempt to define constructs in Stevens, Miller
creates a sequential progression of thought where no such clear
pattern exists in the poet's writings. In praise of Miller, one might
say he brings critical order to ideologic chaos. Such order is, how-

ever, unfair to Stevens, a poet who relished his illogical and contradictory convolutions of thought. The Miller study then performs a genuine service, but categorizes and restricts in the process. The chapter on Stevens is, nonetheless, one of the most definitive and enlightening examinations of Stevens's imagination and reality.

Other critics apparently agree with Miller's hypothesis that Stevens, confronted with the death of god, turned to the interaction of reality and imagination as creative force. Earlier than Miller, Louis L. Martz ("The World of Wallace Stevens," 1950) suggests that Stevens's world is devoid of both the supernatural and mythical. Martz focuses on Stevens's view of man, a creature who according to the poet must find his own salvation and forge his own relationships through the transcending power of the imagination. Although Miller differs with Martz's emphasis on transcendence, the two agree on the imagination as a creative, metamorphosizing power which views an object and thereby enhances, heightens, or intensifies reality. According to this critic, Stevens's imaginative process is a continually renewing process, ever changing the poet's relation to the world of physical objects. Martz describes Stevens's approach to this process as a belief in the ultimate significance of momentary and changing perceptions, and Martz labels this approach the aspect of Stevens's verse that gives his poetry its unique quality. Martz expands these comments in his later "Wallace Stevens: The Skeptical Music" (1966). This more recent study develops from Martz's older assumptions about the Stevens imagination, but adds that Stevens used musical instruments as symbols for the imagination which attempts a "pleasurable metamorphosis" of objects it encounters. Martz notes that in such an imaginative realm, objects do not exist apart from the perceiver because the perceiver makes reality.

Like Martz and Miller, Doris L. Eder in "The Meaning of Wallace Stevens' Two Themes" (*Critical Quarterly*, Summer 1969) defines Stevens's imagination as the poet's substitute for god. Eder disagrees with Martz's contention that the imagination is able to transcend reality, and she proposes instead that the faculty is for Stevens a "spirit," an inward pressure responding to an outward pressure, and the sum of man's faculties. This multiple definition is too general and its components too disparate to provide any clarification of Stevens's term, but Eder's emphasis on the poet's confrontation and reconciliation of the human mind with reality is accurate. Terming reality for Stevens the inert world of matter as well as the world transfigured by the imagination, Eder mistakenly

interjects a value judgment when she says the imagination is not
as great as reality. She contradicts her own assertion when she adds
that for Stevens the imagination became a type of divinity. Stevens never definitively praised one of his dualities at the expense
of the other, and he never assumed nor created divinity in the
modern world. Eder quickly moves from concern with such
divinity into Stevens's second requirement of poetry, the necessity
for a supreme fiction. Her comments on this Stevens construct are
few, but conclude by labeling Stevens a modern because he rejected
traditional religion but nonetheless recognized life's demand for
some supreme sanction. In short, the study adds little to criticism
but unexplained synonyms for Stevens's reality, imagination, and
supreme fiction.

Irving Howe's "Wallace Stevens: Another Way of Looking at
the Blackbird" (1963) is more exact in defining Stevens's imagina-
tion/reality theme. Like Miller, Martz, and Eder, Howe finds at
the base of Stevens's poetry an awareness of man's solitariness and
crisis of belief, both associated with the death of god. To confront
the uncertainty of man's situation, Stevens turns to the interaction
of reality and imagination while calmly accepting the disorder and
dissolution around him. The awareness of the human condition
is for Stevens not the dominant subject one finds in most modern
artists, but a "pressure upon all subjects" (p. 160), to use Howe's
words. Howe also asserts that Stevens uses the reality/imagina-
tion theme to demonstrate the possibilities of consciousness and the
power of the mind, and uses the eye to see and thereby create
external reality. Although Howe's study is too brief to provide
extensive or sustained exegesis of Stevens's ideas, it nonetheless isolates an important problem not noted by other critics. Howe contends that Stevens's use of the reality/imagination theme degenerates into a convention that, like any "formula" or "habit,"
becomes stale with overuse. Noting this, Howe is quick to add
that at his best Stevens manipulates the theme as a way to transform the variations of perception into an affirmation of the self's
power in a disordered world.

Like Howe, R. D. Ackerman ("Wallace Stevens: Myth, Belief,
and Presence," *Criticism*, Summer 1972) focuses on the poet's
perceptions of physical stimuli. Yet, like Eder, Ackerman finds in
Stevens an exaltation of man's imagination as divinity. Ackerman
extends this when he notes in Stevens a rejection of romantic modes
of perception which interfere with the intercourse between reality
and imagination. Ackerman's overall focus varies from previously
discussed critics on this theme. According to him the "ritualized

spontaneity" in Stevens may be associated with primitive myth. To support this, Ackerman examines Stevens's mythic female associated by the critic with the timeless mother, Jung's anima. From this point in his study Ackerman leaves earthly ground behind and moves into spiritual realms, emphasizing the world as a "symbolic figuration of the mind" (p. 270), and the "mysterious point of contact between the physical world and the spiritual imagination" (p. 271). Ackerman becomes even more ethereal when he notes that the mythic aspects of Stevens's poetry provide "an atmosphere wherein the imagination of man-God opens to allow earth-heaven to declare its presence" (p. 273). The study is indeed weakened by such grandiose descriptions which lack explicit reference and resemblance to Stevens's own world view.

Another critic, Adalaide Kirby Morris, has devoted a book to the study of Stevens's mythic background, but Morris focuses specifically on the poet's Christian heritage rather than generally on archetypes. In *Wallace Stevens: Imagination and Faith* (1974), Morris contends that from the faith of Stevens's ancestors, the poet learned a belief in a god who joined the invisible and visible through symbol, ritual, and creed. Stevens's substitute for this is his search for a theory of poetry. For the poet, the imagination becomes god and the merging of self and environment, the joining of invisible and visible that once concerned the church. Unlike his religious refugee ancestors and unlike the American Transcendentalists before him, Stevens depends on physical fact rather than divine force. Morris seeks to prove that this respect for physical fact is often communicated by Stevens through the use of biblical forms. In support of this, the critic discusses elements of parable, anecdote, proverb, prayer, hymn, and psalm as they may be found in various Stevens poems. The comparisons she notes are a bit contrived, but her assertion, that the poet manipulates scriptural phrasing to satirize religious clichés and elevate the mortal to divine status, is well founded. Through their lineage and language, church forms, words, and symbols supply a pattern for the poetic religion Stevens hoped to substitute for Christianity. According to Morris, the poet criticizes the church because it rejects life, doubt, and the self, three important elements in Stevens's world view.

To Morris, then, Stevens did not attempt to question Christian dogma, but more appropriate, through his criticism, juxtaposed the rigid belief of the church with the fluid forces in reality. As a substitute for the rigid, traditional church, Stevens proposed a poetry which would help us live our lives. Yet, according to Morris, he drew on the components of existing religion when he created this new "church" in his poetry. To support this assertion, Morris cites in Stevens's verse biblical images such as the rock; biblical personae such as angels; patterns of history such as the fall, acceptance of grace, and moment of revelation; sacraments such as marriage; and poetic cosmology such as heaven and hell. Morris notes that heaven and hell are useful to Stevens as emblems of psychological disaffection with earth. According to this critic, the poet disdains the hell which is the paralysis of the imagination and the heaven which is an illusion threatening reality, but postulates a paradise on earth in which reality and imagination are balanced.

Morris does make a number of penetrating statements, but her interpretation of the religious theme is often overextended. She suggests that Stevens thinks in proverbs, formulates a theory of poetry that becomes a "mystical theology," applies to poetry the promise of Jesus, creates an imagination that is comparable to divine love, and manipulates his own symbols to function like biblical symbols. All of these assertions are questionable, to say the least. This overextension of thesis coupled with an overreading of many poems is unfortunate, because the study is explicitly structured with clear chapter divisions and a lucid purpose. Yet, a basic flaw mars this purpose from the beginning. Like Miller, Morris focuses on Stevens's reality, but her religious approach to that reality inherently systematizes where Stevens refuted systematization, and inherently questions the validity of earthly experience where Stevens believed in no reality other than that experience. In her symbol hunt for Christian analogs she misses the poetic forest for the doctrinaire trees.

In "Wallace Stevens" (*Contemporary Literature*, Autumn 1975) John V. Hagopian reviews Morris's study and validly questions how useful her analysis of faith is to an understanding of the poetry. Hagopian is scathing in his criticism of her pedantic prose style and deferential treatment of other critics. One might add that such deference is accompanied by an extensive reliance, not fully referenced, on an earlier study by Baird, *The Dome and the Rock* (1968). A much earlier note by Amos N. Wilder (*Modern Poetry and the Christian Tradition: A Study in the Relation of Christianity to Culture*, 1952, pp. 239–42) reviews Stevens's "Sunday Morning" and foreshadows Morris's more lengthy analysis. Wilder concludes that the poem juxtaposes the natural joys of earth and the harshness of Christian life, and that Stevens used it as a vehicle to reject the antinaturalism and antilife tenets of the Christian faith. Stanley Romaine Hopper's chapter, "Wallace Stevens: The Sundry Comforts of the Sun" in *Four Ways of Modern Poetry*

2811 NE Holman Street · Po
503-280-8501 · 800-321-9371 · Fax 5

Wallace Stevens

J. Hillis Miller, The basis of all Stevens' tho't
+ poetry is "the vanishing of god which left
nothing but man and nature, subject and
object. Thus the interaction of the
imagination and reality is the "creative force."

Louis L. Martz,

in WS by Abbie F. Willard, '78, pp 187-189

Irving Howe - the imagination / reality
formula becomes a stale convention, but
in his best poetry WS transcends it
in that "the variations of perception into
an affirmation of the self's power in
a disordered world."

(1965) edited by Nathan A. Scott, Jr., is supposedly a "Christian response" to the twentieth-century literature that defines the sacred in "new" terms. Hopper senses in Stevens a "dropping away of the entire symbolic world of Christendom" (p. 14), but is unable to sustain his analysis in an essay that lacks unity, coherence, and clear emphasis.

H. W. Burtner ("The High Priest of the Secular: The Poetry of Wallace Stevens," *Connecticut Review*, Oct. 1972) is also concerned with defining Stevens's conception of god which Burtner terms a recognition of absence rather than presence. Like Morris, this critic defines the imagination and reality as constructs which may be used in examining the poet's theology. Burtner compares Stevens's moments of interaction between reality and imagination with Joyce's epiphanies, Eliot's moments, and Wordsworth's spots of time, but fails to note that Stevens's interactions lack the transcendence obvious in the other three. Burtner describes the imagination as the shaping spirit which unites reality and mind for Stevens, but adds that Stevens's commitment to reality is so total that the poet functions as a reality priest. By concluding from this that Stevens's poetry is most responsive to the pressures of existence in the here and now, Burtner articulates the obvious and repeats the theme most often emphasized in criticism dealing with Stevens's world view.

Imagination and Reality:
Stevens's Need for a Supreme Fiction

Confronted by Stevens's unorthodox search for meaning in the physical world, other critics focus attention not on the poet's rejection of a traditional god, but on his search for a more tenable fiction. Stevens himself termed this force, which gives meaning to reality, the supreme fiction, while critics to follow him have attempted definitions and descriptions of varying specificity. Among these critics, John William Corrington in "Wallace Stevens and the Problem of Order: A Study of Three Poems" (*Arlington Quarterly*, Summer 1968) is the most exact. Corrington defines supreme fiction as "consciously constructed symbolizations of experience around which some species of assent can cohere, and out of which action, physical or intellectual, can issue" (p. 51). The definition is far more precise than most critics attempt when discussing the term, but as a result it is far more limiting and too narrow to encompass the broad range of fluctuating characteristics that the poet associates with it. Corrington appears to view the supreme fiction as Stevens's synonym for the imagination. Contrary to this critic's opinion, the two are not interchangeable. Corrington also stresses that for Stevens the mode and end of poetry is human order, an order that can be apprehended and comprehended only through the supreme fiction. To support this, the critic examines three poems, "Disillusionment of Ten O'Clock," part VI of "Six Significant Landscapes," and "Anecdote of the Jar," as poetic expressions of Stevens's conceptualization of order. Although Corrington correctly assumes that Stevens's idea of imagination stresses the faculty as integrative force and ordering power, his conclusion, that reality must be approached through the imagination but may never be reached, is false. The poet would find his critic's definitions and conclusions contrary to the interaction of reality and imagination in the poetry and inconsistent with the separate supreme fiction that provides meaning, however fictional, to life.

R. P. Blackmur's "Wallace Stevens: An Abstraction Blooded" reprinted in *Language as Gesture* (1952) provides a more helpful description of the fiction's properties. According to Blackmur, Stevens in *Notes Toward a Supreme Fiction* delineates the three stages through which any idea of supreme being must pass: it must be abstract; it must change; and it must give pleasure. As an abstraction, the supreme fiction must be an initiator and reference of myth. This abstraction must change because change is a condition of vision, perception, and imagination. And, it must give pleasure as a force open to fresh discoveries made by the eye and the imagination. Blackmur's comments are brief, but serve not only to describe requirements of the supreme fiction, but to summarize the theme of the three major sections in *Notes Toward a Supreme Fiction.*

Marjorie Buhr in "Wallace Stevens' Search for Being Through the Supreme Fiction" (*The Carrell*, June 1972) provides an even more general description of the force. Buhr asserts that Stevens was absorbed with the idea of a fiction as an "ontological expression of the twentieth century's effort to find a meaningful substitute for a religious tradition which has lost its vitality" (p. 4). According to Stevens a la Buhr, when man ceases to believe in old dogma he may not merely disbelieve but must create or choose a new belief. Because all men need to believe in something, regardless of its untrue dimension, a fiction supplies for Stevens not a figment of the imagination but all that man knows to be "not true" but nonetheless worthy of belief. As an analogue which "organizes experience in order to attain metaphysical truth," Stevens's fiction is, Buhr suggests, a descendent of fictions in James, Nietzsche,

Jung, Viahinger, Niebuhr, Tillich, Whitehead, Cassirer, and
Kant. In fact, Buhr spends more time paraphrasing such philosophers than relating their ideas to those of the poet. Yet, she is
accurate in her conclusion that Stevens's supreme fiction is the
poet's attempt to inject the unreal into the real and the idea of
god into the idea of man.

Imagination and Reality: Interactional Components

In examining the reality-imagination theme, some critics have
not emphasized its relationship to the death of god or the need
for new fictions, but instead have simply viewed these two components as interactional forces. The most recent of these, *Wallace
Stevens: A World of Transforming Shapes* (1976) by Alan Perlis,
issues from previous studies and attempts to resolve some of the
contradictions in earlier criticism. Perlis defines his parameters by
citing the two extremes of the criticism on Stevens's reality-
imagination theme. According to Perlis, Sister Bernetta Quinn in
1952 (a study to be discussed shortly) introduced the idea that
the poet transforms the world he perceives into imaginary constructs. In opposition to this focus, Perlis places Richard Blessing's
book (discussed in chapter 1) and J. Hillis Miller's study (examined earlier in this chapter). Both Blessing and Miller emphasize
the world of objects rather than their transformation. Perlis not
only claims to reconcile such disparate emphases, but maintains
that he alone stresses the paradoxical conflict between Stevens's
object-in-itself and object perceived. Had this critic read Miller,
among others, more closely, he would have found this emphasis
with multiple variations in much of the Stevens criticism. Perlis
also asserts that he demonstrates for the first time that the act of
transformation at the center of Stevens's poetry relates many disparate themes in the poems. Under this transformation rubric,
then, Perlis discusses many seemingly unrelated topics.

Perlis not only overgeneralizes about his own supposedly
unique ideas, but also overgeneralizes about other criticism. He
contends that every critic who has written about Stevens has noted
relatively few themes coupled with a virtuoso style to maintain
reader interest. And, he suggests that writers who have noted
change in the Stevens canon characterize it as a change in emphasis
rather than idea. Neither assertion is supportable—if one bothers
to read the critics of Stevens. Yet, Perlis does make some insightful comments. He proposes that each of the poet's volumes except
The Rock communicates the belief that the world is a continual

state of flux in which poetic communication issues from the poet's
movement between two poles, defined by Perlis as reality–
imagination, North–South, sun–moon, summer–winter, and death–
life. He extends this analysis of antitheses by noting a conflict
between the individual metaphors in poems and the objects or
phenomena these metaphors attempt to communicate. This latter
extension is an interesting point and exemplifies Perlis at his best.
He is less adequate when he cites poems, well chosen for their
thematic emphasis on reality transformed, but neglects to develop
such citations thoroughly. Because this study draws heavily on
earlier criticism and adds little to it, the scattered perceptive comments might have more successfully been presented in a compact
article rather than a book.

Sister M. Bernetta Quinn's article "Metamorphosis in Wallace
Stevens" is a classic in the reality/imagination criticism. The article
was originally published in the Sewanee Review (Spring 1952),
reappeared in a different form in her book (The Metamorphic
Tradition in Modern Poetry, 1955), and was reprinted by Marie
Borroff in the Wallace Stevens volume of the Twentieth Century
Views series. Quinn early contended that Stevens's poetry is a
verse based on metamorphosis, a force which for the poet joins
the objective and subjective world and connects the realms of
imagination and reality, thereby creating one realm of resemblance.
According to Quinn, Stevens binds all things of man's environment in a relationship based on appearance. In Stevens's poetry
Quinn finds two ways that the poet establishes resemblance:
metaphors and verbal equations. Quinn perceptively examines
these ways in Stevens, and she accurately summarizes the poet's
opinion that poetry satisfies man's desire for resemblance and also
enhances reality. Like Miller and Eder to follow her, Quinn
acknowledges Stevens's imagination as a means of making man
divine, but unlike the later critics, Quinn emphasizes the refashion-
ing of reality into a "terrestrial paradise" rather than the absence
of god in modern reality. If the term paradise is a bit overempha-
tic, Quinn's qualifying assertions save her from undue critical
optimism. She does accurately assess the conflict between Stevens's
desire to face things as they are and his urge to remold them. Such
capsule summaries of the poet's concerns and methods are notably
perceptive for their day.

With only slight shifts of emphasis, many studies have reiterated
many of Quinn's points. L. S. Dembo in "Wallace Stevens: Meta
Men and Para Things" (1966) thinks that Stevens's idea of reality
and idea of man are inherently poetic, facilitating transformations

of the chaotic universe which make it possible for men to satisfy a "will to order." Dembo stresses the transmutations, a version of Quinn's metamorphoses, that create meta-men and para-things; he acknowledges an ideal coexistence of reality and imagination similar to Quinn's terrestrial paradise; and he, like Quinn, finds in Stevens an imagination that is merely responsive to the world at times but actively manipulating it at others.

In a study reviewed briefly in chapter 3, J. V. Cunningham ("The Styles and Procedures of Wallace Stevens," *University of Denver Quarterly*, Spring 1966), like Quinn, describes Stevens's imagination and reality as representatives of the subjective and objective worlds. Similar to Quinn, Cunningham defines Stevens's reality as external things seen and described, but his definition of Stevens's imagination is more lengthy, vague, and inaccurate than Quinn's. According to Cunningham, the imagination may be described as romantic rather than realistic, a fantasy associated with "high-spirited nonsense," a distortion of feeling, and an idea of mythic construction. Yet, similar to Quinn, he also views the imagination as the faculty responsible for the perception of resemblances and the process of abstraction. As noted in chapter 3, this study is extremely negative toward Stevens as a poet who wrote too much bad, tiresome verse. The negativism is excessive as well as contrary to general, critical appraisal, but the most glaring limitation of the article is Cunningham's attempt to discuss too many aspects of a too complex poet. In short, the critic examines Stevens's many faceted approach to his multidefined imagination and reality, but executes the examination without thorough analysis of any one aspect in this demanding subject.

A third critic who follows Quinn's lead, Richard M. Gollin ("Wallace Stevens: The Poet in Society," *Colorado Quarterly*, Summer 1960), defines Stevens's imagination as the organizer of the real world, the force that can reduce the chaos of perception to an aesthetically pleasing order. Gollin suggests, like Quinn, that for Stevens, writing poems was an act that transformed a world without imagination into an imaginative reality. And, like Quinn, Gollin acknowledges Stevens's faith in man founded in the powers of the imagination. Both critics also emphasize Stevens's faith in man's ability, instead of recognizing the poet's belief in human mortality and concomitant mortal limitations.

Charles R. Burns's "The Two Worlds of Wallace Stevens" (*Trace*, Winter 1964) and Joseph N. Riddel's "Wallace Stevens' 'Visibility of Thought' " (*Publications of the Modern Language Association*, Sept. 1962) also repeat earlier expressed Quinn themes. Burns contends that Stevens is concerned with confronting reality through an imaginative process that includes both reflection and perception, while Riddel more thoroughly summarizes Stevens on imagination and reality. As his vehicle, Riddel uses Stevens's "An Ordinary Evening in New Haven" as a summary of poetic ideas including Stevens's imagined reality as a form of natural creation and Stevens's poetic reality as a synthesis of subjective self and objective world. This latter point is a refinement of Quinn's original distinction between objective reality and subjective imagination.

C. Roland Wagner's review of *The Necessary Angel*, "A Central Poetry" (*Hudson Review*, Spring 1952a), supports this same opinion. Wagner summarizes the poetic process in Stevens as the reality of chaos transformed by the imagination into a supreme fiction, creating a central poetry in which the poet's powers of imagination allow insights into reality and place the poet as central creative consciousness. Like others to follow him, Wagner finds in Stevens a human need to master the disorder of reality. Wagner quotes extensively from *The Necessary Angel*, but, rather than review it, lapses into paraphrases of the poet on reality and imagination. However, Wagner's purported review is more seriously weakened by his judgment that this collection of Stevens's essays and lectures presents a "precise and clear-sighted doctrine." Any careful reading of this collection reveals arguments that are at best ambiguous or contradictory.

Stevens in Poetry: The Practice

In a study that resembles in focus those which attempt to define Stevens's poetic world view, Frank Lentricchia (*The Gaiety of Language: An Essay on the Radical Poetics of W. B. Yeats and Wallace Stevens*, 1968) interprets the poetics of Yeats and Stevens in light of three questions: how do they define the reality within which imagination must operate; what are the powers and limitations of the imagination; and what do they understand to be the nature and value of a poem? The study is explicit in answering these questions and is itself an example of defined and precise order: chapters 1 and 2 review the philosophical heritage of both poets; chapters 3 and 5 examine the explicit poetic theories noted in the three questions; and chapters 4 and 6 analyze the implicitly theoretical poems by the two authors. Aside from its extensive structuring, this study is distinguished from many examinations of

world view by its discussion of world view as it is realized in
poetic practice. Lentricchia believes that for Stevens and Yeats
poems are not simple statements about a theory of poetry, but are
poems for their own sake. According to Lentricchia, Stevens
sensed the primarily verbal nature of poetry while he recognized
that his commitment to a world of particulars could destroy him
as a poet by enslaving him to a secretarial function. To counter
this, Stevens asserts the freedom of the imagination and attempts
to establish a linguistic interrelationship between denotative language, more favorable to reality, and connotative language, more
favorable to the imagination.

Such specification of the relationship between message and
means in Stevens exemplifies Lentricchia at his strongest. The
critic adds that the irrational energy of the imagination aids in the
aesthetic ordering or creating of what Stevens termed a fiction, a
"cultivated illusion made by the process of 'abstracting' or consciously distorting the chaos of the real into a palatable image" (p.
139). Yet, Lentricchia also notes that the poet was not satisfied
with either reality or imagination and therefore did not maintain
a static attitude toward either. Because Stevens views reality itself
as changing, language falsifies it because language tends to fix it. In
conclusion, Lentricchia places both poets in the "poetics of will"
tradition which defines imagination as finite energy that seeks to
ground the self in a linguistic medium. Like many critics who
examine Stevens's theory. Lentricchia bases many of his comments
on the poet's philosophical heritage, and like most critics who
examine Stevens's techniques, Lentricchia devotes more attention
to paraphrasing poems than to explaining them. Both approaches
distort the poetry itself because both tend to neglect combined
philosophy and technique, the poetic embodiment of theory.

Techniques in the Use of Language:
Vocabulary and Parts of Speech

In a study, "Examples of Wallace Stevens" reprinted in *Language as Gesture* (1952), R. P. Blackmur provides a far more
specific look at the poet's use of language-related techniques.
Blackmur notes that the most striking aspect of Stevens's verse is
its vocabulary that exudes "an air of preciousness," but the critic
qualifies this assertion by suggesting such words are chosen not
for that preciousness, but for their exact meaning. Stevens's use of
language then is perfectly precise within the context of the poem,

but becomes diluted when the words are extracted from the content and analyzed by critics. The point is well taken, as is Blackmur's comment that in poems such as "Disillusionment of Ten O'Clock" the light tone increases the gravity of the subject because the wit in the word choice juxtaposition creates a "poignancy of meaning." In other poems such as "Sea Surface Full of Clouds" language is used to create a tone and atmosphere which are nearly equivalent to substance and meaning. Blackmur extends his astute analysis by noting the "intentional ambiguity" produced when the poet uses two figurative statements in combination, and by noting that in Stevens's use of trope, abstractions are rendered concrete by their association with concrete words. The difficulty in Stevens's verse Blackmur lodges in the poet's seemingly impenetrable words or phrases. The rhetorical language manipulated by the poet, language which in a nondramatic meditative way carries the "real substance" of the poetry, Blackmur describes as creating a surface equivalent to an emotion. According to the critic, such language creates such an equivalent by its escape from the "purely communicative function of language" (p. 243).

Blackmur concludes his study with an examination of "The Comedian as the Letter C," a poem with a rhetorical form in which language is used for its own sake but with a content of concrete experience not usually found in such rhetoric. In this poem, Stevens's subject becomes nothing but words, words which to the poet are everything. The study is helpful, not only because it identifies the simple and complex reasons for the difficulty in Stevens's style, but also because it lucidly describes how the poet's word choice, tropes, and rhetoric work.

Josephine Miles's comments in *The Continuity of Poetic Language: Studies in English Poetry from the 1540's to the 1940's* (1951, pp. 403-9), are minimally helpful. She, like Blackmur, looks at Stevens's language, but, more specifically than Blackmur, notes the proportion of parts of speech in Stevens's verse. According to Miles, nouns predominate in Stevens and reflect the typical vocabulary of the 1940s, an era concerned with "death," "mind," "thing," "time," and "world." That this period, more than other eras, is more concerned with such words is certainly debatable, but Miles partially redeems her study by accurately noting the poet's reliance on passive verbs and participial modifiers which extend and suspend action. The most glaring inadequacy in this study, however, is the date at which Miles establishes the end of her concern. In the 1940s Stevens had much of his poetry yet to write. Her sampling of his art is therefore limited.

Techniques in the Manipulation of Language:
Metaphors and Images

Among those critics who concern themselves with Stevens's techniques, most confine their emphasis to three manifestations of the poet's use of language: metaphor, image, and more generally, overall style. Of these three concerns, metaphor has attracted the most attention.

J. Hillis Miller's previously cited study, *Poets of Reality*, attempts to relate the poet's use of metaphor to his ideas about reality and imagination. Astutely, Miller notes that many of Stevens's poems are comprised of a series of "fluid transformations in which objects modulate into one another by a process which is not metaphorical because all of the elements in the series are on the same level of reality" (pp. 226–27). Such images do not refer to any "beyond" and are not symbolic, but are directly related to the poet's concern with reality and things as they are. Because such images lack reference in depth, referential vibrations occur horizontally between the images themselves. These images are nonetheless universalized because each one interacts with others in the series and is a part of a reality characterized by universal change. This results in poems in which a unifying flow among images progresses simultaneously with the unreconciled tension between imagination and reality, self and world.

Miller then moves quickly into a discussion of Stevens's metaphors, but never clearly defines how such metaphors differ from the images he has discussed. The critic suggests that, for a poet concerned with perspectives, metaphor supplies a way of exploring resemblances and a way of creating a new reality that heightens and extends existing dimensions of old reality. Noting that some of Stevens's poems are pure studies of metaphor, Miller describes these as a search for the real which fails because it loses itself in ever multiplying resemblances, never touching the thing itself. For this reason Stevens ultimately rejects metaphor as evasive and unreal and accepts reality as the most important member of the imagination-reality conflict. Miller's emphasis is inaccurate when he notes that the poet ultimately rejects metaphor as a technique of resemblance that betrays itself by evading reality. This critical assumption fails to distinguish the two types of metaphor Stevens postulates: the desirable one which enhances reality; and the contrived one which is superimposed on and therefore untrue to reality. The critic is far more accurate when he contends that in Stevens metaphor is not just a horizontal relation between the particulars of reality, but a trope composed of horizontal analogies that contribute to a vertical metaphor in which "the world is transformed into an expression of the poet's mind" (p. 245).

Miller's assessment of Stevens's techniques in the late poetry is also more exact than his lack of distinction between image and metaphor and his lack of recognition when faced with two types of metaphors. Miller suggests that Stevens's late poetry captures a sense of the fleeting moment through a variety of linguistic strategies including images such as the aurora borealis; phrases such as "gawky flitterings"; sequences of images which are metamorphoses of one another; and phrases in opposition that restate terms in rapid succession. And Miller, appropriate to the poet he discusses, ultimately describes a poetry of "flittering metamorphosis" as the only poetry that for Stevens is true to both reality and imagination.

Suzanne Juhasz takes a similar approach. In *Metaphor and the Poetry of Williams, Pound, and Stevens* (1974) she clearly defines her use of the term metaphor as a technique in which meaning is "created by and contained within the relation established between 2 terms" (p. 32). Her thesis is that Williams, Pound, and Stevens emphasize metaphor as a structuring element in their poetry and use the trope as a means of dealing with aesthetics dependent on the imagination. In Stevens the function of this metaphor is to effect a relation between abstract and concrete elements of language. According to Juhasz, all three poets share basic assumptions about metaphor and poetry, including a common description that metaphor is not ornamental but central to poetic vision; a belief in the intrinsic truth of metaphoric transfer; a stress on metaphor as a form of language; manipulations of metaphor as a power to achieve in poetry what is impossible in thought or action alone; and utilization of metaphor to indicate the relation of elements central to poetry. In Stevens, this relationship exists between abstract and concrete elements, and takes the form of metaphors arranged in a series of parallel statements that define a concept in terms of its complications and resemblances.

To support her thesis, Juhasz interprets a long poem by each of the poets. Her Stevens selection, "Notes Toward a Supreme Fiction," provides Juhasz with an example in metaphors that create structuring patterns and communicate the crucial relationship between imagination and reality. According to this critic, "Notes" is built upon a pattern of metaphors placed in opposition to literal, abstract statements that they modify. They are usually parallel to one another, forming series of metaphors that in their language move back and forth from the concrete to the abstract. The totality of metaphors (or resemblances, to use one of Stevens's terms) defines the concept in question; it also creates the poem. In addition, the poem sometimes achieves extended, or total metaphors, which are what Stevens calls "fictions," and which are "the supreme moments of poetry" (p. 132). Using as her basis Stevens's statements about metaphor in "Three Academic Pieces," "Poem Written at Morning," "The Motive for Metaphor," and the "Adagia," Juhasz applies this theory randomly to sections of "Notes." This random approach to various sections in the poem as well as her judgment that the poem is an attempt at definition flaw her argument. The very title of "Notes Toward a Supreme Fiction" intentionally indicates the poet's lack of belief in definitive statement.

Her interpretation of Stevens on metaphor is also marred by the intrusion of her own opinion on the nature of abstract language; by her failure to develop potentially enlightening contentions; and by her reluctance to define or resolve the contradictions in Stevens's theory of metaphor. She repeatedly urges the reader of Stevens to "keep track" of the poet's "stance toward metaphor," but she describes neither the stances nor how they differ. However, she accurately notes that Stevens uses series of metaphors in opposition to an abstract statement in order to make the abstract more concrete; and she appropriately identifies Stevens's tendency to describe with metaphors his antimetaphorical moments. Although her interpretations are scattered and erratic, her selections from the verse more often quoted than explicated, and her argument developed without reference to preceding critics, her study is strongest in its conclusion when she distances herself from the poetry in question. Juhasz's summary relating metaphor to experience is apt: she asserts that patterns of metaphor provide a nondiscursive method by which a poet may link and develop images, and she contends that metaphor reveals the dual aspects of experience (inner and outer) while concentrating on reality itself.

Juhasz's total lack of reference to other critics on Stevens's metaphoric theory is puzzling because of the number and contribution of such critics. Donald Sheehan's "Wallace Stevens' Theory of Metaphor" (*Papers on Language and Literature*, Winter 1966) is an example of meaningful work on this subject. Sheehan suggests that Stevens's concept of metaphor is intimately related to his view of reality as dualistic, but that Stevens makes no attempt to resolve the dualism which is interpreted by his critics as confusion. To counter the confused critics, Sheehan contends that Stevens never constructed a formalized theory of metaphor. but displayed a consistent point of view toward the trope. In short, Stevens's inexactness reflects for Sheehan not a muddiness of thought, but a vitality. Stevens's only sustained discussion of metaphor, "Three Academic Pieces," expresses a reliance on resemblance between things, but fails to define precisely what the term "metaphor" itself means. Sheehan correctly isolates the two poles between which the techniques of metaphor must operate: an unknowable, irreducible, external reality; and a coalescence of subject-perceiver and object-perceived that is metaphoric reality in which being and knowing are one. Between these poles the poet searches for resemblance, distrusting metaphoric reality but refusing to accept unknowable reality. Stevens consistently states and implies that things as they are cannot be known by a fixed view, but must be seen by a perspective in constant flux appropriate to a world in continual flux. Because of this interaction of object and perceiver, Sheehan finds at the base of Stevens's theory the question, "how do we know?" The poet confronts epistemological dualism by proposing metaphor as an answer. Knowledge, then, derives from perceiving resemblances, and perceiving resemblances is the process of creating metaphors. But Sheehan, like the poet, recognizes the limitations of the trope. If metaphor is a prelude to knowledge of relationships, it may also become an evasion of reality when it accepts these relationships as actual and complete descriptions of reality. Sheehan's article is excellent because it explicitly clarifies the poet's position on this complex theory.

Like Sheehan, Northrop Frye in an earlier study, "The Realistic Oriole: A Study of Wallace Stevens" (*Hudson Review*, Autumn 1957), describes Stevens as a poet for whom metaphysics, poetic vision, and a theory of knowledge are interrelated. And, like Sheehan to follow him, Frye suggests that the poet's theory of metaphor depends on the term "resemblance." Frye extends this, asserting, like Quinn, that Stevens's metaphors depend on metamorphosis and develop out of a theory of likeness and parallelism. Frye quarrels with Stevens's poems in which metaphor is pejoratively presented as a shrinking from immediate experience, and uses his differences of opinion as a springboard into his own critical theory. According to Frye, in metaphor objects maintain their own identity while being identified with each other, an illogical occurrence and therefore opposed to logical likeness or similarity. Stevens's poetry is termed "apocalyptic" by Frye because "the theoretical postulate of Stevens's poetry is a world of total metaphor, where the poet's vision may be identified with anything it visualizes" (p. 173). Yet, the limitations of Frye's comments must be acknowledged. Although his theory of metaphor provides an interesting approach to this poet's technique, it fails, in its emphasis on identity, to account for the tension created between terms in the trope. Frye also cites and explains only those comments by the poet which are pejorative in attitude toward metaphor. In this emphasis the critic ignores Stevens's positive and often explanatory comments on the trope.

William Bevis's "Metaphor in Wallace Stevens" (*Shenandoah*, Winter 1964) agrees with Frye's and Sheehan's studies. Bevis's approach is based on the premise that metaphor in Stevens is not just a stylistic device but an entire theory of reality and art. Bevis acknowledges that Stevens contradicts himself on metaphor, but Bevis, lacking the sophistication of Sheehan, sees this as pure confusion; and Bevis, lacking the insight of Sheehan, attempts to distinguish categories of reality in Stevens rather than differentiate between approaches to metaphor. In this way, Bevis superimposes three types of reality on the poet's work: the "res" or external physical reality; the harmonium, reality in a union of self and external world; and the *ding an sich*, an ultimate abstract reality. According to Bevis, metaphor is allied with the harmonium because metaphor is the basis of art and art the basis of harmonium. Stevens, then, lauds metaphor when he is in search of harmonium, but rejects it in his attempts to find the "res" or *ding an sich*. Like Frye, Bevis thinks that metaphor is for Stevens the human function of grasping relationships among externals, but unlike Frye and Sheehan, Bevis finds in Stevens's metaphors a substitute for knowledge that is "one of the tragedies of the human situation" (p. 38). If Bevis is inaccurate here, he is also incorrect in contending that the concrete in Stevens exists only through the abstractions of metaphor. Yet, he is more thorough in his description of the metaphoric process, because, unlike Frye, he recognizes that metaphor depends on the concrete in a relationship with the abstract that is not mere identity but a circular exchange of meaning between the concrete and abstract.

Although such a distinction is clear, Bevis's total thesis is not. Precisely how Stevens's theory of metaphor fits into Bevis's three types of reality is not clarified. The study attempts two separate tasks: to define the reality types in Stevens; and to examine metaphorical function. The two are uncomfortably combined when Bevis superimposes his three types on Stevens's multiple descriptions of trope function. Bevis's compartmentalization is far too rigid a system for Stevens's reality, metaphor, and art, three terms that the poet fluidly merges. Hayden Carruth best summarizes this fluidity when, in his review of "Three Academic Pieces" ("Ideality and Metaphor," *Poetry*, Aug. 1948), he suggests that, according to Stevens, "Reality is perceived through metaphors: life is known through metaphors in reality: life is ideal in metaphors of itself. Thus every metaphor is, in the broadest sense, an experience of life" (p. 271).

Like Frye before him, M. J. Collie ("The Rhetoric of Accurate Speech: A Note on the Poetry of Wallace Stevens," *Essays in Criticism*, Jan. 1962) praises Stevens's rhetorical skill and emphasizes metaphor as the poet's primary technique. Collie's assessment, however, moves toward the inaccurate when he comments that Stevens safeguarded the purity of our language—a glaring error when one considers some of the poet's effective but flamboyant wordplay. The critic is also off base when he suggests that Stevens, in attempting to avoid overstatement in rhetoric or misrepresentation through false metaphor, writes dry poems. The approach of this study in general is superficial. Although Collie accurately notes that Stevens's poetics include a concern with the appropriateness of language, the critic never develops his potentially elucidating hypothesis that Stevens attempts to achieve an order in language which is related to his sense of order in reality and his search for the supreme fiction, itself a nonstatic ultimate order.

Daniel P. Tompkins's study, " 'To Abstract Reality': Abstract Language and the Intrusion of Consciousness in Wallace Stevens" (*American Literature*, Mar. 1973), is more exact in specifying stylistic components in the poet. Unlike critics on metaphor such as J. Hillis Miller, Tompkins thinks Stevens is concerned primarily with abstraction rather than concrete reality. According to Tompkins, this concern is manifested in three elements of language which communicate abstraction: abstract diction, aphoristic statements, and the verb "to be." Tompkins defines abstraction in Stevens as "the act of seeking out resemblances in a group of heterogeneous items, and summarizing them in an 'abstract' noun" (p. 85). This technique, Tompkins suggests, resembles metaphor in that it establishes a resemblance between two classes and thereby creates a third class. But, Tompkins asserts, when this abstraction pushes toward identification, the poet reaches the "vanishing point of resemblance" where metaphor and the imagination fail. The study is strongest in such attempts to relate the poet's mechanics and ideas.

A final approach to Stevens's use of metaphor may be found in critics who focus on individual poems and the trope as primary technique in these poems. Price Caldwell's "Metaphoric Structure in Wallace Stevens' 'Thirteen Ways of Looking at a Blackbird' " (*Journal of English and Germanic Philology*, Spring 1972) is one of the best of these. Caldwell examines the structure of the much anthologized Blackbird poem and analyzes it as a demonstration of the poet's ideas on the nature and use of metaphor, a subject which, according to Caldwell, reveals the principle behind the stanza orderings. Caldwell cites passages from Stevens in which the poet discusses a theory of metaphor based on resemblance, but Caldwell extends the poet's comments and astutely suggests that the interaction of reality and imagination in Stevens is comparable to the interaction between two terms of a metaphor. In the poem itself, each stanza is a metaphor with two terms corresponding to imagination and reality, idea and thing, invisible and visible; and each interaction of terms resolves itself into thing as idea or idea as thing. By specifying this interaction, Caldwell's study provides a unique and absorbing perspective on the poem, but approaches overreading when it suggests dialectical, symmetrical, logical, parallel, and pyramidal methods of development. Stevens would have quaked at such a rigid structure, but would have delighted in Caldwell's approach which reads the poem as a survey of ways metaphor works.

I

Among twenty snowy mountains,
The only moving thing
Was the eye of the blackbird.

II

I was of three minds,
Like a tree
In which there are three blackbirds.

III

The blackbird whirled in the autumn winds.
It was a small part of the pantomime.

IV

A man and a woman
Are one.
A man and a woman and a blackbird
Are one.

V

I do not know which to prefer,
The beauty of inflections
Or the beauty of innuendoes,
The blackbird whistling
Or just after.

VI

Icicles filled the long window
With barbaric glass.
The shadow of the blackbird
Crossed it, to and fro.
The mood
Traced in the shadow
An indecipherable cause.

VII

O thin men of Haddam,
Why do you imagine golden birds?
Do you not see how the blackbird
Walks around the feet
Of the women about you?

VIII

I know noble accents
And lucid, inescapable rhythms;
But I know, too,
That the blackbird is involved
In what I know.

IX

When the blackbird flew out of sight,
It marked the edge
Of one of many circles.

X

At the sight of blackbirds
Flying in a green light,
Even the bawds of euphony
Would cry out sharply.

XI

He rode over Connecticut
In a glass coach.
Once, a fear pierced him,
In that he mistook
The shadow of his equipage
For blackbirds.

XII

The river is moving.
The blackbird must be flying.

XIII

It was evening all afternoon.
It was snowing
And it was going to snow.
The blackbird sat
In the cedar-limbs.

Caldwell concludes that the poetic exercise of using metaphor in "Thirteen Ways" operates as an interaction of external and internal world viewed here as thirteen structured portraits of a bird, but also thirteen vignettes of imagination and reality mingling metaphorically.

Confronted by Stevens's concern with language, other critics have approached its poetic manifestation through the poet's images rather than through his metaphors. Edward Kessler's book-length study, *Images of Wallace Stevens* (1972), suggests that Stevens employs images purely for themselves but arranges his poems around recurring patterns of imagery. Kessler borrows Suzanne Langer's term "art symbols" to describe Stevens's images as figures that carry import rather than meaning, but he foolishly strays from his defined emphasis when he asserts that in Stevens metaphors become symbols because repeated images evoke associations which increase a metaphor's work load. The equation of metaphor and symbol is misleading as are many of Kessler's explications. He accurately isolates many of Stevens's more important image clusters—north and south, sun and moon, music and sea, statue and wilderness, and colors—but when he attempts to discuss these in individual poems, his interpretations are faulty. Kessler simplistically views "Farewell to Florida" as a poem written when the poet was in a bad mood; "The World as Meditation" as a hymn to Penelope's immortality; "The Idea of Order at Key

West" as an invocation of music; and the late rock poems as testaments that Stevens's definition of nobility is also a definition of god.

Although Kessler is able to define the parameters of Stevens's images such as the female and the statue, he is more troubled by complex images such as the sun-moon constellation, music as art form, and varying referents of color. Kessler contradicts himself by noting that the sun is associated in Stevens with the imagination; the moon is associated with the romantic imagination; the moon is stripped of its romantic associations; and the two images are in opposition. Then he attempts to extricate himself from his critical entanglement by psychoanalyzing Stevens as a poet whose conscious mind resented any subconscious identification with the female moon. He reviews Stevens's "The Comedian as the Letter C" and "Peter Quince at the Clavier" as examples of musical theme, but neglects the poet's use of music in the form, composition, word choice, and rhythm of the poems. In this way Kessler misses one of the most obvious and most important extensions of the poet's images: Stevens's images are often reified because they are thematically embodied and technically evoked through the re-creation of the image's original form. And, even in his examination of color imagery, Kessler superficially counts the occurrence of color combinations but is apparently unable to perceive the complexity of the poet's nonsymbolic color manipulations.

In general, Kessler's method of looking at bits of poems, intermingling quotes from widely scattered years, and symbol-hunting is inadequate. This method obviously takes words and phrases out of context, distorts the meaning of the poem as a whole, lacks unity and cohesiveness necessary for readability, and fails to reintegrate the decreated pieces, leaving the reader with more questions than answers. Thoroughness is sacrificed for thematic unity, but Kessler's thematic emphasis fails to expose or penetrate a meaning in many of the cursorily viewed poems. Encompassing generalizations are formulated on the basis of selected quotes which may or may not be consistent with images elsewhere in the poetry. A reader unfamiliar with Stevens could be greatly hampered by all but Kessler's table of contents. The delineation of subjects in this table is as enlightening as its often inaccurate expansion in the study. And, in the table of contents, one can at least be spared the out-of-context quotations and extended overreadings that characterize the chapters.

Eugene Paul Nassar's *Wallace Stevens: An Anatomy of Figuration* (1965) also examines Stevens's images, but terms them figures, and approaches them through purported explications of the text.

Nassar chooses the label "figure" for Stevens's images because he
describes them as emblems lacking the reverberations of metaphoric or symbolic associations. According to Nassar, Stevens limits rather than expands his figures when he chooses this nonasso-
ciational mode. The poet abstracts from a figure its essence which
then serves a doctrinal function. Such figures the critic divides into
types: figures of the mind—imagination and reason; figures of
disorder—reality and chaos; figures of order—all arrangements; and
figures of change such as the wheel and fire. Throughout each of
the chapters which discusses these types, Nassar relies heavily on
overgeneralizations and direct symbolic equations. The critic himself warns against such one-to-one correspondences, but only after
he has described white and black as pernicious polarities of the
mind's mood. He falsely concludes that all arrangements such as
coiffures, crowns, and bouquets are false, but inconsistently suggests that unarranged elements of reality "get out of control."
Even more irritating are the critic's meaningful comments which
are never expanded. In his discussion of figures of change, Nassar
notes that the poet manipulates archetypal figures to represent eter-
nal change. The idea is an interesting one, and certainly a potentially useful one. Nassar briefly mentions examples of a few archetypal symbols, but fails to provide any discussion of these.
    After identifying such figures, the critic turns, in part 2 of his
study, to an examination of structural figurations as they are manifested in the duplicity of Stevens's attitudes and emotions evident
in some of his best poems. In this part Nassar contends that poems
such as "Peter Quince at the Clavier," "Le Monocle de Mon
Oncle," "The Comedian as the Letter C," "Credences of Summer," and "Notes Toward a Supreme Fiction" express a double
vision. In "Peter Quince" this duplicity takes the form of two con-
current themes, the fate of man and the process of the imagination.

I

Just as my fingers on these keys
Make music, so the selfsame sounds
On my spirit make a music, too.

Music is feeling, then, not sound;
And thus it is that what I feel,
Here in this room, desiring you,

Thinking of your blue-shadowed silk,
Is music. It is like the strain
Waked in the elders by Susanna.

Of a green evening, clear and warm,
She bathed in her still garden, while
The red-eyed elders watching, felt

The basses of their beings throb
In witching chords, and their thin blood
Pulse pizzicati of Hosanna.

II

In the green water, clear and warm,
Susanna lay.
She searched
The touch of springs,
And found
Concealed imaginings.
She sighed,
For so much melody.

Upon the bank, she stood
In the cool
Of spent emotions.
She felt, among the leaves,
The dew
Of old devotions.

She walked upon the grass,
Still quavering.
The winds were like her maids,
On timid feet,
Fetching her woven scarves,
Yet wavering.

A breath upon her hand
Muted the night.
She turned—
A cymbal crashed,
And roaring horns.

III

Soon, with a noise like tambourines,
Came her attendant Byzantines.

They wondered why Susanna cried
Against the elders by her side;

And as they whispered, the refrain
Was like a willow swept by rain.

Anon, their lamps' uplifted flame
Revealed Susanna and her shame.

And then, the simpering Byzantines
Fled, with a noise like tambourines.

IV

Beauty is momentary in the mind—
The fitful tracing of a portal;
But in the flesh it is immortal.

The body dies; the body's beauty lives.
So evenings die, in their green going,
A wave, interminably flowing.
So gardens die, their meek breath scenting
The cowl of winter, done repenting.
So maidens die, to the auroral
Celebration of a maiden's choral.

Susanna's music touched the bawdy strings
Of those white elders; but, escaping,
Left only Death's ironic scraping.
Now, in its immortality, it plays
On the clear viol of her memory,
And makes a constant sacrament of praise.

After this introduction, Nassar's comments on the poem deteriorate when he describes Susanna as the raped and murdered heroine, and when he fails to describe any of the sensual and musical elements in the verse. This omission reduces the poem and its characters to figures representing unexplained, theoretical constructs. At best the explications to follow this one are uneven in quality. Nassar accurately identifies the dual dramatic and doctrinal progression in "The Comedian as the Letter C," but inexcusably superimposes a rigid symbolic interpretation on the four daughter figures of the poem. Similarly, he appropriately suggests the complexity of meaning in the three section labels of "Notes Toward a Supreme Fiction," but assesses the poem as a fragmentary, unsure, uncommunicative piece about desperation and chaos. At his strongest when he attempts to isolate in the poetry the ambiguities and inconsistencies in Stevens's attitude toward language and

poetry, Nassar errs significantly when he strays from this subject
into speculations about the poet's mind. In such moments of weakness he suggests that Stevens's mind cannot help create images of
itself; that in Stevens metaphor is always evasive; and that Stevens
himself longed for a religious belief that promised transcendence.
This study in its very theoretical framework is also flawed: Nassar
attempts to formalize a theory of poetic figures as representational
and definable counters, then he builds on this assumption, explicating poems as accumulations of such counters. The critical method
approaches allegorical interpretation, but the poet never wrote allegory. Even more weakening is an early and damaging omission;
Nassar never defines what he means by the word "figure."

Northrop Frye's discussion of Stevens's images ("Wallace Stevens and the Variation Form," 1973) is far more to the point. In
an analysis of Stevens's variation form Frye suggests that this form
is a "generic application of the principle that every image in a
poem is a variation of the theme or subject of that poem" (p. 396).
Frye cites Stevens's own opinion, voiced in "Effects of Analogy,"
that every image restates the attitude of the poet toward the subject of the image, and that every image is the image maker's intervention in reality. Images and poems then become variations
wrought by the imagination on the theme of reality. This image
making process depends for constancy on reality as a stabilizing
principle amid all of the poetic variations. While describing this
process, Frye accurately lists some of the characteristics of Stevens's reality-imagination interplay. According to the critic, these
two elements may be in opposition; the imagination may intensify
reality by emphasizing unreal aspects; it may function as the informing principle of reality; and it may inform reality through fictions and myths.

Mildred E. Hartsock in "Image and Idea in the Poetry of Stevens" (*Twentieth Century Literature*, April 1961) is less concerned with the theory behind the poet's image making, and more
concerned with identifying recurrent images as well as their relationship to the poet's belief. She defines the real for Stevens as
a dichotomy which includes the inner world of the mind and
poetic image as well as the external word. To Hartsock, the nature
of this reality, the theme of many poems, is expressed in images
which are associated with certain aspects of reality. As examples of
how Stevens's images and ideas merge, she cites the image of winter associated with the reality of bare fact and the image of ironi-
cal, professional clergymen associated with Stevens's doubt of traditional religion. Rather than suggest symbol equations, Hartsock

suggests associations: a concern about mortality with images of hair; a confrontation of man's mortality with images of nothingness; a preoccupation with reality in images of fruit, flowers, and exotic birds; and a similar preoccupation with imagination in images of music, clouds, and air. She perceptively notes Stevens's late search for value in the "idea" of things, a search which creates the weakness of the late poetry, too obsessed with belief in ideas and unable to objectify such abstractions in concrete imagery.

Morton Zabel's early study, "Wallace Stevens and the Image of Man" (originally published in the *Harvard Advocate*, December 1940, but revised and expanded to be reprinted in *Wallace Stevens*, ed. Marie Borroff, 1963), is even more specific in its approach to Stevens's imagery. According to Zabel, Stevens's poetry is distinguished from that of his contemporaries by the richness of his imagery and the confidence of his rhetoric. These images balance the intellectual and realistic functions of metaphor in a style that combines Mallarmé's imagery of "disciplined intuitive intellection" and Hopkins's imagery of "instinctual actuality" (p. 154). It is, according to Zabel, imagery of "aesthetic fastidiousness, tropical splendor, and privileged taste" (p. 154), yet imagery communicating a sense of chaos, confusion, decadence, and waste. Stevens handles these antithetical forces in life by forging images to communicate man's rage for order in conflict with images of man's confusion amid his phenomenal experience. According to Zabel, the early images are saved from elaborate triviality by the poet's use of wit, irony, urbanity, and compassion, while the later images move away from the early sensory realism toward speculation and abstraction. Zabel also suggests that as Stevens's verse became more philosophic, his images lost the wit and inventiveness that characterized them earlier. And, ultimately, to Zabel, the goal of Stevens's poetic search is an image of man, who, denied recourse to a superhuman authority, could make the human position credible by using the imagination. In this final thought Zabel laid the groundwork for future studies on Stevens's image of man as hero and mortal.

Techniques Reflecting a Comic Vision: Poetic and Dramatic Wit

Critics who examine Stevens's view of man have attempted to explain why the poet lacks the pessimism of many other twentieth-century writers. Among these critics, two have completed book-length studies on the comic vision which allows Stevens his opti-

mistic view of man. Both of these critics turn to the poetic techniques in search of stylistic evidence for this optimism. The earliest
of these studies, Robert Pack's *Wallace Stevens: An Approach
to His Poetry and Thought* (1958), asserts that Stevens regards
the antinomy of reality and imagination as a flourishing of human
consciousness which demands a comic rather than academic or
aesthetic approach. As defined by Pack, the comic imagination
fixes itself on common, practical things of ordinary life. Stevens's
world is itself comic because it contains no tragic necessity. The
characters, Pack continues, operate as abstractions in the mind
rather than the real world, and transfer the reader's focus from the
self of persona into a larger poetic context. Pack extends this comic
theme in his discussion of secular mystery in Stevens, a subject the
poet faced with comic vision when he recognized that man might
be dwarfed by reality, but had to find his paradise in this real
world. And, Pack finds the unity typical of comedy in Stevens's
view of reality as correspondences and resemblances. Yet, when
Pack attempts to relate this comic spirit to poetic practice, he
names many of the poet's techniques—irregular rhymes, sound clusters, invented or combined words, verbal wit, ironic tone, variation structure, imitation of musical form—but is unable to conclude
how these contribute to or compose the "comic spirit." Pack obviously uses "comedy" in its broadest sense, but by labeling Stevens a comic poet, the critic by emphasis ignores the darker, more
pensive ruminations of this poet. Stevens's comic vision becomes
for Pack a blind but joyful poetic acceptance of the world as it is.
This opinion not only falsely limits the scope of the poet, but exemplifies the critic's limit in dealing with poetic complexity. Because of this limitation and an attempt to label too many disparate
aspects of Stevens as "comic," Pack leaves his reader with little
more than the superficial conclusion that Stevens proposes, in his
witty verse, a version of earthly paradise.

Daniel Fuchs (*The Comic Spirit of Wallace Stevens*, 1963)
also dilutes his study with considerations other than the comic
strain in the poet. Taking Pack's lead, Fuchs thinks that Stevens
achieved comic effect through language that asserts the power of
poetry. But, unlike Pack, Fuchs traces this comic mode to what
he terms Stevens's alienation from and scorn for an American lack
of refinement, as well as to what he considers Stevens's uneasiness
at being a poet. To cope with such alienation and uneasiness the
poet develops comic masks typical of a dandy. According to
Fuchs, these masks provide an affected way of communicating

what is genuine, but they also provide a sense of drama issuing from the tension between seriousness and the deflation of grandeur. Although Fuchs accurately describes this style as a method of wit, he judges it "hypercivilized, perverse, confusing, and erudite" (p. 29) without explaining his scathing comments. And, although Fuchs attempts to relate this wit to the style of Baudelaire, Laforgue, Meredith, Molière, and Eliot, he confuses the dandyism he finds in the poetry with Stevens's own way of life. Tangentially he cites the poet's expensive clothes as evidence of Stevens's affectation, which translates, according to Fuchs, into the "bizarre" style of *Harmonium*.

After establishing what he believes to be Stevens's comic milieu, Fuchs examines "The Comedian as the Letter C" as a spiritual autobiography and mock-heroic *Prelude*, but ignores the contradictions in these two labels and fails to resolve his inconsistent characterizations of Crispin as Stevens himself and Crispin as a man retreating from poetry. More emphasis by Fuchs on "The Comedian" as a comedy and Crispin as a comic hero would have been helpful. With this and other poems, Fuchs, like so many Stevens critics, quotes and paraphrases extensively. The critic would like to let the poetry speak for itself, but in so doing, he evades definitive statement about the verse.

The study is marred, however, by a more serious problem. If the reader accepts the title of Fuchs's book as an indication of the critic's focus, that reader is sorely disappointed. Fuchs leaves his avowed subject for wanderings into the definition of modern poetry, into Stevens's concern with imagination and reality, into the inadequacies of the romantic imagination, and into the poet's platonic and antiplatonic ideas. If the latter three themes are related in passing to Stevens's comic spirit, the first one, modern poetry, is discussed more fully but only in an indirect way. According to Fuchs, modern poetry is a poetry opposed to the verse which preceded it but a poetry based on the rejection of attitudes implicit in that older poetry. It is also, according to Fuchs, modern in a historical sense, having been written in the last fifty years. In developing this discussion, Fuchs inconsistently, at various times, calls Donne, Wordsworth, Coleridge, and Whitman modern. If one is able to wade through an inadequate definition and multiple misapplications of the term, Fuchs's ultimate point—that Stevens's satiric wit issues from a juxtaposition of modernity's outdated moral idealism and the mundane contemporary world—is a valid one.

In a far more honorific assessment of early Stevens, Harriet
Monroe (*Poets and Their Art*, 1926, pp. 39–45) more concisely
states what Fuchs expands into diluted half truths and misreadings. According to Monroe, Stevens is a profound humorist in the
company of Cervantes and Shakespeare; his poem "The Comedian
as the Letter C" is the poet's most complete assertion of "cosmic
humor"; and his recognition of beauty amid mortal imperfection
is confronted with laughter.

Techniques in General Style: Interaction of Theory, Poet, and Reader

More generally, critics have attempted to summarize not just
Stevens's comic mode, but his overall style. One of these, Lionel
Abel ("In the Sacred Park," *Partisan Review*, Winter 1958), disagrees with Fuchs's later emphasis on Stevens's firm place in the
modernist tradition. Abel contends that Stevens's poetry, unlike
other modern poetry, is unconcerned with a vindication of the poet's vocation. This freed Stevens to focus on the content of his art.
The conclusion that Stevens did focus on his art is accurate, but
the premise, that he was not concerned with the poet's vocation,
is erroneous. Abel also misjudges the poet when he labels him an
amateur in need of inspiration, but establishes an acceptable approach to the poet when he identifies Stevens's techniques and
examines how they interact with the poetry's content. The most
notable of these techniques Abel defines as characterized by
archaic and foreign vocabulary, heavy pigmentation, meditative
and leisurely mood, juxtaposition through verbs, and abundance of
figures with positive associations. Abel thinks that through such
techniques Stevens's subject matter is transformed into a light and
frivolous "language of vacations." This hypothesis in no way accounts for the meditative Stevens of the later years.

Samuel French Morse's "Wallace Stevens: Some Ideas About
the Thing Itself" (*Boston University Studies in English*, Spring
1956) precedes Abel's article in asserting that Stevens's strategy
includes combining poetic theory and practice in a playful, somewhat odd vocabulary. Morse extends this by describing Stevens's
use of language and by concluding that the combined theory and
practice imply a respect for poetry as process and poet as maker.
The point is well taken, as is Morse's undeveloped but critically
popular idea that Stevens belongs to the tradition of comedy.

Adding a third dimension to the critical concern with the role
of poet and poetic technique in the poem, some more recent

critics have included the reader as an active participant in Stevens's poetic manipulations. Richard Blessing in "Wallace Stevens and the Necessary Reader: A Technique of Dynamism" (*Twentieth Century Literature*, Jan. 1972), asserts that the twentieth-century artist must attempt to symbolize life that is motion in order to communicate concretely the dynamic energy in modern experience. Stevens is, according to Blessing, the most successful modern poet in creating an artistic experience infused with this "motion of life." This dynamism is achieved in Stevens's poems when the poet forces the reader to participate.

As an example of this technique, Blessing cites "The Snow Man," a poem in which the reader is forced to think about and thereby participate in the reality of imagined winter. Stevens plays the same game in "Study of Two Pears," a poem, according to Blessing, in which the language of description becomes more alive, the individual poems themselves take on life, and the narrator as well as the reader become obsessed with proliferating resemblances. In this way both narrator and reader learn that observation is active rather than passive. The technique in these poems reminds Blessing of Stevens's dynamic relationship between objects and observers. These poems become symbols of the ever changing relationship between mind and world, and therefore depend on the reader's mind for completion. By summarizing this technique as a trick in Stevens's illusionist's act, Blessing sells the poet short. According to Blessing, Stevens uses this trick to conjure a symbolic structure made of nothing but moving space. This conclusion is not supported by evidence Blessing cites in his study, nor is it supported by the verbal and visual maneuvers of a poet who delves into many dimensions of art. Blessing's remarks provide an interesting and refreshing approach to the poems through their readers, but hardly equal the sum of his conclusion.

Stevens on Man: The Hero

Frank Doggett in "Wallace Stevens' Secrecy of Words: A Note on Import in Poetry" (*New England Quarterly*, Sept. 1958) preceded Blessing in his thesis that many of Stevens's poems resemble discourse with the reader. Doggett relates this not to the verbal trickery Blessing intimates, but to a concept of selfhood found in Stevens. In brief, Doggett thinks that many of Stevens's poems are about the relation of the interior self with the external world. This focus is indicative of critics who search for Stevens's

view of man, a view they usually find expressed in the term
"hero."

The Hero as Human

One critic, James E. Mulqueen ("Man and Cosmic Man in
the Poetry of Wallace Stevens" *South Dakota Review*, Summer
1973) goes so far as to suggest that the subject of all Stevens poetry
is man, a figure symbolized as archetypal Cosmic Man. According
to this approach, many Stevens poems attempt to reconcile the
symbolic human who contains the entire cosmos, Cosmic Man,
with the embodiment of each individual's awareness of self. Syn-
onymously, Mulqueen uses man, giant, and poem as one concept,
"the sum of all the individual expressions of man's concept of himself" (p. 17), and draws on poems such as "Chocourua to Its
Neighbor," "A Rabbit as King of the Ghosts," "The Man with
the Blue Guitar," and "A Thought Revolved" to describe the
different aspects of man-giant-poem. In times of war this Cosmic
Man takes the form of a heroic soldier, a hero who, according to
Stevens, is not a human embodiment, but an essence of heroism.
To Mulqueen then, a hero is an idea, emotion, or feeling; a part of
each self and not one figure; and one stage of the self's imaginative
journey toward self-recognition. Mulqueen summarizes his argument by stating that Stevens uses the Cosmic Man as a modern
version of an ancient and universal symbol. If this conclusion and
the description on which it is based are accurate, Mulqueen's distinctions between man, Cosmic Man, and hero are never clearly
defined. He relates the hero of modern war to nationalism and
individualism, but fails to note how this hero differs from the
mythic, cosmic figure he describes.

John Warren Beach in "The Hero" (1960) describes the concept of hero as it is used in the American poetry written in periods
of twentieth-century war. Like Mulqueen, Beach interprets Stevens's "Examination of the Hero in a Time of War" as an examination of the heroic image created by the popular imagination, and
like Mulqueen, Beach defines this figure as greater than life-size
but associated with feeling. Stevens himself refuses to pass judgment on this figure because, according to Beach, as poet he is too
"cold." This assessment is incorrect. The dualism of imagination
and reality as well as the human need for fictions, such as heroes,
preclude for Stevens the need to judge the rightness or wrongness
of these issues. Aptly comparing Stevens's hero to Marianne

Moore's, Beach unfortunately wanders into an assessment of Stevens's aesthetic preciosity and thereby abandons any thoroughness in his definition of Stevens's hero.

The Hero as Spirit

All critics do not agree that this hero is a greater than life composite of feeling. While some emphasize the humanity of this figure, others emphasize a spiritual quality. Alan Perlis (*Wallace Stevens: A World of Transforming Shapes*) and Hi Simons ("The Humanism of Wallace Stevens," *Poetry* Nov. 1942) contend that Stevens creates a hero who is a part of daily life. Simons suggests this early by emphasizing the trivial acts in which the hero participates, and Perlis extends it by emphasizing the ordinary and real in the figure. According to Perlis, Stevens's hero evolves out of man, from the "quintessence" of his place and time, and as a part of all Stevens's personae. Trying to balance the best of both worlds, Perlis also notes that the Stevens hero is bodiless, a point at which the imagination and reality can meet, and therefore an ideal poet. In the entire *Collected Poems* Perlis finds only two figures who achieve this ultimate physical and spiritual stance, Santayana in "To an Old Philosopher in Rome" and Stevens himself as old poet in the autobiographical poems of *The Rock*.

Robert Pack's "The Abstracting Imagination of Wallace Stevens: Nothingness and the Hero" (*Arizona Quarterly*, Autumn 1955), emphasizes the spiritual side of this figure. According to Pack, "Wallace Stevens' hero is not a man among us, but an idea beyond us," existing as an abstraction that encompasses all individuals and all human possibilities. Pack confuses this hero with Crispin, Stevens's comedian, because according to Pack the hero is all things to all people, a reflection of the world, a myth of self, a concretization of the ideal, and a reflection of belief in the infinite possibilities of man and his imagination. Crispin is hardly such a symbolic—or totally serious—figure.

The Hero as Poet

Sounding a note Perlis's very recent study echoes, critics such as Arthur M. Sampley ("Wallace Stevens: Executive as Poet," *Midwest Quarterly*, Jan. 1972); Thomas B. Whitbread ("The Poet-Readers of Wallace Stevens," 1962); Denis Donoghue (*The Ordinary Universe: Soundings in Modern Literature*, pp. 267–90); and

Joseph N. Riddel ("Wallace Stevens' 'Notes Toward a Supreme Fiction'," *Wisconsin Studies in Contemporary Literature*, Spring-Summer 1961) emphasize not the human or spirit but the poet in the hero figure. Sampley's study is multiple in purpose: he relates Stevens's position as insurance executive to a need for imaginative power; reviews the poet's concepts, evil and pain, as materialistic; and finally attempts a definition of Stevens's hero. To unify this topic with his subject, executive as poet, Sampley must speculate about Stevens's business philosophy. Because of this questionable approach, Sampley judges the Stevens hero pragmatically dictated by the poet–executive's opinion that important matters should be assigned to "superior men." The source of Sampley's inside information is never revealed. The Stevens major man is to Sampley a combination of Plato's philosopher–king. Nietzche's superman, and Stevens's own aspirations as creative poet. To Sampley, major man gives form to reality but also inspires enthusiasm for reality by providing life with a "national image," "zest," and "sparkle." Sampley's word choice is inane. Stevens would shudder at the adjectives this critic uses to describe a confabulated major man who in this study appears as a well-polished, public-relations-oriented, cardboard Mr. America.

Thomas B. Whitbread also finds the ideal poet and complete hero in Stevens's poetry, but examines this figure in one of Stevens's more unfamiliar and less successful poems, "Large Red Man Reading." The large red man for Whitbread expresses the faithful rendering of imagination and reality, exemplifies being, and communicates the life of feeling. Denis Donoghue finds the same poet–hero in "Notes Toward a Supreme Fiction," and accurately defines this major man as an issue of the meditative imagination, a portion of each individual, and a concept that defies fixity of name or limitation. Joseph N. Riddel's brief discussion of this figure is one of the earliest and the most cogent. According to Riddel, the major man who takes the name of MacCullough in "Notes" is a humanistic combination of finite man and infinite idea; a merging of poet and poetic creation; part of the search for a man–hero to replace god–hero; and a symbol for intercourse between the self and world.

Stevens on Man: The Mortal

This emphasis on interacting self and world is also noted by critics who emphasize not the superhuman but the very human in

Stevens's verse. Most of these critics find in the poet a concern with mortality. Frederick J. Hoffman ("Mortality and Modern Literature," 1959) offers some basic assumptions about death in modern literature. According to Hoffman, in the twentieth century death is no longer a moment in our progress to eternity. Denied immortality, individuals are lodged in and concerned with time which has become spatial rather than lineal, an ontology of objects and experiences that replaces the metaphysics of the infinite. In this state, death artistically takes the form of realistic images such as the conqueror-worm and physical dissolution, or of idealistic images in which physical dissolution is replaced by spiritual beginnings. These assumptions Hoffman applies to Stevens's "Sunday Morning," a poem in which death is a state in time associated with the beauty and experience of present objects. For Hoffman, Stevens, like other twentieth-century writers, creates such a state because post mortem paradise is no longer believable.

Michael Zimmerman, in "The Pursuit of Pleasure and the Uses of Death: Wallace Stevens' 'Sunday Morning' " (*University Review, Winter* 1966), also discusses Stevens's general approach to mortality as the theme is expressed in a poem such as "Sunday Morning." He finds in the female persona of the poem a fear of death coupled with a desire for immortality complicated by her alienation from traditional religion. The persona's conflict he attempts to explain using theory from Norman O. Brown's *Life Against Death*. This psychoanalytic approach adds nothing to the poem and adds nothing to Zimmerman's basic assumption that the poem expresses a tie between man's experience of pleasure and recognition of death. Zimmerman accurately summarizes Stevens's belief that to affirm the pleasure of life one must affirm death as an inherent part of that life. But Zimmerman's specific conclusion, that the poem is a sermon on the inseparableness of life and death rather than a hedonistic exercise, gains little from a psychoanalytic approach.

In other poems such as "Flyer's Fall" and "The Owl in the Sarcophagus," Thomas Whitbread ("Wallace Stevens' 'Highest Candle'," *Texas Studies in Literature and Language,* Winter 1963), looking at specific examples of a general view, finds a more reverential awe in the poet's attitude toward death. According to Whitbread, death becomes a godlike power that inspires in Stevens the creation of a mythology of modern death. Confusingly, Whitbread thinks Stevens himself did not believe in the figure of death he as poet created for his source and end of belief. This seeming ambiguity is never clarified by the critic.

Death in the Cemetery

Most critics who attack the issue, Stevens's approach to mortality, do so not through general statement of theme but by explicating specific poems such as "Like Decorations in a Nigger Cemetery," "The Emperor of Ice-Cream" or selections from the late volume, *The Rock*. The most cogent statement on "Decorations" is made by Helen Hennessy Vendler in "Stevens' 'Like Decorations in a Nigger Cemetery'" (*Massachusetts Review*, Winter 1966). Vendler thinks that the title of the poem is an ellipsis for "My poems are like decorations in a Nigger Cemetery," and that the poem itself is an experiment in poetry as epigram. According to Vendler, the subject of the poem is not just physical death but a death that means simply not living in the physical world. The odd, epigrammatic quality of the poem is produced by an omission of verbs which contributes to a sense of incompleteness and aridity. In expanded form, most of Vendler's comments may also be found in her later study, *On Extended Wings* (1969), discussed in chapter 1.

Paul McBrearty provides a more extended but less precise analysis of "Decorations" in his "Wallace Stevens's 'Like Decorations in a Nigger Cemetery': Notes toward an Explication" (*Texas Studies in Language and Literature*, Summer 1973). Like Vendler before him, McBrearty contends that the poem is about death and dying, but unlike Vendler and untrue to Stevens's emphasis, McBrearty asserts that death in Stevens is a passage to nothingness and an end of everything. McBrearty also disagrees with Vendler in his assessment of the poem's structure, according to McBrearty, a series of meditations. Vendler criticizes the same poem for its lack of progressive, meditative development. McBrearty, however, accurately notes that Stevens interweaves the theme of death with his reality and imagination theme, a natural combination because of the poet's belief that the imagination is the power by which man contemplates reality, including death, with calmness and resignation. The fifty fragmentary poems are, in McBrearty's view, representative of the littering leaves associated with death and the shabby, broken monuments found in a cemetery, all attempts to give death meaning. McBrearty takes the poem stanza by stanza and provides an interpretation that draws from glossary comments Stevens made in various letters that discussed the poem; and he concludes that the "resigned stoicism" at the poem's end is indicative of Stevens's optimistic approach to death, an approach that acknowledges death's ugliness but in the face of it, asserts the advantages of living.

Long before McBrearty's study, Ardyth Bradley suggests many of the same ideas. In "Wallace Stevens' Decorations" (*Twentieth-Century Literature*, Oct. 1961) Bradley cites four major themes in Stevens: the omnipresent dichotomy and interdependence of life and death; the interactional reality and imagination; the loss of the imagination's vitality in the twentieth century; and the necessity of living and creating in the present. Having noted these, Bradley explicates "Decorations" as a poetic example of such themes.

Death and the Emperor

While "Decorations" has attracted scattered critical attention to its death theme, another poem, "The Emperor of Ice-Cream" has also been the object of similar analyses. One of the earlier examinations of the poem is provided by Richard Ellmann in "Wallace Stevens' Ice Cream" (*Kenyon Review*, Winter 1957). In poems such as "The Death of a Soldier," "Cortège for Rosenbloom," and "The Emperor of Ice-Cream," Ellmann locates the poet's approach to death and describes it as feelings of horror and fear coupled with an acceptance of death's place apart from life. This latter opinion is wrong; Stevens repeatedly intimates that death is a part of life. Ellmann confines most of his comments to Stevens's earliest volume *Harmonium* in which "Cortège" specifies the wrong way to conduct a funeral and "The Emperor" balances it with suggestions for the right way. To Ellmann, *Harmonium* is a volume unified by the poet's theme, the acceptance of death. Ellmann is so convinced that this is a pervasive concern that he describes all of Stevens's late poetry as verse about the major presence of death.

"Wallace Stevens' Emperor" (*Criticism*, Winter 1960) by Taylor Culbert and John M. Violette is concerned entirely with "The Emperor of Ice-Cream," but is a study filled with incorrect assumptions and inaccurate interpretive statements. In a too literal reading, this study describes the emperor as a ruler of a land filled with people he does not respect. Through this interpretation Culbert and Violette reaffirm the respect for death in the poem, though they never stipulate how their absurdly contemptible subjects reveal the poet's respect for death.

Michael Zimmerman's "Wallace Stevens' Emperor" (*English Language Notes*, Dec. 1966) acknowledges earlier critics who have stressed the emperor's relationship with death, but proposes another alternative, an emperor related to the imagination. According to Zimmerman, Stevens shows the reader a man imagining a funny funeral. This interpretation places the entire poem within a persona's mind, but Zimmerman fails to describe this persona, and he fails to explain the passages in the poem that are obviously not funny. Zimmerman suggests that the imagination is a force that presses against death, a harmless suggestion until one reads Zimmerman's definition of the imagination as an abnormal force. Apparently Zimmerman read only selectively and superficially in Stevens. If most of the Stevens canon belies this "abnormal force" label, Stevens's individual poems such as "Cortège for Rosenbloom" clearly contradict Zimmerman's opinion that funerals in Stevens provide appropriate social forms for purging death of its terror.

Stuart Silverman's "The Emperor of Ice-Cream" (*Western Humanities Review*, Spring 1972) is also inadequate but for different reasons. Silverman accurately notes that "The Emperor," like many of Stevens's shorter poems, lacks a clear statement of the poem's subject, and that in this poem a tension exists between reality and appearance, beauty and ugliness, life and death. Out of this promising beginning, Silverman moves into symbol hunting, but even worse, exemplifies a critical inability to explain problematic images. As one of the most criticized and explicated of Stevens's poems, "The Emperor" suffers not only from simplistic disagreements about symbol referents but from overreadings that extend into and pollute other poems. Edward Neill's "The Melting Moment: Stevens' Rehabilitation of Ice Cream" (*Ariel*, Jan. 1973) goes ice-cream tasting and finds the "sugared void" not only as death in "The Emperor" but as an unexplained image in "The Comedian as the Letter C." The study is mentioned only as an example of critical perversion and as an inducement to laughter, for when Neill suggests that the corpse in "The Emperor" is a dead person who is too dead, we, like Stevens, must smile at man's inability to cope with the concept of mortality.

Death and the Rock

More generally, critics lodge Stevens's concern with mortality primarily in his last poems of *The Rock* period. In a book-length study examined in chapter 1, Merle Elliott Brown (*Wallace Stevens: The Poem as Act*, 1970) devotes an entire chapter to the characteristics of old age, a subject Stevens inherently bound with his thoughts about death. According to Brown, Stevens's poems of old age are written with a "savage and joyous imaginative awareness" (p. 176) of the withering process at the end of life. Brown tends to see shriveled bodies where there are none, and in so doing misreads poems such as "An Ordinary Evening in New Haven" as an expression of the "garrulousness" in old age. In such late poems, Brown isolates the poet's tendency to withdraw from objects around him and to merge opposing forces he had earlier placed in a dualism.

Ralph J. Mills in "Wallace Stevens: The Image of the Rock" (*Accent*, Spring 1958, reprinted with revisions in *Wallace Stevens*, ed. Marie Borroff, 1963) contends that the last poems are meditations on death in which the theme is time as death's instrument. Tracing the rock image through earlier poetry, Mills accurately associates the rock symbol with death and with reality, and states that man is able to "interpenetrate" life and death with his mind because the imagination imposes itself on and gives meaning to all that is real. Mills strays into speculations about Stevens's theology, rationalizing this digression as necessary to the understanding of Stevens's ideas on death. The relationship is, however, not clarified.

Isabel G. Maccaffrey's "A Point of Central Arrival: Stevens' *The Rock*" (*Journal of English Literary History*, Winter 1973) provides the most lucid and helpful explanation on this death topic. Maccaffrey views *The Rock* as "a final soliloquy, the concluding movement in the dialogue of a mind with itself" (p. 606), and as poems of old age that are about ends, beginnings, and ends that are beginnings. She describes the volume as "intimations of mortality [which] unite poet and reader in concern for their common fate" (p. 607). In Stevens's contemplations of his own death, Maccaffrey finds echoes of the dyings and rejuvenations of all men and all cultures. To Maccaffrey this death on a cosmic level is best embodied in *The Auroras of Autumn*, a volume in which the concerns of autumn, voiced as early as *Harmonium*, appear in the dying of day, year, and self. Finally, in *The Rock*, Stevens attains, for Maccaffrey, his final place, his completion metaphorically presented as a mountain vista from which the poet surveys the world of the past. And, in conclusion, she appropriately emphasizes that in late life Stevens did not turn to the sinister prophecy and apocalypse in a poet like Yeats, but to a Wordsworthian calmness, soberness, and certainty.

Frank Doggett's "Wallace Stevens' River that Flows Nowhere" (*Chicago Review*, Summer-Autumn 1962) more specifically relates these ideas to the passage of time when Doggett finds in Stevens a sense of the world "continually passing away." Doggett explains that because of the incessant passage of the present moment, the world is seen the moment after. Doggett's poet finds his own mortality in this flux because the passing of time is evidence of the approaching close of life. Thus, for Stevens, the life of experience is a life of changing self and each moment, a fresh beginning. Doggett develops this thesis when he describes the flux as characterized by paradoxes: moments in which an end and a beginning coexist and a flux progresses but never advances. This critic also perceptively notes that Stevens does not name this flux, but uses images that inspire a sense of change.

Nothingness

Extending the emphasis on mortality, transience, change, and death, several critics have looked beyond the "river that flows nowhere" described by critics like Doggett and Maccaffrey, and found what they term the "nothingness" in Stevens's poetry. Like the concept of death which must ultimately be described by critic and poet as an absence of certain qualities we term life, or as an unexpressible variation of that life, the concept of nothingness becomes for its reviewers an exercise in negative assertion: it can only be described by what it is not. The semantics of the subject are therefore inherently abstruse and imprecise. Two critics who attempt to explain the phenomenon of nothingness in Stevens must be noted. Early in the criticism, C. Roland Wagner's "The Idea of Nothingness in Wallace Stevens" (*Accent*, Spring 1952b) introduced the theory issue to the critical world. Wagner contends that Stevens uses the words "nothing" and "nothingness" to define an entire range of mortal man's moral and spiritual life, but Wagner directs the idea upward, suggesting that "nothing" in Stevens is a poetic expression of a supreme idea or god, a Plotinian means of fulfillment and extinction through and beyond the human. In brief, "nothingness" in Stevens is a blank, inhuman, amoral absolute, but according to Wagner this "nothingness" functions as a mediation between spirit and imagination; includes the religious notion of depletion for the sake of fulfillment; embodies the metaphysical notion of reality as purposeless and valueless; and emphasizes the necessity of stripping the self of comforting illusions in order to prepare the self for the contemplation of truth. Wagner fails to see that Stevens does not seek religious fulfillment, does not find reality purposeless, and does not posit belief in some form of truth. Finally, Wagner lists the possible meanings for "nothingness" and attempts to find these in various poems. As a term which to this critic may mean blank spirit, ultimate contemplation, absolute peace, self in awareness of others, moral disillusionment, objects of imagination with being but no existence, reality, and life, the term is meaningless. Wagner's comments about Stevens's "nothingness" are therefore ambiguous because they fail to explain the perceived conflicting uses of the term.

William Bevis's more recent "Stevens' Toneless Poetry" (*Journal of English Literary History*, Summer 1974) ties Stevens's ideas about nothingness with a purification of consciousness. According to Bevis, nothingness in Stevens is akin to a mood of ecstasy, a term defined by Bevis as a "state of consciousness lasting certainly no more than two hours and almost always less than one, during which the person feels independent of time and space" (p. 261). To Bevis this is an ecstatic experience also associated with a blurring of the border between self and world, and may be associated with either a joyous or detached mood. Bevis attempts to relate this altered state of consciousness to the poet's tone, or lack of it, and brazenly asserts that Stevens's poems are toneless because they articulate a nonfeeling state of consciousness. The critic translates this as communications from a poet who does not affirm, deny, and indeed, does not care.

If this all sounds rather murky and surreal, the reader should fear not, for Bevis explains the inability to understand this tone in Stevens as a function of reader naiveté about altered states of consciousness. Bevis's own state of consciousness (and presence of mind) must have been altered because the original focus on nothingness disappears amid the smoke of Bevis's theoretical issues, all more related to the metaphysics and psychology of mystical states than to the poetry itself. One might also quarrel with Bevis's basic assumption that a poem may be toneless and exemplify a total absence of feeling. And, one might question his emphasis on the mystical in the poet. Mystical carries with it an associated transcendence of reality which Stevens never expressed. By calling on modern, transcendental, drug-culture type metaphysics and perceptual psychology, Bevis's focus shifts away from Stevens to an intellectualizing on the ecstatic experience available to poet or abstract self. At best such external systems and interdisciplinary associations provide an unusual if tangential perspective on the poetics. While Bevis sheds light on neither the poet nor the poem, he does possibly illuminate his own sense of the mystical potential within man's consciousness. Stevens's own world view has, along the way, slipped into the smoke.

Perhaps it is fitting that a poet moves from an enthrallment with the vibrant, sensual world of youth to the somber considerations of mortality that age brings. Or perhaps it is even more fitting that a poet who accepts that mortality as one more aspect of life's experience should still look to some realm for a type of nonexperiential idea. Here, though the critics have yet to locate it, Stevens delved into nothingness. If the critics are more inadequate here, perhaps that too is expected because of the difficulty inherent in defining another's world, especially when that world includes that which cannot be rationally described. Stevens's theory of poetry, his practice of that art, his disembodied physical hero, and his mortality of aging, death, and nothingness—in short his views on the world—often defy paraphrase or critical exegesis. For this reason, chapter 5 addresses the poet's "criticism," the man speaking about his world view and about himself in that world.

References

Abel, Lionel
  1958. "In the Sacred Park." *Partisan Review* Winter, pp. 86–98.
Ackerman, R. D.
  1972. "Wallace Stevens: Myth, Belief, and Presence." *Criticism* Summer, pp. 266–76.
Beach, John Warren
  1960. "The Hero" In *Obsessive Images,* ed. William Van O'Connor, pp. 208–13. Minneapolis: Univ. of Minnesota Pr.
Bevis, William
  1964. "Metaphor in Wallace Stevens." *Shenandoah* Winter, pp. 35–48.
  1974. "Stevens' Toneless Poetry." *Journal of English Literary History* Summer, pp. 257–85.
Blackmur, R. P.
  1952. "Examples of Wallace Stevens"; "Wallace Stevens: An Abstraction Blooded." In *Language as Gesture,* pp. 221–49, 255–59. New York: Harcourt, Brace.
Blessing, Richard
  1972. "Wallace Stevens and the Necessary Reader: A Technique of Dynamism." *Twentieth Century Literature* Jan., pp. 251–58.
Bradley, Ardyth
  1961. "Wallace Stevens' Decorations." *Twentieth Century Literature* Oct., pp. 114–17.
Brown, Merle Elliott
  1970. *Wallace Stevens: The Poem as Act.* Detroit: Wayne State Univ. Pr.
Buhr, Marjorie
  1972. "Wallace Stevens' Search For Being Through the Supreme Fiction." *The Carrell* June, pp. 1–15.

Burns, Charles R.
  1964. "The Two Worlds of Wallace Stevens." *Trace* Winter, pp. 295–96, 336–38.
Burtner, H. W.
  1972. "The High Priest of the Secular: The Poetry of Wallace Stevens." *Connecticut Review* Oct., pp. 34–45.
Caldwell, Price
  1972. "Metaphoric Structures in Wallace Stevens' 'Thirteen Ways of Looking at a Blackbird'." *Journal of English and Germanic Philology* Spring, pp. 321–35.
Carruth, Hayden
  1948. "Ideality and Metaphor." *Poetry* Aug., pp. 270–73.
Collie, M. J.
  1962. "The Rhetoric of Accurate Speech: A Note on the Poetry of Wallace Stevens." *Essays in Criticism* Jan., pp. 54–66.
Corrington, John William
  1968. "Wallace Stevens and the Problem of Order: A Study of Three Poems." *Arlington Quarterly* Summer, pp. 50–61.
Culbert, Taylor, and John M. Violette
  1966. "Wallace Stevens' Emperor." *Criticism* Winter, pp. 38–47.
Cunningham, J. V.
  1966. "The Styles and Procedures of Wallace Stevens." *University of Denver Quarterly* Spring, pp. 8–28.
Dembo, L. S.
  1966. "Wallace Stevens: Meta Men and Para Things." In *Conceptions of Reality in Modern American Poetry*, pp. 81–107. Berkeley: Univ. of California Pr.
Doggett, Frank
  1958. "Wallace Stevens' Secrecy of Words: A Note on Import in Poetry." *New England Quarterly* Sept., pp. 375–91.
  1961. "The Poet of Earth: Wallace Stevens." *College English* Mar., pp. 373–80.
  1962. "Wallace Stevens' River that Flows Nowhere." *Chicago Review* Summer-Autumn, pp. 67–80.
Donoghue, Denis
  1968. *The Ordinary Universe: Soundings in Modern Literature.* New York: Macmillan.
Eder, Doris L.
  1969. "The Meaning of Wallace Stevens' Two Themes." *Critical Quarterly* Summer, pp. 181–90.
Ellmann, Richard
  1957. "Wallace Stevens' Ice Cream." *Kenyon Review* Winter, pp. 89–105.
Frye, Northrop
  1957. "The Realistic Oriole: A Study of Wallace Stevens." *Hudson Review* Autumn, pp. 353–70.

1973. "Wallace Stevens and the Variation Form." In *Literary Theory and Structure*, ed. Frank Brady, pp. 395–414. New Haven: Yale Univ. Pr.

Fuchs, Daniel
   1963. *The Comic Spirit of Wallace Stevens*. Durham, N.C.: Duke Univ. Pr.

Gollin, Richard M.
   1960. "Wallace Stevens: The Poet in Society." *Colorado Quarterly* Summer, pp. 47–58.

Hagopian, John V.
   1975. "Wallace Stevens." *Contemporary Literature* Autumn, pp. 500–3.

Hartsock, Mildred E.
   1961. "Image and Idea in the Poetry of Stevens." *Twentieth Century Literature* April, pp. 10–19.

Hoffman, Frederick J.
   1959. "Mortality and Modern Literature." In *The Meaning of Death*, ed. Herman Feifel, pp. 133–56. New York: McGraw–Hill.

Hopper, Stanley Romaine
   1965. "Wallace Stevens: The Sundry Comforts of the Sun." In *Four Ways of Modern Poetry*, ed. Nathan A. Scott Jr., pp. 13–31. Richmond, Va.: John Knox Pr.

Howe, Irving
   1963. "Wallace Stevens: Another Way of Looking at the Blackbird." In *A World More Attractive*, pp. 158–67. New York: Horizon.

Juhasz, Suzanne
   1974. *Metaphor and the Poetry of Williams, Pound, and Stevens*. Cranbury, N.J.: Bucknell Univ. Pr.

Kessler, Edward
   1972. *Images of Wallace Stevens*. New Brunswick, N.J.: Rutgers Univ. Pr.

Lentricchia, Frank
   1968. *The Gaiety of Language: An Essay on the Radical Poetics of W. B. Yeats and Wallace Stevens*. Berkeley: California: Univ. of California Pr.

Maccaffrey, Isabel G.
   1973. "A Point of Central Arrival: Stevens' *The Rock*." *Journal of English Literary History* Winter, pp. 606–33.

Martz, Louis L.
   1950. "The World of Wallace Stevens." In *Modern American Poetry*, ed. B. Rajan, pp. 94–109. London: Dennis Dobson.
   1966. "Wallace Stevens: The Skeptical Music," In *The Poem of the Mind*, pp. 183–223. New York: Oxford Univ. Pr.

McBrearty, Paul
   1973. "Wallace Stevens's 'Like Decorations in a Nigger Cemetery':

Notes toward an Explication." *Texas Studies in Literature and Language* Summer, pp. 341–56.

Miles, Josephine
1951. *The Continuity of Poetic Language: Studies in English Poetry from the 1540's to the 1940's.* Berkeley: Univ. of California Pr.

Miller, J. Hillis
1969. *Poets of Reality.* New York: Atheneum.

Mills, Ralph J., Jr.
1958. "Wallace Stevens: The Image of the Rock." *Accent* Spring, pp. 75–89; reprinted in *Wallace Stevens,* ed. Marie Borroff. Englewood Cliffs, N.J.: Prentice-Hall, 1963.

Monroe, Harriet
1926. *Poets and Their Art.* New York: Macmillan.

Morris, Adalaide Kirby
1974. *Wallace Stevens: Imagination and Faith.* Princeton, N.J.: Princeton Univ. Pr.

Morse, Samuel French
1956. "Wallace Stevens: Some Ideas About the Thing Itself." *Boston University Studies in English* Spring, pp. 55–64.

Mulqueen, James E.
1973. "Man and Cosmic Man in the Poetry of Wallace Stevens." *South Dakota Review* Summer, pp. 16–27.

Nassar, Eugene Paul
1965. *Wallace Stevens: An Anatomy of Figuration.* Philadelphia: Univ. of Pennsylvania Pr.

Neill, Edward
1973. "The Melting Moment: Stevens' Rehabilitation of Ice Cream," *Ariel* Jan., pp. 88–96.

Pack, Robert
1955. "The Abstracting Imagination of Wallace Stevens: Nothingness and the Hero." *Arizona Quarterly* Autumn, pp. 197–209.
1958. *Wallace Stevens: An Approach to His Poetry and Thought.* New Brunswick, N.J.: Rutgers Univ. Pr.

Perlis, Alan
1976. *Wallace Stevens: A World of Transforming Shapes.* Lewisburg, N.J.: Bucknell Univ. Pr.

Quinn, Sister M. Bernetta
1963. "Metamorphosis in Wallace Stevens." In *Wallace Stevens* (Twentieth Century Views series), ed. Marie Borroff, pp. 54–70. Englewood Cliffs, N.J.: Prentice Hall.

Riddel, Joseph N.
1961. "Wallace Stevens' 'Notes Toward a Supreme Fiction'," *Wisconsin Studies in Contemporary Literature* Spring–Summer, pp. 20–42.
1962. Wallace Stevens' 'Visibility of Thought'," Sept., pp. 482–98.

Sampley, Arthur M.
    1972. "Wallace Stevens: Executive as Poet." *Midwest Quarterly*
    Jan., pp. 213–28.
Sheehan, Donald
    1966. "Wallace Stevens' Theory of Metaphor." *Papers on Lan-
    guage and Literature* Winter, pp. 57–66.
Silverman, Stuart
    1972. "The Emperor of Ice-Cream." *Western Humanities Review*
    Spring, pp. 165–68.
Simons, Hi
    1942. "The Humanism of Wallace Stevens." *Poetry* Nov., pp.
    448–52.
Southworth, James G.
    1950. "Wallace Stevens." In *Some Modern American Poets*, pp.
    88–106. Oxford: Basil Blackwell.
Stern, Herbert J.
    1966. *Wallace Stevens: Art of Uncertainty.* Ann Arbor: Univ. of
    Michigan Pr.
Sukenick, Ronald
    1967. *Wallace Stevens: Musing the Obscure.* New York: New
    York Univ. Pr.
Tompkins, Daniel P.
    1973. " 'To Abstract Reality': Abstract Language and the Intrusion
    of Consciousness in Wallace Stevens." *American Literature* Mar.,
    pp. 84–99.
Vendler, Helen Hennessy
    1966. "Stevens' 'Like Decorations in a Nigger Cemetery'." *Massa-
    chusetts Review* Winter, pp. 136–46.
Wagner, C. Roland
    1952a. "A Central Poetry." *Hudson Review* Spring, pp. 144–48.
    1952b. "The Idea of Nothingness in Wallace Stevens." *Accent*
    Spring, pp. 111–21.
Wells, Henry W.
    1964. *Introduction to Wallace Stevens.* Bloomington: Indiana
    Univ. Pr.
Whitbread, Thomas B.
    1962. "The Poet-Readers of Wallace Stevens." In *In Defense of
    Reading: A Reader's Approach to Literary Criticism*, ed. Reuben
    A. Brower and Richard Poirier, pp. 94–109. New York: Dutton.
    1963. "Wallace Stevens' 'Highest Candle'." *Texas Studies in Liter-
    ature and Language* Winter, pp. 465–80.
Wilder, Amos N.
    1952. *Modern Poetry and the Christian Tradition: A Study in the
    Relation of Christianity to Culture.* New York: Scribner.
Zabel, Morton
    1963. "Wallace Stevens and the Image of Man." In *Wallace*

Stevens, ed. Marie Borroff, pp. 151–60. Englewood Cliffs, N.J.: Prentice Hall.

Zimmerman, Michael

1966. "The Pursuit of Pleasure and the Uses of Death: Wallace Stevens' 'Sunday Morning'." *University Review* Winter, pp. 113–23.

1966. "Wallace Stevens' Emperor." *English Language Notes* Dec., pp. 119–23.

Own Work

He gripped more closely the essential prose
As being, in a world so falsified,
The one integrity for him, the one
Discovery still possible to make,
To which all poems were incident, unless
That prose should wear a poem's guise at last

WALLACE STEVENS "THE COMEDIAN AS THE LETTER C"

Wallace Stevens was himself very much a critic in that he occasionally analyzed his own work and, even more frequently,
used his verse as a springboard into a discussion of aesthetic theory.
Although he never adhered to the rigors of logic demanded by
philosophy or criticism, he nonetheless in verse, prose, and drama
discussed or demonstrated principles of poetry. His statements in
their varied forms not only annotate his own theory and practice,
but reveal something of the modern era's aesthetics as well. His
poems are the most masterful and numerous examples of theory in
practice or art by demonstration in the twentieth century, but
themselves could and have inspired volumes of critical attention.
This study will make no attempt to redefine the relationship of
poetic and critical genres, and will therefore not discuss the poetry
for two reasons: obviously, to be thorough, a discussion of Stevens's verse would require a lengthy, separate volume; and second,
although Stevens delves in his poetry into issues common with an
aesthetic critic's concern, this poet, above all else, writes poetry. To
label it criticism and dissect it accordingly would grossly under-
estimate the mastery of its technique. His plays are also basically
poetry and will be left to more appropriately poetic analysis.

On the other hand, much in Stevens's aphorisms, essays, and letters lends itself far more easily to analysis as criticism and reveals
far more about the poet's stated approach to poetry than the
poems themselves in their complexity and ambiguity do.

"The Necessary Angel"

Stevens's collected prose appeared first in 1951 as a volume of
essays, The Necessary Angel. As the poet himself relates in his
introduction to the volume, all but one of these essays were pre-

pared for oral delivery. Yet, when the collection appeared, critics praised it as a homogeneous presentation of the poet's theory. Three reviews of *The Necessary Angel* seem to exemplify the volume's reception. Bernard Heringman, a student who corresponded with and completed a dissertation on the poet, published a review, "The Critical Angel" (*Kenyon Review*, Summer 1952), stipulating that the essays develop ideas in a less explicit and systematic way than the poems do. Heringman is accurate in describing Stevens's method as free association and his pattern as fugal; and he is even more apt in describing Stevens's ontology as a tentative discussion rather than a philosophical construction. Heringman suggests that Stevens's definitions of reality and imagination in dichotomy and synthesis manifest themselves in the essays, while in the poetry the two constructs alternate as dichotomic and are presented only seldomly and indirectly as synthesis. This critic's review is the best on *The Necessary Angel* because Heringman, unlike many Stevens reviewers, understands the convolutions of the poet's thought, and even more important, is able to specify how Stevens's constructs—reality, imagination, poetry—metamorphose and interchange in their definitions.

Byron Vazakas's review, "Three Modern Old Masters: Moore, Stevens, Williams" (*New Mexico Quarterly Review*, Winter 1952), is less successful because Vazakas merely attempts to paraphrase Stevens's oblique and often ambiguous prose. According to this critic, the social upheaval of the early twentieth century compelled Stevens to write essays as both a "requiem" and a "resurrection." Contrary to Vazakas's view, Stevens certainly alludes indirectly to the mood of the era, but his essays respond to his personal, aesthetic concerns as poet, rather than to the political or social demands of his external environment. Yet, this critic accurately describes Stevens's tendency in these essays to argue with himself.

A third, even more unsuccessful review, "Duologue of Two O'Clock" by P. LeBrun (*Essays in Criticism*, April 1961), appeared after the 1960 British printing of *The Necessary Angel*. As if taking Vazakas's lead, LeBrun attempts to mimic Stevens's arguments with himself by structuring his review as a dialogue. If LeBrun's mimesis is irritating because of its stream of consciousness development, his assertions are even more disconcerting because they only tangentially relate to the poet's thought. Although LeBrun notes some incongruities in Stevens's ideas, the critic is unable to isolate the complexities and development of these incongruities. LeBrun inaccurately suggests that Stevens defines rather than argues a stance, but the critic at least partially redeems himself by correctly identifying a crucial problem in the essays: Stevens manipulates words in his prose as he does in his poetry, without realizing that the demands of the two genres differ. Unfortunately, the emphasis of LeBrun's comments mars the review. When the critic compares Stevens to Bergson, Langer, and I. A. Richards, and thereby finds the poet inadequate, LeBrun overlooks Stevens's role, not as aesthetic philosopher, but as poet explaining his concept of art.

That very concept of art is the focus of *The Necessary Angel*. To Stevens, the papers collected in the volume are "disclosures of definitions of poetry" (p. vii), and are bound together only in their contributing role to the theory of poetry. Contending that these essays are not philosophy or criticism but "enlargements of life," Stevens nonetheless admits that they seek to reveal his thoughts and feelings about poetry. Written in response to Frank Church's invitation for Stevens to speak at the *Mesures* lecture at Princeton University in 1941, the first essay, "The Noble Rider and the Sound of Words," is the best in the collection. The essay was written during the period in which Stevens created some of his most theoretic poems, collected in the 1942 volume, *Parts of a World*. Using metaphor in the essay as a unifying trope, Stevens borrows Plato's figure from the *Phaedrus* in which the soul is an immortal, noble, animate horse traversing the heavens, but in tension with a second chariot team horse which pulls toward the ground. After criticizing this figure as lacking an imaginative adherence to the real, Stevens moves into a discussion of Verrocchio's statue of Bartolommeo Colleoni, Clark Mills's Andrew Jackson statue, and a painting titled *Wooden Horses*. From this brief description of statuary and painting, Stevens concludes that nobility exists in art only in a degenerate form caused by an imbalance in the relationship of reality and imagination. The imbalance is itself caused by the pressures of reality. As a statement about the relationship of reality and imagination, the essay is interesting for several reasons. First, it early exposes the poet's interest in visual stimuli as they are expressed through nonverbal media. This interest in statuary and especially painting influences not only the poet's choice of imagery for his verse, but also the very mode of creation he chooses for that poetry. A second interest revealed by the essay exemplifies Stevens's manipulation of psychological terms. He was attracted by popular notions of psychology and the psychological interaction between poet, language, and reader.

However, far more important than the poet's general concern

with visual art and popular psychology is his voiced desire, in
this essay and in many poems, to define the poet's role. Toward
this end he constructs, in "The Noble Rider and the Sound of
Words," the figure of a poet who must abstract himself from
reality and abstract reality into the imagination; must recognize
the inseparableness of the imagination and reality; must help people live their lives; must give life meaning through the creation of
a supreme fiction; and must absolve himself from social obligations
of a too political world. This figure of a poet is the key to Stevens's
voice as poet in his first-person poems, and is the key to distinguishing his positive personae (adherents to this role) from his
negative personifications. Finally, in this essay Stevens defines many
of his terms. He describes reality as more than solid, static objects
and as life lived in an external scene; poetry as words and words
as sounds; and the nature of poetry as the interdependence of reality and imagination.

In reviewing *The Necessary Angel*, Richard Eberhart ("The
Stevens Prose" *Accent*, Spring 1952) characterizes the entire volume as "a poetry of rational notions systematically expressed" (p.
122), and describes this first essay as deficient in logic, somewhat
confessional, but basically poetic in "the overtones and nuances of
thought" (p. 123). The same might be said of the second essay,
"The Figure of the Youth as Virile Poet." The essay was written
when Jean Wahl invited Stevens to present a paper in the summer
of 1943 to a conference at Mount Holyoke College. The essay is
important primarily because it specifies the relationship based on
contrast between poetry and philosophy. According to Stevens,
philosophy approaches truth through reason, while poetry approaches truth through the imagination. The poet is distinguished
from the philosopher because the former is a part of life while the
latter is alien. Stevens further indicts philosophers by assuming that
they are unable to agree on philosophic truth, a lack of consensus
implied by the poet as absent among artists.

If Stevens's assessment of the two professions is less than objective, his essay is less than overtly unified in the variety of subjects he discusses. He moves into a description of poetry as a type
of metamorphosis and a process of the poet's personality; then
from the poet's personality he jumps into psychological considerations of the poet's mind manifesting itself in the poet, the poet's
sensitivity as a factor in the creative process, and the poet's act
of creation as a psychologically liberating experience. He yokes
this speculation to philosophy by calling for a poetic truth and by
suggesting that poetry must satisfy the reason as well as the imagi-

nation. Through comparing and contrasting the roles of philosophy and poetry, Stevens is able to move beyond the poet's task—to create the unreal out of the real—into the imagination's role in this process. With this final subject, the poet himself seems most comfortable. Like the personality of the poet, the imagination is important as a process in the act of creating. This imagination, the sum of man's faculties, is for Stevens, like light because "it adds nothing except itself" (p. 61). The imagination as defined here, like the figure of poet described in "The Noble Rider and the Sound of Words," is an important key to the imagination that recurs constantly in the verse.

The third piece, "Three Academic Pieces," is composed of one essay and two poems prepared for a 1947 lecture at Harvard. The essay is based on the premise that to formulate a theory of poetry, one must examine reality because, in Stevens's words, "reality is the central reference for poetry" (p. 71). In the three pieces, Stevens attempts to analyze one component of reality's structure, the resemblance between things. Stevens's discussion of resemblance in poetry is a discussion of metaphor, to him "the creation of resemblance by the imagination" (p. 72). From a discussion of resemblance in reality and poetry, the poet concludes that man's need for resmblance is inherent in his nature but satisfied by poetry; and that the structure of reality and the structure of poetry, both based on resemblance, are the same. Poetry and reality are therefore one.

The first poem of the piece, "Someone Puts a Pineapple Together," exemplifies this theory of metaphor and resemblance, while the second poem, "Of Ideal Time and Choice," exemplifies man's capacity to see resemblance and thereby recognize the structure of reality common in all things. In the total "Three Academic Pieces," as in most of his other essays and poems, Stevens manipulates a tried and true mode: he states a proposition, then restates it metaphorically in what might be called an example, but in Stevens is a figurative representation extending the original statement. This is the technique that confounds the syntax in his poetry and the technique that dilutes the rhetoric of his prose. But it is also the technique that gives a poetic quality, a resounding, proliferating depth of figurative associations, to all he utters. "Three Academic Pieces" is then crucial to an understanding of his verse because it not only specifies his theory of resemblance/metaphor, but epitomizes his metaphoric technique. It is the key to all of his poetry, and as such, without one word of overt interpretation or paraphrase, is criticism at its most lucid.

In the next essay, "About One of Marianne Moore's Poems,"

Stevens follows the lead of "The Figure of the Youth as Virile
Poet," and discusses poetic truth. The Moore essay, unlike all of the
others in the collection, was written for publication. It appeared in
the *Quarterly Review of Literature* in the summer of 1948 as an
attempt to relate Marianne Moore's technique in a poem "He
'Digesteth Harde Yron," to H. D. Lewis's ideas in "On Poetic
Truth," a paper published in *Philology* (July 1946). Like Lewis,
Stevens calls for an appraisal of poetic truth not on moral or religious grounds but with aesthetic standards. Poetry, measured in
this way, is valuable when it penetrates and reveals reality. Moore's
description of an ostrich, never naming the bird, provides an aesthetic integration of reality's fact and, according to Stevens, creates "a reality of her own particulars" (p. 95). Although Stevens's
comments on Moore are critically apt, they reveal more about his
definition of reality as perceived appearance than about her general
technique or Lewis's approach to poetic truth. The indirect method
of evoking an object through extensive detailed but ambiguous
metaphoric description of that object's characteristics is a technique Stevens obviously admired in Moore's poetry and utilized
in his own.

The subject of resemblance introduced by Stevens in "Three
Academic Pieces" and the perceptive use of imaginative imagery
defined in "About One of Marianne Moore's Poems" are discussed more extensively in "Effects of Analogy," delivered by
Stevens at the Yale University Bergen lectures in March 1948.
Analogy for Stevens is synonomous with a symbol's power to
evoke multiple associations which become the reflections and refractions of the original object. Analogy then is a "likeness," a
"resemblance between parallels," but also is a technique that must
be approached by its effect, the associations it inspires. While the
poet maintains that his essay is no more or less than an attempt to
isolate a few effects of analogy, he emphasizes this subject because
he contends that poetry itself is one effect of analogy. Although he
repeats several ideas from "The Figure of the Youth as Virile
Poet" and "Three Academic Pieces" when he discusses the personality of the poet, poetry as inherently bound to the imagination,
metaphor and poetry as interrelated, and metaphor as metamorphosis, he also expands earlier comments about the poet's role. By
asserting in this lecture that a poet's personality is manifested by
his choice of subject and style, Stevens makes a noteworthy acknowledgment: a writer's work cannot avoid autobiography.

He also discusses imagery as analogy and develops his thesis by
describing an image as a pictorial restatement that illustrates, ex-

plains, or gives definition to the original thing stated. This statement and restatement constitute an analogy. The definition leads him to three generalizations about imagery: "Every image is the elaboration of a particular of the subject of the image" (p. 127); "Every image is a restatement of the subject of the image in the terms of an attitude" (p. 128); and "Every image is an intervention on the part of the image-maker" (p. 128). Although such conclusions illuminate the poet's use of imagery in his verse, they are presented in an essay that is certainly not Stevens's best. In "Effects of Analogy" the poet relies on general, often undefined, terms, unexplained and only tangentially related generalizations, and a mode of development that exceeds associational progression and approaches simple rambling. Yet, in this imprecise essay, Stevens includes his most workable definition of poetry as a "transcendent analogue composed of the particulars of reality, created by the poet's sense of the world, that is to say, his attitude, as he intervenes and interposes the appearances of that sense" (p. 130).

In Stevens's next lecture, "Imagination as Value," presented at the Columbia English Institute in the fall of 1948, the poet repeats his often discussed theme, imagination as "the power of the mind over the possibilities of things" (p. 136). More specifically in this selection, Stevens distinguishes an imagination that is metaphysical force from an imagination as the practical power of the mind over external objects. Stevens contends that if the imagination is to be viewed as vital and valuable, it must be approached as a metaphysical force, but that its value as metaphysics is not the same as its aesthetic value to arts and letters. To summarize his position, he tells his audience that the imagination enables us to live our lives because it is man's way of projecting the idea of god into the idea of man; and it is the power that enables man to find order amid chaos.

Although the subject of this lecture is one of the most important ones in all of Stevens's poetry and prose, its execution is seriously flawed. With a subject that requires explicit definition and logical development as well as simple, expository prose, the poet speaks in mixed metaphors and describes tangentially related undefined constructs. He wanders into concerns of logical positivism, Freud, and communism in an attempt to broaden his definition of the imagination and relate it to the entire modern world. He thereby dilutes his discussion with global generalities that must relate his ambiguous terms to vague descriptions of modern movements.

The final essay of the collection, "The Relations between Poetry

and Painting," is far more successful. Originally prepared as a
lecture, these comments were delivered at the Museum of Modern
Art in January 1951. Stevens introduces his subject by shunning
speculation about some fundamental and common aesthetic basis
for poetry and painting, then moves instead into consideration of
the details (common to poets and painters) that are important to
their media. These common denominators he lists: selection of
composition as an element in creation; the labor of composition as
a consummating exercise of the imagination; the uncompromising,
plausible, and bigoted nature of both; possible division into two
types, one interested primarily in form, the other interested in
mode of expression; the shared basis in a modern reality of decreation; and an ability, in an age of disbelief, to compensate for
what has been lost. This last idea is the most important one, according to Stevens, because it demonstrates that the poet and painter
may use the imagination as a replacement for faith, may project
reality beyond its present boundaries, and may enlarge the human
spirit. Stevens's entire discussion is enlightening, not because it
exposes previously unexpressed similarities, but because it reflects
a concern, obvious in his verse still lifes and landscapes, with combining visual and verbal techniques in order to create a new poetic
reality.

About the collection in general, several conclusions may be
drawn. Stevens's method of development in the essays is like the
method of development in most of his poems. He alternates specific but metaphoric descriptions of constructs with questions of
import or value, also couched in metaphoric terms. This juxtaposition works best in poems and essays where an object, scene, or
idea is described concretely then expanded with philosophical
issues of value made concrete by further external description. In
essence, as he tells us in "Three Academic Pieces" and "Effects of
Analogy," the creation of an image and ultimately of a poem (or
essay) is the establishment, through juxtaposition of concrete and
abstract, of a metaphor. This structure is the key to his poems and
his criticism because it embodies his theory of creation which
depends on perceptions of reality juxtaposed in extraordinary
imaginative relationships.

While the weaknesses in these selections must be acknowledged,
their contribution to the understanding of Stevens must also be
emphasized. Certainly, they suffer from vague word choice, am-
biguously developed descriptions, contradictory assertions, logic
of generalities and absolutes, and speculative syntax. But, if the
thought occasionally verges on the irrational, the language con-

comitantly moves toward the poetic. Although these essays never focus on a particular poem or explain a specific allusion, as detailed examples of Stevens's thought, they reveal qualities of his poetic mind. And, like any criticism that provides revelation, should be studied.

"Opus Posthumous"

No other collections of Stevens's prose were compiled until after the poet's death when Samuel French Morse, Stevens's biographer, gathered some uncollected poems, plays, prefaces, speeches, essays, and miscellaneous statements for a volume, *Opus Posthumous*. In a scathing review, "Mind all Alone" (*New Statesman*, Jan. 9, 1960), G. S. Fraser criticizes the Stevens of this volume for the poet's "high-grade copy-writing" which is not only vague but repetitious and pretentious as well. Although a bit overzealous, Fraser's criticism is not without merit, and his praise of Morse's role in the volume certainly well founded. In fact, Morse's introduction to *Opus Posthumous* is beyond a doubt the strongest section of the book. Morse accurately identifies Stevens's subject as a theory of poetry and correctly notes that the poet was concerned in all he wrote with a principle of order. True to his purpose, Morse successfully displays not the best of Stevens's work, but the range of the poet's varying attempts. Morse's collection then provides the best of two worlds, an indication of the poet's breadth combined with an objective, editorial selectivity and discrimination in the introduction and presentation of the poet's scope. And, Morse performs a genuine critical service by reprinting many of Stevens's previously uncollected early poems, later poems completed after the publication of the *Collected Poems*, two of the poet's three plays, and the original version of the infamous "Owl's Clover."

One of the most interesting sections of *Opus Posthumous*, the "Adagia," is a selection of Stevens's aphoristic statements concerned with topics such as happiness, consciousness, life, poetry, thought, literature, art, imagination, and the poet. Morse himself describes the "Adagia" as *pensées* in the manner of Braque's *Notebook*, the *materia poetica* of an artist not unlike Paul Valéry's "Litterature." Morse earlier published "A Note on the 'Adagia' " (*Poetry*, Mar. 1957) in which he more extensively discusses the source of Stevens's statements. According to Morse, the poet maintained three notebooks: "From Pieces of Paper," a workbook of titles, metaphors, and notes; *Sur Plusieurs Beaux Sujets*, passages from studies Stevens admired; and the "Adagia," written over a span of twenty years. Suggesting that these pithy statements indicate a literary heritage traceable to the eighteenth century, Mallarmé, Thoreau, and Santayana, Morse more specifically in his *Opus Posthumous* introduction praises them as indicative of Stevens's anecdotal style and interest in economy. They are, to Morse, Shakespearean in tone; exemplary of one who defines meaning in terms of style; related to Stevens's manipulations of vocabulary in order to forge extraordinary relationships; and reminiscent of Pope's exploitive language.

Adagia such as "Poetry and materia poetica are interchangeable terms" (p. 159); "A change in style is a change in subject" (p. 171); or "God and the imagination are one" (p. 178), exemplify Stevens at his most terse. Other more developed, less arbitrary samples communicate basic premises identifiable in much of the verse. "The final belief is to believe in a fiction, which you know to be a fiction, there being nothing else. The exquisite truth is to know that it is a fiction and that you believe in it willingly" (p. 163); or "There is no such thing as a metaphor of a metaphor. One does not progress through metaphors. Thus reality is the indispensable element of each metaphor. When I say that man is a god it is very easy to see that if I say that a god is something else, god has become reality" (p. 179). As disparate as the "Adagia" subjects are, common themes, however, pervade. Throughout, Stevens is concerned with material for poetry; the role of belief; the function of the mind; the importance of imagination, reality, and metaphor; and ultimately, through these concerns, with a definition of poetry. In their interrelationships, such issues are indications of Stevens's search for order, a hallmark of his verse.

While many of the selections in *Opus Posthumous* were specifically prepared as remarks for award acceptances, prefaces to works by other artists, or occasional program pieces, they often repeat ideas and themes found in *The Necessary Angel* and the *Letters* (to be discussed later in this chapter). Yet, four essays in *Opus Posthumous* are worth further investigation because of the poet's emphasis. These include "A Collect of Philosophy,' "Two or Three Ideas," "The Irrational Element in Poetry," and "A Note on *Les Plus Belles Pages*.

One of Stevens's most ambitious essays, "A Collect of Philosophy," was prepared for print and submitted for publication in a professional philosophical journal. After its rejection, Stevens never resubmitted it. His premise, that the concepts of philosophy are often poetic, is expanded by an argument in which Stevens maintains that poetic concepts result when philosophers attempt to explain cosmic reality, a reality that defies ordinary discourse. A philosophic idea is also poetic when it "gives life to the imagination," a phrase Stevens uses to mean it transforms reality. Although he compares poetry and philosophy as genres because both confront problems of perception and both probe "for an integration," he contrasts the two because: philosophy searches for integration for its own sake while poetry searches because of the quality that integration possesses; a philosopher's world always remains to be discovered while a poet's remains to be celebrated; and a philosopher's world is a combination of present world and thought, while a poet's is a combination of the present world and imagination.

The essay is weakened by Stevens's very focus. Rather than explore the philosophy of poets, a subject with which he was intimately concerned, Stevens attempts to analyze the poetry of philosophers. This emphasis places him, as poet, out of his element. As a poet he has neither the experience nor the psychological bent to write the logical, explicit, discursive prose demanded by a philosophical argument. Yet, in this very weakness the essay resembles his verse in which the poetry is too heavily burdened by the theoretic concerns that frequently confuse aesthetics and metaphysics.

Back in his own poetic realm, Stevens is more readable in "Two or Three Ideas," a paper presented at the spring 1951 meeting of the College English Association. The three ideas are statements about style: "The style of a poem and the poem itself are one" (p. 202); Gods are a creation of style; and poets, in an age of disbelief, must "supply the satisfactions of belief" (p. 206) by creating a style that helps one bear reality. From all of this Stevens concludes that "we use the same faculties when we write poetry that we use when we create gods or when we fix the bearing of men in reality" (p. 216). Although the poet's logic in the essay is faulty, his comments may be applied to his own poetry. When he voices a belief in style that enlarges, enriches, and liberates language, he articulates the principle behind his use of non-English terms and his creation of "hierophantic" phrases. And, when he notes that style is not applied but is inherent, he specifies the basis for his own associational stanza arrangements that reflect the convolutions of his own thought and the basis for his variation form reflecting the nuances and shifts in the reality he perceives.

This interaction of reality and perceiver is the subject of his comments, "The Irrational Element in Poetry," which preceded a rare public reading of his own poetry. By irrational element in poetry, Stevens means the "transaction between reality and the sensibility of the poet from which poetry springs" (p. 217). The subject of that poetry, its choice and development, are unpredictable chance occurrences. To the question why does one write irrational poetry, Stevens responds, "because one is impelled to do so by a personal sensibility and also because one grows tired of the monotony of one's imagination" (p. 221). His definition of irrational seems to be nonrational, but his comments communicate his need, unexplained to himself and thereby irrational, to write poetry about topics, themselves irrational because of their chance selection. If this all seems a bit circular in its reasoning, its relevance to his poetry must still be acknowledged. Stevens's subjects almost always "occurred" to him as random stimuli from his environment. His early trips to Florida appear in the tropical vegetation images of his *Harmonium* years; his concern with genealogy is voiced in ancestral allusions of the middle years; and the autumn auroras of the Hartford sky become subject and image in the more mature verse. Stevens, like all poets, picked randomly from the reality around him, but, unlike most, he found a theoretical construct, irrationality, to explain this.

Finally, in "A Note on *Les Plus Belles Pages*," Stevens provides a rare commentary on his own work. Although most of his comments on his poems may be found in his letters, this brief note provides a capsule statement about the poem of the title. According to Stevens, the poem "means" that the "inter-relation between things is what makes them fecund" (p. 293). He develops this interpretation only minimally by citing interaction as the source of poetry and by noting that the interrelation between reality and the imagination is the basis of literature. In short, he repeats here in direct criticism what he indirectly reveals about his verse in *The Necessary Angel*. While his equation stating that the poem "means" one thing is a bit simplistic, his concise comments here must be commended for their brevity and direct statement.

"Letters of Wallace Stevens"

The third volume of interest, *Letters of Wallace Stevens*, reveals much about the poet's life and ideas. These letters combined with his daughter's brief but penetrating introductory comments to each period of his life might be term. 1 a biography in installments. From over thirty-three hundred letters spanning sixty years Holly Stevens selected and edited, choosing those samples concerned with poetry, those written to other poets, some of interest because of their style, and many that contain pertinent biographical information.

The critical reception of the *Letters* was appropriately positive. One of the more detailed reviews, "Wallace Stevens: Business and a Sonnet" (*Nation*, Jan. 16, 1967) by A. Walton Litz, provides one of the most complete overviews of their development. According to Litz, the *Letters* provides tentative connections between the poet's private personality and his poetic aesthetics. Litz scans the early letters as examples of Stevens's pervasive concern with sound and rhythm; considers the poet's journal entries that almost surreptitiously mention his poetry as well as his business endeavors; summarizes the letters of the poet just beginning to publish as more external and revealing; reviews the defensive letters of the thirties as more concerned with criticism; and emphasizes the forties letters, in the most productive decade of Stevens's life, as some of his most varied and vital. Litz convincingly relates the progression of thought detectable in the letters to the evolution of poetics evinced in the verse. As a summary of the poet's development or his daughter's purpose in compiling these samples, Litz's review is first-rate.

A second review, "The Poet Behind the Desk," (*Saturday Review*, Nov. 19, 1966) by William York Tindall, also relates the letters to the poems. Tindall suggests that the elegance, gaiety, and fastidiousness of the verse is also evident in the poet's correspondences. Like Litz, Tindall emphasizes the importance of letters that discuss Stevens's own poems, but more specific than Litz, Tindall notes that the correspondence with Hi Simons, Renato Poggioli, and Ronald Latimer provides "a kind of handbook to the more difficult poems" (p. 42). George S. Lensing, in "Wallace Stevens' Letters of Rock and Water" (1970), not only describes the letters as a source for the poetry, but also as a source for Stevens's prose essays. Lensing's emphasis differs from Tindall's and Litz's because Lensing writes an article rather than a short review, and because the latter emphasizes the man behind the letters rather than the letters' poetic affinity. Stevens's letters offer to Lensing a glimpse of the private man as insurance executive, attorney, and poet, and a method whereby the poet distanced himself from his friends. As Lensing accurately notes, the letters became Stevens's way of exploring a world in which he seldom traveled for other than business reasons; and they became "a store from which the poetic imagination could generously draw" (p. 321). Lensing's conclusion, that the *Letters* should be perused "as the actual workshop for the creation of his poetry," is the most perceptive comment made by any critic examining the volume.

Joseph N. Riddel ("Wallace Stevens' 'It Must Be Human'," *English Journal*, April 1967), unlike Lensing, deemphasizes the contribution made by the letters. While noting that they reveal an orderly, ordinary life, he quickly admits that the new information they provide (the poet's lengthy commentaries on his own work), is quite significant. Riddel compares the importance of those letters to that of the poetry, when in his later study, "Blue Voyager" (*Salmagundi*, Winter 1968), he clearly prefers the poetry's "discovery of reality" to the prose's "matter of facticity." Disagreeing with Lensing, Riddel asserts that the letters provide biographers with little information, but are noteworthy because they expose something of the poet's humanity.

Donald E. Stanford's "The Well-Kept Life: The Letters of Wallace Stevens" (*Southern Review*, Summer 1967) emphasizes not this individual humanity, but the genuine contribution to the history of American poetry made by this volume. Stanford is quick to note the prevalence of biographical information; the important critical comments in notes to Simons, Latimer, and Poggioli; and the human eccentricities of the man Stevens, all elements of the letters cited by other critics. Unlike others, though, Stanford also isolates the importance of dates, citing letter comments that refute critical speculation. As examples, Stanford notes that "The Emperor of Ice-Cream" could not have been written for Stevens's daughter, as Richard Ellmann contends (*Kenyon Review*, Winter 1957), because the poem, according to the letters, was published in a 1922 issue of the *Dial*, while Holly Stevens was not born until 1924. Similarly, Stanford claims that "The Comedian as the Letter C" was not an answer to Eliot's *The Waste Land* as Roy Harvey Pearce (*The Continuity of American Poetry*, 1961) and Joseph Riddel (*The Clairvoyant Eye*, 1965) note because the Stevens poem was being written before *The Waste Land* appeared. These points will certainly not change the great stream and direction of Stevens criticism, but such attempts at precision and accuracy of detail are not without merit.

Like Stanford, Stanley Kunitz in "The Hartford Walker" (*New Republic*, Nov. 12, 1966) notes the volume's general contribution to American literary history and its value as a gloss on the poet's verse. Like Riddel, Kunitz also describes Stevens as a walker who, in his verse and prose, strolls through Hartford with an energy and eye for detail impossible in motorized vehicles. And, like Riddel, Kunitz seems a bit embarrassed by and apologetic for Stevens's conservatism, revealed in his letters about New Deal politics and, more specifically, in his pro-Mussolini stance.

Roy Fuller ("Both Pie and Custard," *Shenandoah*, Spring 1970) repeats much of what was established by early reviewers such as Kunitz, but extends Stanford's "contribution to literature" theme by specifying the *Letters'* likeness to similar modern volumes. According to Fuller, this book may be ranked with Freud's letters and Gide's journal, and must certainly be acknowledged as extraordinarily interesting because it delineates the two themes of Stevens's life, reality and imagination. Labeling Stevens one of the three greatest English-speaking poets of the century, then describing his correspondence as always polished and intelligent, Fuller balances with praise what a British critic, V. S. Pritchett, ("Truffles in the Sky," *New Statesman*, Mar. 31, 1967) provides in blame. Describing the poet as a royalist romantic, affected and prone to vulgarity, who lives in an artificial world where he demonstrates the "tetchiness and pathos of a sycophant" (p. 439), Pritchett finally labels Stevens a colonist with a dull life. The sarcastic tone of the review is equalled only by its vehement dislike for the American poet. One might say of Pritchett as the critic himself says of Stevens: he was "lazy-minded," and possessed "a great energy and wit that have created their own monotony" (p. 440).

After the dust of the early reviews and studies on the *Letters* has settled, a careful perusal of the volume reveals first the chronicle of a twentieth-century everyman, and it reveals the format for the workings of a master poet's sensibility. About the man, various readers find varying evidence in the volume. To Fuller, Stevens surfaces as a connoisseur of language, while to Stanford he becomes an epicurean gourmet. Riddel envisions a respectable lawyer and esthete who bordered on the provincial ordinary in his conservative politics. Tindall is more beneficent in his portrait of a warm, kindly, orderly Republican, though Pritchett is most scathing in his description of an inadequate, homespun insurance tycoon. For Litz, Stevens reveals himself as a secretive, remote man, but for Kunitz he is so remote as to be an embodied voice, a distant human who exuded a "superior presence." The speculation is possible, indeed encouraged, by Stevens's reticence to become a public figure. If the letters provide only brief glimpses behind this, they nonetheless present the poet's mind in its many convolutions of aesthetic thought.

From the earliest letters one detects the poet's interest in wordplay; his attentiveness toward nature coupled with a dislike of a city's grime; his belief in a theory of art that is "part of the system of the world" (p. 24); and his delight in the specificity of his environment but his comparable need for a force beyond fact.

They divulge, from beginning to end, much about his family life, his business career, his personal idiosyncrasies, but more importantly for criticism, they reveal much about his poetry. The barren period of his publishing life after the appearance of *Harmonium*, much bemused by critics as mysterious, is quite explainable using his correspondence. His developing insurance career, the birth of his daughter, and his somewhat cramped and noisy living conditions combined to create an environment unconducive to poetic creation. The family names and childhood places evident in the verse of his middle years, though somewhat incongruous with the early gaiety of *Harmonium* and the late introspection of *The Rock*, issue naturally out of his concern, as he aged, with genealogy. Such bits of biographic trivia provide a new dimension for the poetry in general, but very seldom elucidate any one poem in particular. Stevens's annotations on his own poems commence with the correspondence between the poet and Harriet Monroe. This exchange was initiated in 1914 when Stevens began publishing in *Poetry*, then edited by Monroe. A similar interchange occurred later between Stevens and Hi Simons, a Chicago critic and publisher who became interested in Stevens while preparing a Stevens bibliography. Later, toward the end of his life, Stevens maintained an extended and helpful correspondence with Renato Poggioli, who translated selected Stevens poems into Italian. Responding to Poggioli as he once did to Simons, Stevens clarified symbols and allusions, and occasionally wrote lengthy explanations and interpretations of his own work.

Although the poet responded selectively and discriminately to those who wrote him, he often furnished explanatory comments on his poetry to students and critics who contacted him. In letters from various periods of his life, he praises Morton Dauwen Zabel's "The Harmonium of Wallace Stevens" as "uncommonly sensitive and intelligent"; notes that Howard Baker's "Wallace Stevens and Other Poets" is an "extremely intelligent analysis"; commends Hi Simons' " 'The Comedian as the Letter C': Its Sense and Its Significance" as "correct" and "keen"; suggests that Bernard Heringman's "Wallace Stevens: The Use of Poetry" is a skillful example of textual explication; and labels C. Roland Wagner's "A Central Poetry" a "remarkable," "solid," and "masterpiece" review of *The Necessary Angel*. Stevens was flattered by positive comments about his work and often, when contacted, responded directly and favorably with praise and information. However, when confronted by a negative assessment such as Yvor Winter's "Wallace Stevens or the Hedonist's Progress" or Stanley Burnshaw's "Turmoil in the Middle Ground," Stevens refused to respond directly or responded indirectly in his verse. In short, because he was human, he was not an objective evaluator of criticism about his own work.

Yet, Stevens provides a criticism of his own. In his typically confounding fashion he notes that once a poem has been explained it has been destroyed, because a reader can no longer "seize it." To this he adds that a critic should work with what the author says, not what he meant to say, and should therefore not ask the poet for explanations. But Stevens is asked and does provide explanations. He rightly acknowledges that, when criticism is involved, the final authority is not the poet, but the poem itself; and develops this point in a letter (to John Pauker) also stating that meaning is a question of philosophy irrelevant to him because of his belief in poetry for its own sake.

The two most detailed explications of meaning that he provides appear in letters to Hi Simons and Renato Poggioli, and seek to elucidate sections of "The Man with the Blue Guitar" and "Notes Toward a Supreme Fiction." The paraphrase of "Blue Guitar" amounts to little more than an explication of personal allusions and a description of the poet's choice of connotative meanings for his diction, but the poet also mentions referents for symbols that would have been discerned by most serious students of Stevens. "Blue Guitar" is similarly the subject of a detailed letter to Renato Poggioli in which Stevens discusses selected images and figures but also concisely summarizes his subject in the poem: "The general intention of the 'Blue Guitar' was to say a few things that I felt impelled to say 1. about reality; 2. about the imagination; 3. their inter-relations; and 4. principally, my attitude toward each of these things" (p. 788).

While his comments on "Blue Guitar" were written in response to inquiries, his interest in "Notes" increased as he created it and inspired excited yet thoughtful letter comments to many of his acquaintances. In letters, he wrote frequently during and after the poem's completion, then cooperated willingly with Simons's request for explanations. Stevens's notes on this poem reveal the growing obscurity of his images; his ambiguous definition of the "supreme fiction"; his feeling that "Notes" was a tentative, initial statement about a few of the supreme fiction's characteristics; and his conviction that to clarify the enigma of the supreme fiction would destroy the poetry of the idea. In this last admission, Stevens provides a retort to all of those critics who would neatly define and categorize the elusive poetics of his verse.

These selective annotations of "Blue Guitar" and "Notes" exemplify Stevens's criticism at its most helpful. Similar clarifications of purpose and theme may be found in his summary of "To the One of Fictive Music" as a poem about the imaginative world as the only real world; "Sailing After Lunch" as a theory of poetry that requires poetry to be romantic, constantly new; and "Angel Surrounded by Paysans" as a response to Tal Coat's *Still Life* which Stevens acquired through his Paris art dealer. Unfortunately, like most critics, Stevens also has his weaknesses manifested in simplistic quips and laborious rationalizations. When he writes that "Cortège for Rosenbloom" "comes down to the proverbial six feet of earth in the end," or notes that "Sunday Morning" is simply an expression of paganism, one must fault him for gross simplistic reductions. And, when he interprets "Mr. Burnshaw and the Statue" as a reversal of the critic's method, turning poetry on communism rather than the reverse, one must grant that the poet was neither so objective nor so systematic in his reply to the Marxist.

When one reads the *Letters* for details on the poems, the frequent perceptiveness of the poet's insight prevails over such weaker statements. Indeed, one can find elements of criticism at its best when Stevens specifies a relationship between theory and practice, and in so doing not only clarifies aspects of the poem, but also tantalizes the reader into further investigation. In this vein the poet tells us that "Earthy Anecdote" is a presentation of theory in a poem devoid of symbolism but inhabited by animals that are concrete; and that "Le Monocle de Mon Oncle" is a certain point of view, a retrospective glance, and a cacophony of sound.

As such a chronicle of the poet and his art, the *Letters* reveals several characteristics of Stevens. He was a poet influenced significantly by his environment—the letters he received, the paintings he purchased, the objects he viewed in his daily walks. All of these become a part of the process and product of his poetry. He was a poet with a visual orientation; and because of this he obsessed over the purchase of minor paintings, composed detailed vignettes of occasional pleasing scenes, and was extremely concerned with the printing format used for his volumes. If he was a philosopher, he was a relatively unread one, exposed to such men of thought only by the times in which he lived. He did not seek out such theory, but came to considerations of theory only through the what and why of poetry. Painting to him, on the other hand, was pursued in exhibition catalogs, museum visits, personal art acquisitions, and the replication of painted detail in verse. And, he was not a consistently reliable critic. He lacked the objectivity and predisposition for any sustained exegesis of his own work; he lacked the time

and energy for systematic analysis of other's work; and he lacked
the definitive finality required in general of most critics. He
evolved, or as he might say, metamorphosed, in his interpretations
and ideas. If this marred his critical decisiveness, it enriched the
flickering variations of his verse. As his reputation increased, he
received many volumes of poetry, sent to him by hopeful poets
who often received in return superficial comments about the
book's appearance, the general quality of its printing, or the simple delight inspired by the young poet's thoughtfulness. Stevens
was clearly pleased and flattered, according to the very letters that
lack the substantive comments and directions sought. To one such
poet, Delmore Schwartz, Stevens wrote a responsive letter about
poetic language, poetic order, poetic theory, the experience of
reality—in summary, about many of Stevens's career-long concerns. About the interrelationship of poetry and criticism, he
briefly but perceptively comments: "The analysis and interpretation of poetry are perceptions of poetry" (p. 591). For a poet who
dealt primarily with perceptions and an order in which they could
become meaningful, analysis and interpretation belonged to his
reality—as well as to his imagination.

"Souvenirs and Prophecies: The Young Wallace Stevens"

What has been billed as the final, definitive collection of Stevens's
prose, has been collected and published by his daughter, Holly
Stevens. The volume, *Souvenirs and Prophecies: The Young Wallace Stevens* (1977), was assembled from journals the poet kept
and previously unpublished letters that he wrote during a sixteen-
year period commencing in 1898 with Stevens's sophomore year at
Harvard. Helen Vendler maintains that Holly Stevens's volume
provides the literary world with "a relatively complete portrait of
the artist as a young man." Vendler's review, "Portrait of Wallace
Stevens as a Young Artist: *Souvenirs and Prophecies*" (*New York
Times Book Review*, Jan. 30, 1977), emphasizes the coexistence
of the visual and the ruminative in the poet; his rapport with the
weather and landscape; and the solitary character of the poet's life.
Vendler also accurately acknowledges the unfortunate loss of the
most personal sections in many of the journal entries and letters.
These sections, excised years earlier by the poet or his wife, might
have provided illuminating information on the Stevens who in this
volume emerges as both reclusive and enigmatic.

Souvenirs and Prophecies, however, adds significantly to the public's knowledge of Stevens as man, because it gathers together the poetic juvenilia and many of the previously unpublished letters. For continuity, Holly Stevens reprints some letters published earlier in the *Collected Letters*, and she provides commentary, linking much in the early journals and letters with the later poems. To recreate his childhood, she describes Stevens's parents and the house in Reading where he was born, but she extends the meaning of this description beyond mere biographical fact when she relates that in his house all windows and doors faced west, a fact from the poet's youth that enhances the meaning of his poem subtitle, "The Westwardness of Everything." Similarly, her comments are helpful when she exposes early journal selections and publications as antecedents of the later verse. Stevens's 1898 short story, "Her First Escapade," though sophomoric, provides an interesting first draft of lines to appear much later in "Extracts from Addresses to the Academy of Five Ideas" (1940). A journal entry from 1901 is particularly relevant to a much later poem "The Poem That Took the Place of a Mountain" (1952):

August 24
    Walked from Point Lookout (which I reached by trolley and train and boat from Mineola) on the South Shore to Long Beach today: a very short walk perfect in itself but contemptible to get to and to come away from. I am not at home by the sea; my fancy is not at all marine, so to speak; when I sit on the shore and listen to the waves they only suggest wind in treetops. A single *coup d'oeil* is enough to see all, as a rule. The sea is loveliest far in the abstract when the imagination can feed upon the idea of it. The thing itself is dirty, wobbly and wet. But today, while all that I have just said was true as ever, towards evening I saw lights on heaven and earth that never were seen before. The white beach (covered with beach-fleas etc.) ran along behind and before me. The declining sun threw my shadow a frightful length on the sand. The clouds began to become confused and dissolve into a golden mist into which the sea ran purple, blue, violet. The sun went down lighting the underworld and gilding a few clouds in this one. The West filled with a blue city mist etc. Turning to the East I saw that a storm was creeping up, and suddenly then I caught sight of two rainbows swinging down. Walking over the beach under this lowering sky was like stepping into a cavern. Two women-one dressed in yellow, one in purple moving along the white sand-relieved the severity of the prospect.   (p. 107)

There it was, word for word,
The poem that took the place of a mountain.

He breathed its oxygen,
Even when the book lay turned in the dust of his table.

It reminded him how he had needed
A place to go to in his own direction,

How he had recomposed the pines,
Shifted the rocks and picked his way among clouds,

For the outlook that would be right,
Where he would be complete in an unexplained completion:

The exact rock where his inexactnesses
Would discover, at last, the view toward which they had edged,

Where he could lie and, gazing down at the sea,
Recognize his unique and solitary home.   (p. 108)

As Holly Stevens accurately notes, the two selections are similar
not only in theme but also in the improvisational style common to
journal entries and Stevens's poetic mode. Although the poet's
daughter admits that she cannot explain the great leap from the
juvenilia to poems such as "Extract," "The Poem That Took the
Place," and "Sunday Morning," she intimates that we can antici-
pate the later masterful poems in the earlier descriptions of place
and event. A 1904 journal entry on an April Sunday morning
exemplifies such anticipatory description ultimately resulting in the
poem "Sunday Morning."

> April 30.
>   I am in an odd state of mind today. It is Sunday. I feel a
> loathing (large & vague!), for things as they are; and this is the
> result of a pretty thorough disillusionment. Yet this is an
> ordinary mood with me in town in the Spring time. I say to
> myself that there is nothing good in the world except physical
> well-being. All the rest is philosophical compromise. Last
> Sunday, at home, I took communion. It was from the worn,
> the sentimental, the diseased, the priggish and the ignorant that
> "Gloria in excelsis!" came. Love is consolation, Nature is con-
> solation, Friendship, Work, Phantasy are all consolation. [The
> last sentence, about seven words, of this entry has been crossed
> out and is illegible.]   (p. 146)

While Holly Stevens's commentary often relates her father's early self-disclosure to his later art, she also leaves to the student of Stevens the task of finding many relationships between and associations to the poet's images.

Wednesday Evening.

My Dearest Bo-Bo:-
   A little phantasy to beguile you—a bit of patch–work—and about music . . . What is the mysterious effect of music, the vague effect we feel when we hear music, without ever defining it? . . . It is considered that music stirring something within us, stirs the Memory. I do not mean our personal Memory—the memory of our twenty years and more—but our inherited Memory, the Memory we have derived from those who lived before us in our own race, and in other races, illimitable, in which we resume the whole past life of the world, all the emotions, passions, experiences of the millions and millions of men and women now dead, whose lives have insensibly passed into our own, and compose them. —It is a Memory deep in the mind, without images, so vague that only the vagueness of Music, touching it subtly, vaguely awakens, until

"it remembers its august abodes,
And murmurs as the ocean murmurs there."

But I need not solve any theme—so I drop poetry. There is enough magic without it.
   I hang prose patches to my introduction and say that "great music" agitates "to fathomless depths, the mystery of the past within us." And also that "there are tunes that call up all ghosts of youth and joy and tenderness;—there are tunes that evoke all phantom pain of perished passion;—there are tunes that resurrect all dead sensations of majesty and might and glory,—all expired exultations,—all forgotten magnanimities." And again, that at the sound of Music, each of us feels that "there are answers within him, out of the Sea of Death and Birth, some eddying immeasurable of ancient pleasure and pain."
   While I had always known of this infinite extension of personality, nothing has ever made it so striking as this application of Music to it . . . So that, after all, those long chords on the harp, always so inexplicably sweet to me, vibrate on more than the "sensual ear"—vibrate on the unknown . . . And what one listens to at a concert, if one knew it, is not only the harmony of sounds, but the whispering of innumerable responsive spirits within one, momentarily revived, that stir like the invisible motions of the mind wavering between dreams and

sleep: that does not realize the flitting forms that are its shadowy
substance.—A phantasy out of the East Wind, for meditation.

With love,

WALLACE (pp. 212–13)

This letter, presented by Holly as an "interesting meditation," is
far more important than a mere letter to "Bo-Bo," Stevens's pet
name for his late wife. The interplay of phantasy, music, and
memory becomes artfully shaped into the *Harmonium* poem,
"Peter Quince at the Clavier."

A second important contribution made by Holly Stevens in this
volume is her publication of information written by Stevens in his
post-Harvard, prepoetry years. The poet's heretofore unpublished memoirs from this period reveal a young man whose opinions about the city, about life, and about people are continually
changing. We read the first person account of a sensitive individual
learning to cope with a dull journalism job, becoming familiar with
the diversity and debris of big city New York, and experiencing
the pathos of industrialized "girls making flowers in a dirty factory
near Bleecker St." (p. 101). What emerges for the reader of these
bits and pieces is a figure of a young man attempting to define
himself, his goals, and the world around him. The forces and influences that affected the later verse also surface as, through
Holly's careful selection, we follow the poet through his stultifying
newspaper job into his decision to change careers. The decision is
an important one, for it is followed by distinguishable changes in
his views of the world. The journal entries become immediately
more poetic in their imagery and emphasis.

September 15.
    Suddenly it has become Autumn. The hollows at twilight are
like charming caves—mists float in the air—the heat of the sun
is that bracing Septembery heat straight from the star without
any gusts from the earth. I was in the woods yesterday (never
mind where I walked). The fact is I have discovered a solitude—
with all the modern conveniences. It is on the Palisades—about
opposite Yonkers, reachable by cutting in from the Alpine road
at the proper place. Silver ropes of spiders' weaving stretched
over the road, showing that my retreat had had no recent
visitors. There was no litter of broken bottles or crushed egg-
shells on the brown needles—but a little brook tinkled under a
ledge into a deep ravine—*deep* en vérité—; two thrushes fidgeted
on the logs and in the boughs; stalks of golden rod burned in
the shadows like flambeaux in my temples; I thought I heard a

robin's strain. Oh! I can fancy myself at my ease there How
often I shall stretch out under those evergreens listening to the
showers of wind around me—and to that tinkling bit of
water dripping down among those huge rocks and black
crevices! It is really very undisturbed there.

I was saying it had become autumn. The sumach leaves are
scarlet, and there are other weaklings that have turned in these
chill nights. Yet the world is still green. Witness: that mighty
promontory bathed in the light of the next to latest declining sun.

Item: At noon I lay on a rock taking a bake. Was startled
upon gazing into the heavens to find them swarming with birds
whirling about at an immense height. Think they were crows.

October 1. 1902.

Ran home a week ago. Found Livingood just back from one
of his flights, Heilig just from Europe, Lee Smith in England.
Weather stupefied me. Yet a trip of the kind is a benefit: here
I can polish myself with dreams, exert myself in hard work,
live in a fine, false way; there dreaming is an effort in itself and
hard work is merely meritorious—not instructive, and the way
of the world is neither fine nor false. Fate carves its images there
in a tedious fashion, and neither beautifully nor well. And the
very wings of Time hang limp in the still air. Alas! it did nothing
but rain. Once I got a few miles into the country. I sat on a stone
wall facing a pool of rain-water in a field of green wheat watching a few plover feed near by. The sun shone for a short time
on the pool. The wind covered the pool with reflections of
gold. Far off the hills lay blue in the mist. Again I visited the
Wilys who (with their angels) grow more and more pathetic.
More, I visited Kuechler on his hill-top and found him still
and pale—his beautiful beard spread over his bosom, the gleam
of an invisible sword darting about him. Called on Miss Lewis
and found her to be without manners: that is without any more
than I myself. (pp. 109–10)

While the reader is independently able to discern such changes in
the evolving poet, Holly Stevens's introductory and transitional
comments further elucidate influences on the poet such as his 1904
trip to the Canadian Rockies, the death of his mother in 1912, and
the 1913 acquisition of a piano for his wife Elsie to play. The
volume is valuable then for Holly Stevens's own contribution as a
critic who recognizes such important events as the poet's publication of the Carnet de Voyage group of poems, the group which
clearly marks Stevens's transition from juvenilia to mature poetry.
Throughout, she exudes a warmth and affection for the man she
hopes to elucidate in print; but like the reader of this volume, she

approaches the poet with a certain awe inspired by the ambiguity of how, in the early years of this century he became a masterful artist. This "how" is appropriately and tantalizingly left to our imaginations.

Much also exists in *Souvenirs and Prophecies* for the reader's imagination. Journal entries and letters frequently abound with the rich visual detail that typifies much of Stevens's verse.

> In the sunset tonight I tried to get the value of the various colors. The sun was dimmed by a slight mistiness which was sensitive to the faintest colors and thus gave an unusual opportunity for observation. In this delicate net was caught up first of all a pure whiteness which gradually tinted to yellow, and then to heavy orange and thick, blazing gold; this grew light again and slowly turned to pink. The feathery deer-grass before me twinkled silverly in a little breeze, the ordinary blades of green-grass and wheat stubble glittered at their tips while the ragweed and clover were more dark and secret. The middle-distanced remained stolid and indifferent. The horizon, on the contrary, was deepening its blue—a color to which the outermost clouds were already turning. The pink in the sky brightened into a momentary vermilion which slowly died again into rose-color edged with half-determined scarlet and purple. The rose-color faded, the purple turned into a fine, thin violet—and in a moment all the glow was gone.
>
> My feelings tonight find vent in this phrase alone: Salut au Monde!   (p. 55)

Although such self-conscious revelations characterize the young Stevens, they nonetheless resemble the attention to perception and detail that pervades all of Stevens's later work. And, although the samples of his work provided here hardly compare in artistic quality with the verse to follow, they expose a poet who very early examined the role of his art and its interaction with criticism.

> I've started "Endymion" and find a good many beautiful things in it that I had forgotten, or else not noticed. I wonder if it would be possible for a poet now-a-days to content himself with the telling of a "simple tale." With the growth of criticism, both in understanding and influence, poetry for poetry's sake, "debonair and gentle" has become difficult. The modern conception of poetry is that it should be in the service of something, as if Beauty was not something quite sufficient when in no other service than its own.   (p. 237)

Poetry was for Stevens an avocation sufficient in itself, and "in no other service than its own." That much of his life is still a mystery is appropriate because much of his theory will always remain elusive and many of his poems will fortunately evade final analysis. In the sufficiency of this art rests the ambiguity of one man's imaginative perceptions of reality—an ambiguity that both attracts critics to this poet, and at the same time reveals the poet's own mastery of his art.

References

Eberhart, Richard
  1952. "The Stevens Prose." *Accent* Spring, pp. 122–25.
Fraser, G. S.
  1962. "Mind All Alone," *New Statesman* Jan. 9, pp. 43–44.
Fuller, Roy
  1970. "Both Pie and Custard." *Shenandoah* Spring, pp. 61–76.
Heringman, Bernard
  1952. "The Critical Angel." *Kenyon Review* Summer, pp. 520–23.
Kunitz, Stanley
  1966. "The Hartford Walker." *New Republic* Nov. 12, pp. 23–26.
LeBrun, P.
  1961. "Duologue of Two O'Clock." *Essays in Criticism* April, pp. 226–32.
Lensing, George S.
  1970. "Wallace Stevens' Letters of Rock and Water." In *Essays in Honor of Esmond Linworth Marilla*, ed. Thomas Austin Kirby and William John Olive, pp. 320–30. Baton Rouge: Louisiana State Univ. Pr.
Litz, A. Walton
  1967. "Wallace Stevens: Business and a Sonnet." *Nation* Jan. 16, pp. 85–87.
Morse, Samuel French
  1957. "A Note on the 'Adagia'." *Poetry* Mar., pp. 45–46.
Pritchett, V. S.
  1967. "Truffles in the Sky." *New Statesman* Mar. 31, pp. 439–40.
Riddel, Joseph N.
  1967. "Wallace Stevens' 'It Must be Human'." *English Journal* April, pp. 525–34.
  1968. "Blue Voyager." *Salmagundi* Winter, pp. 61–74.
Stanford, Donald E.
  1967. "The Well-Kept Life: The Letters of Wallace Stevens." *Southern Review* Summer, pp. 757–63.
Stevens, Holly
  1977. *Souvenirs and Prophecies: The Young Wallace Stevens.* New York: Knopf.

Stevens, Wallace
  1951. *The Necessary Angel.* New York: Knopf.
  1957. *Opus Posthumous.* New York: Knopf.
  1966. *Letters of Wallace Stevens.* New York: Knopf.
Tindall, William York
  1966. "The Poet Behind the Desk." *Saturday Review* Nov. 19,
  pp. 42–43.
Vazakas, Byron
  1952. "Three Modern Old Masters: Moore, Stevens, Williams."
  New Mexico Quarterly Review Winter, pp. 434–39.
Vendler, Helen
  1977. "Portrait of Wallace Stevens as a Young Artist: *Souvenirs
  and Prophecies." New York Times Book Review* Jan. 30, pp. 2
  and 16.

Additional Study Guides

Bibliographies and Checklists

Anonymous. "A Supplemental List of Items in the Wallace Stevens Collection at Dartmouth College." *Dartmouth College Library Bulletin* Dec. 1961, pp. 67–71.

Bryer, Jackson R., and Riddel, Joseph N. "A Checklist of Stevens Criticism." *Twentieth Century Literature* Oct.-Jan. 1963, pp. 124–42.

Edelstein, J. M. *Wallace Stevens A Descriptive Bibliography*. Pittsburgh: Univ. of Pittsburg Pr., 1973.

Eder, Doris L. "A Review of Stevens Criticism to Date." *Twentieth Century Literature* April 1969, pp. 3–18.

Ford, William T. "Some Notes on Stevens' Foreign Bibliography." *Wallace Stevens Newsletter* Oct. 1969, p. 3.

Huguelet, Theodore L. *The Merrill Checklist of Wallace Stevens*. Columbus, Ohio: Charles E. Merrill, 1970.

Kuntz, Joseph M. *Poetry Explication: A Checklist of Interpretation Since 1925 of British and American Poems Past and Present*. Denver, Colorado: Swallow, 1962.

Mariani, Paul L. "In Review: The Critic As Friend from Pascagoula." *Massachusetts Review* Winter 1971, pp. 162–67.

Mitchell, Roger S. "Wallace Stevens: A Checklist of Criticism." *Bulletin of Bibliography* Sept.-Dec. 1962, pp. 208–11.

Morse, Samuel French. *Wallace Stevens: A Preliminary Checklist of His Published Writings: 1898–1954*. New Haven: Yale Univ. Library, 1954.

Morse, Samuel French; Bryer, Jackson R; and Riddel, Joseph N. *Wallace Stevens Checklist and Bibliography of Stevens Criticism*. Denver, Colorado: Swallow, 1963.

Riddel, Joseph N. "The Contours of Stevens Criticism." *English Literary History* Mar. 1964, pp. 106–38.

———"Wallace Stevens." In *Fifteen Modern American Authors: A Survey of Research and Criticism*, ed. Jackson R. Bryer, pp. 389–423. Durham: Duke Univ. Pr., 1969.

Collections of Essays and Criticism

Borroff, Marie, ed. *Wallace Stevens: A Collection of Critical Essays.* Englewood Cliffs, N.J.: Prentice-Hall, 1963.

Brown, Ash.ey, and Haller, Robert S., eds. *The Achievement of Wallace Stevens.* New York: Lippincott, 1962.

Ehrenpreis, Irvin, ed. *Wallace Stevens: A Critical Anthology.* Middlesex, Eng.: Penguin, 1972.

McNamara, Peter L., ed. *Critics on Wallace Stevens.* Coral Gables, Fla.: Univ. of Miami Pr., 1972.

Pearce, Roy Harvey, and Miller, J. Hillis, eds. *The Act of the Mind: Essays on the Poetry of Wallace Stevens.* Baltimore: Johns Hopkins Pr., 1965.

Periodicals

Dartmouth College Library Bulletin. A Stevens Issue. Dec., 1961.
Harvard Advocate. A Stevens Issue. Dec., 1940.
Perspective. A Stevens Issue. Autumn, 1954.
Southern Review. A Stevens Issue. July, 1971.
Trinity Review. A Stevens Issue. May, 1954.

Books

Culler, Jonathan D., ed. *Harvard Advocate Centennial Anthology.* Cambridge, Mass.: Schenkman, 1966.

Hall, Donald, ed. *The Harvard Advocate Anthology.* New York: Twayne, 1951.

Stevens,. Holly, ed. *The Palm at the End of the Mind.* New York: Vintage, 1967.

———*The Young Wallace Stevens.* New York: Knopf, 1977.

Walsh, Thomas F. *Concordance to the Poetry of Wallace Stevens.* University Park, Pa.: Pennsylvania State Univ. Pr., 1963.

Index

PS3537.T4753 .Z95   CU-Main
c. 1
Willard, Abbie F./Wallace Stevens : the poet and h

3 9371 00029 5494